S0-BYF-564

Realism and Imagination
in Ethics

REALISM AND IMAGINATION IN ETHICS

Sabina Lovibond

University of Minnesota Press · Minneapolis

Copyright © 1983 by Sabina Lovibond

All rights reserved.

Published by the University of Minnesota Press,
2037 University Avenue Southeast, Minneapolis MN 55414

Printed in Great Britain

ISBN 0–8166–1268–4
0–8166–1269–2 (pbk.)

The University of Minnesota
is an equal-opportunity
educator and employer.

For Roger Cash

Acknowledgement

This book was written during my tenure of the Mary Somerville Research Fellowship at Somerville College, Oxford in 1979-82. My warmest thanks are due to the College for its support over that period.

Analytical Table of Contents

Abbreviations

recognize no legitimate intellectual authority in respect of morals. Dissatisfaction with non-cognitivist ethical theory situated against this background $\qquad$ 90

have already noted the material obstacles to his living a life in defiance of that culture. Yet the idea of the historicity of our own particular form of life seems none the less to entail that any future 'reintegration of subjective and objective standpoints' on our part will have to be a critical reintegration – i.e. that we shall never again be able to participate ingenuously in any language-game unless we can regard it as *rational* ('find ourselves in it'). The tension resolved by reference to the notion of 'recessive formulae' of rationality: deviant schemes of values which, while themselves grounded in the total form of life of a community, enable dissident individuals to sustain their identity as rational persons even though they may disengage themselves from the dominant institutions of that community. This situation arises out of the imperfect internal coherence of a social practice   *120*

31 Is the social world we actually inhabit such as to allow a reflective reintegration of subjective and objective standpoints? This (ethical) question gains urgency from our new insight into the role of *coercion* in sustaining all those forms of discourse which are regulated by the norms of *truth* and *rationality*   *132*

32 What is the relation between our idea of the immanent critique of a form of life, and the supposedly Wittgensteinian view that such forms do not lend themselves to evaluative comparison? The philosopher *qua* 'describer of language-games' can do no more than record the development and decay of specific configurations of intellectual authority. Examples of this kind of subject-matter: how social practices can 'go off the rails'   *137*

33 It is certainly implicit in Wittgenstein's later philosophy that any value-judgement concerning a form of life will necessarily be made from some definite historical standpoint, i.e. from within some world-view which is itself embedded in a historically specific form of life. (Denial of culture-transcendent values.)   *140*

34 But this 'value-free' account of the process of change in consensual norms might be held to suffer from the same *phenomenological* defect which was laid at the door of non-cognitivism, viz. refusal to acknowledge at the philosophical level those differences of objective value that we think we perceive in ordinary life. (Conflict between 'outside' and 'inside' with respect to the idea of a 'shared form of life which is constitutive of rationality itself'.)   *144*

35 The conflict resolved – and in a manner strongly reminiscent of its resolution within non-cognitivism. (Our language-games *display*, but do not *describe*, the fact of our 'agreement in judgements'. The relation of consensus to critical concepts compared with that of pain-behaviour to pain-discourse.) This way of reintegrating subjective and objective standpoints will, however, prove innocent of the irrationalism which marred the non-cognitivist strategy, since it rests upon an expressivist conception of the whole of our discourse, not just of one area   146

36 'Absolutism' versus 'relativism' with regard to confrontations between forms of life. Do rival belief-systems compete in respect of *truth*, or merely in respect of *material dominance*? This question forestalled by the expressivist idea that any extensive theoretical confrontation is also a practical confrontation, if it matters at all. Instances of such confrontation as seen (a) from the objective, (b) from the subjective standpoint   151

37 The 'descent' from objectivity to subjectivity, or from *mention* to *use* of critical concepts. The 'trust' which ultimately characterizes our relation to any world-view within which we consent to operate. Role of this concept in Hegel, Wittgenstein and non-cognitivist ethical theory   154

38 A topic in the 'linguistic phenomenology of dissent': the ironic or 'purely descriptive' use of value-terms. Its historical origins in non-alienated usage; and conversely, the prefigurative character of irony, in that it gets its point by opposition to the idea of a 'redeemed' language-game within which we should once again be able to use critical concepts in a non-alienated way. 'Dialectical reason'   159

39-40 Resumption of our inquiry into the relation between expressivist doctrines and moral conservatism. Wittgenstein's conception of philosophy as the attempt to dispel fetishistic misunderstanding of the workings of language (i.e. refusal to recognize these as manifestations of our own subjectivity). Failure to assimilate this aspect of the expressivist position allows that position, and the moral realism grounded in it, to be misrepresented as offering support to a conservative ethics and/or politics. (Reification of existing institutions.) Bradley's essay, 'My Station and its Duties', as a case-study. Instances of expressivist views divorced from conservatism: Nietzsche, etc.   165

41 'Conservatism' and 'liberalism' as contrasting *policies* with respect to moral anomalies: what degree of deviancy do we regard as a justification for ceasing to treat the deviant as a 'soul' (i.e. as a rational person)? The criteria of 'rationality' are determined by our practice. The expressivist view of language, *per se*, yields no practical lesson in this connection   *172*

42   A 'symptomatic reading' of the refusal to acknowledge indeterminacy (i.e. incompleteness of intellectual authority) within the moral language-game, and of the associated impulse to objectify dissenting persons   *179*

43   How does the objectification of the moral dissident proceed at the level of theory? The technique of 'divide and rule': resistance to the authorities who currently specify where the 'ideal moral observer' is to stand is interpreted as outright rejection of the public point of view (i.e. as mere selfish individualism). However, opinions can differ as to where one needs to stand to get a good view of moral reality   *185*

44   Another theme within realist ethics, which converges with the above: that of 'curbing imagination'. The process of moral degeneration feared by philosophers who emphasize 'narrowness', simple virtue, etc. appears to be identical with that of 'rational value-change' as celebrated by the theorists of dialectical reason   *189*

45   Moral 'imagination' as the critical scrutiny of existing institutions by 'seeing new aspects', and – arising logically out of such scrutiny – the speculative construction of alternatives. A quasi-verificationist objection: how can imagination transcend experience with respect to morals? (How can there be *Moralität* as well as *Sittlichkeit*?) Reply: speculative thought in the practical sphere can be defended against this objection without abandoning realism, by an argument analogous to that used in the theoretical sphere. The fact of syntactic structure in language ensures that as competent speakers about ethics, we can represent to ourselves moral justifications for replacing existing institutions by others –even though this competence is itself grounded in our personal history of incorporation into the existing institutions. Imagination as a linguistic capacity   *194*

46   The 'breakdown of ethical substance' as a *conscious* exercise. How far this can be carried, within the matrix of a given form of life, is a matter of experiment. The renunciation of a ponderous array of (moral) 'certainties' might be seen as a mode of *asceticism*

201

Abbreviations

The following abbreviations are used in references to works by Wittgenstein:

T   *Tractatus Logico-Philosophicus*, trs. D. F. Pears and B. F. McGuinness (1961)

PI   *Philosophical Investigations*, trs. G. E. M. Anscombe, 3rd edn (1967)

BB   *The Blue and Brown Books*, 2nd edn (1969)

OC   *On Certainty*, ed. G. E. M. Anscombe and G. H. von Wright, trs. Denis Paul and G. E. M. Anscombe (1969)

RFM   *Remarks on the Foundations of Mathematics*, ed. G. H. von Wright, R. Rhees and G. E. M. Anscombe, trs. G. E. M. Anscombe, 3rd edn (1978)

CV   *Culture and Value*, ed. G. H. von Wright in collaboration with Heikki Nyman, trs. Peter Winch (1980)

Z   *Zettel*, ed. G. E. M. Anscombe and G. H. von Wright, trs. G. E. M. Anscombe, 2nd edn (1981)

Other abbreviations used:

PAS   *Proceedings of the Aristotelian Society*

PASS   *Proceedings of the Aristotelian Society: Supplementary Volume*

read 12-22-89

——— 1 ———

For some decades now, Anglo-Saxon moral philosophy has been governed by a certain distinctive set of metaphysical presuppositions. These presuppositions have given rise to an essentially uniform treatment of questions belonging to the 'metaphysics of morals': questions concerning the foundations of duty, the objectivity of values, the status of moral judgements, and the relation of moral thinking to other kinds of thinking. The orthodoxy thus generated is called the *non-cognitivist* theory of ethics.

Non-cognitivism, as its name announces, is the thesis that there is no such thing as moral cognition or knowledge. The reason there is no moral knowledge, according to this view, is that knowledge logically requires a real object set over against the knowing subject: but there is no objective moral reality; consequently, as far as morals are concerned, there is nothing to know.

An alternative way of stating the non-cognitivist position is in terms of answerability to truth. Moral judgements, it is claimed, lack truth-status – they are not the sort of utterance which can be true or false – because there is nothing in the world which *makes* them true, in the way that the physical condition of the world makes remarks about material objects true. Of course this ontological formulation of non-cognitivism is intimately connected with the epistemological formulation, since we cannot be said to *know* something unless it is *true*.

Non-cognitivism, then, may be characterized initially as the view that there is no truth about values, whether in morals, politics or art. The theory may be seen as an expression of the liberal-individualist notion of freedom as the condition in which no one can order you about. In the present context, this notion yields the thought that no one can tell you that you are mistaken in your moral (or other) values. Thus R. M. Hare refers to the 'conviction, which every adult has, that he is free to form his own opinions about moral questions'; and he asserts also that 'we are free to form our

1

own moral opinions in a much stronger sense than we are free to form our own opinions as to what the facts are.'[1] (We shall see later, however, that Hare's idea of what counts as a 'fact' derives from a distinctive metaphysical position.)

We can give greater precision to our initial characterization of non-cognitivism by saying: the theory denies that there are any truths about *intrinsic* values. The concept which is jettisoned by non-cognitive theorists is that of a value which is both objective and intrinsic. Such theorists are quite ready to allow that there can be propositions, in the strict logical sense of the word, about *instrumental* value: it can perfectly well be a 'fact', on their view, that such and such means are conducive to such and such an end, and hence that the means are good, given the end as determined. Conversely, the notion of intrinsic value is still admitted, but it is no longer taken to have impersonal validity: it becomes something of which individuals are the ultimate arbiters. That is to say, judgements of intrinsic value are held to be warranted not by the actual obtaining of a certain state of affairs which they declare to obtain, but by some phenomenon which, pending a better use for the word, can be called 'subjective': candidates for this role include desires, reactive attitudes, personal decisions or prescriptions.

Non-cognitive theorists also recognize a realm of fact as regards what *is valued*, or *is desired*, for its own sake. Such facts would belong to the domain of empirical psychology or sociology. But G. E. Moore's diagnosis of the 'naturalistic fallacy' has been respected by his successors; non-cognitivism in the twentieth century has avoided using the fact of a thing's being desired as a criterion of its desirability. Rather, it asserts – as stated above – that there is no such thing as a fact about the desirability or otherwise of any object.

It might be felt that what had no objective existence was not worthy, or not logically suited, to be a topic of serious discussion. But non-cognitivism tells us that we should not think of language merely as a medium for the communication of truths. It has another function which is equally important –

---

[1] R. M. Hare, *Freedom and Reason* (1963), p. 2.

namely, the expression of attitudes, or dispositions of the *unconstrained attitudes or dispositions* will. These functions are held to be distinct: specifically, our attitudes are held to be logically unconstrained by the facts. Given any state of affairs, I am 'free' (in Hare's sense) to adopt any attitude I please, to feel whatever I like about it.

Neither is there supposed to be any relation of precedence between the two functions. Reacting to the condition of the world is not admitted to be a less important human capacity than determining what that condition is. Indeed, non-cognitive theorists have consistently spoken out in defence of affectivity. 'Reasons serve not to bring our attitudes into being,' writes C. L. Stevenson, 'but only to redirect them . . . If we initially distrust all our attitudes . . . our reasons will not *give* us attitudes; but an initial distrust of all our attitudes is so fantastic that we need not, surely, take it seriously.'[2] Philippa Foot, too, has emphasized the need for us to affirm our own moral commitments. We should have less reason to fear defection from the moral cause, she argues, 'if people thought of themselves as volunteers banded together to fight for liberty and justice and against inhumanity and oppression.'[3]

The idea of moral judgements, not as statements of fact, but as expressions of the moral orientation of the individual, leads to a conception of morality itself as a kind of *partisanship*. *morality as partisanship* This answers to the common-sense view that you have to stand up for your own values in the face of competition from the rival values endorsed by others. Individuals are pictured as struggling to defend their own moral convictions, either within an institutional framework, or (possibly) by a trial of brute strength. Our 'factual' beliefs are not considered to need a militant defence of this kind, since they after all are (we *defence* hope) *true* – and, as such, can take care of themselves to some extent.

This theme of partisanship, or voluntarism, might be *voluntarism* regarded as the crux of the non-cognitivist theory of ethics:

---

[2] C. L. Stevenson, 'Relativism and Non-Relativism in the Theory of Value' (1962), in *Facts and Values: Studies in Ethical Analysis* (1963), p. 90.
[3] Philippa Foot, 'Morality as a System of Hypothetical Imperatives' (1972), in *Virtues and Vices* (1978), p. 167.

its 'moral', so to speak. Accordingly, we can see non-cognitivism as an attempt to set morality on a firmer, because more psychologically accessible, basis. Rather than seeking, with Kant and his followers, to represent the requirements of morality as binding upon any rational being *qua* rational, non-cognitivism says that morally acceptable behaviour is commended by our reason (where it is so commended) in the same way as any other kind of behaviour: namely, as a means to satisfying the desires we actually have. This is the only sense in which any action can be shown to be rationally indicated, if our conception of rationality is a technical one – that is, if we define a rational individual as one who acts in such a way as to maximize his[4] utilities (get as much satisfaction as possible, relative to his output of resources). And that conception of rationality is characteristic of the philosophical tradition to which non-cognitivism belongs.

Admittedly, the robust foundation of morality in our spontaneous desires is secured at the cost of founding it in something contingent – in 'fortuitous or escapable inclinations'[5] to defend the cause of justice, liberty, or whatever. But the contingency which thus infects moral motivation is counterbalanced by the idea of partisanship which we have

---

[4] I hope women readers will not be offended by my failure to challenge the conventional use of 'he', 'him', 'his' where a pronoun is needed to refer to an 'individual' of indeterminate gender – a need which will arise frequently in this book on account of the attention we shall be paying to the relation between individuals and linguistic communities. I considered the possibility of writing 'he or she', etc. but eventually rejected this, not only because of the threatened increase in verbiage, but also – and more importantly – because the 'abstract individual' of philosophical literature *is*, after all, a male individual with a distinctively masculine set of problems and concerns, and it seems preferable at the moment to maintain an explicit awareness of this fact, rather than try to gloss it over with futile reformist turns of phrase. Indeed, I would go further and suggest that the emotional distance established by a policy of self-conscious conservatism on this point can sometimes be a help rather than a hindrance to women in our attempt to come to grips with the philosophical tradition. But the problem cannot be said to admit of a 'correct' solution, and the above remarks are intended simply to explain my own usage.

I have of course avoided referring to 'a man' when I mean 'a person'.

[5] Cf. Thomas Nagel, *The Possibility of Altruism* (1970), p. 6.

4

seen to be central to non-cognitive theories. No doubt there will be those who lack the desires which make it rational to behave decently; however, the rest of us, who do possess these desires, can defend ourselves against the delinquents by means of any sanctions (psychological or physical) that may seem appropriate. In this way we shall constitute the 'party of humankind against vice and disorder, its common enemy'.[6]

sanctions

Hare, for example, is anxious to reassure us that 'the moral philosopher has no reason to be disturbed by the logical possibility of people becoming fanatics without self-contradiction.'[7] The reassurance is found in a discussion of practical reasoning, where it is pointed out that anyone who undertakes a justification of his own behaviour by reference to practical principles can always be pressed, by the determined questioner who wants a *complete* answer, to give a *complete* specification of the way of life in which those principles are embedded. However, Hare continues, if the questioner then proceeds to ask for reasons why he should live like that, there is nothing more to be said, since the way of life specified by the first speaker is the source of all the potentially justifying considerations to which that speaker can appeal. When this happens, 'We can only ask him' – that is, the questioner – 'to make up his own mind which way he ought to live; for in the end everything rests upon such a decision of principle. He has to decide whether to accept that way of life or not. . . . If he does not accept it, then let him accept some other, and try to live by it. *The sting is in the last clause.*'[8]

way of life

decision of principle

---

[6] Cf. David Hume, *An Enquiry Concerning the Principles of Morals,* ed. L. A. Selby-Bigge, 3rd edn (1975), p. 275.

[7] Hare, *Freedom and Reason,* p. 199. ('Fanatic' is a name which, if I accept the doctrine of *Freedom and Reason,* I shall give to persons whose moral orientation is fundamentally at odds with my own, and who cannot be won over by moral arguments constructed on the model proposed by Hare in that book, even though they acknowledge the correctness of that model as a representation of what we understand by 'rationality' in ethics.)

fanatic

[8] R. M. Hare, *The Language of Morals* (1952), p. 69 (emphasis added).

mistrust of 'freedom' However, there are those who mistrust the 'freedom' extolled by non-cognitivism, seeing it instead as an 'irresponsible and undirected self-assertion'; an 'inconsequential chucking of one's weight about'.[1] They believe that there are compelling reasons not to accept any meta-ethical theory which legislates *possibility of moral thinking & argument* away the possibility of moral *thinking* and of moral *argument*, as A. J. Ayer did in his exposition of emotivism: 'We hold that one really never does dispute about questions of value,' he wrote.[2]

Obviously, the opponents of non-cognitivism understand by 'thinking' something more rigorous than the expression of *rigorous* unmotivated attitudes and unconstrained decisions, and by 'argument', again, something more rigorous than the attempt to elicit congruent attitudes or decisions from others by a process of persuasion. Both these procedures are recognized by non-cognitive theorists – indeed, required by them in order to account for the appearance (sometimes) that moral deliberation or argument is taking place. What their opponents mean by thinking, however, is an activity governed by *truth and validity* the norm of truth; and by argument, one governed by the norm of validity. The objection to non-cognitivism is that it places the moral side of life beyond the reach of these critical concepts. Moral philosophy is thus lured into what A. T. *'subjectivistic suicide'* Kolnai describes as the 'subjectivistic suicide of thought'.[3]

This critique of non-cognitive theories may be entered *resistance to irrationalism* under the general heading of resistance to irrationalism. There is an honourable and long-standing tradition of such resistance – and a broadly-based one: for although it has sometimes been inspired by authoritarian motives (Kolnai's colourful remark about subjectivism occurs in the same paragraph as an assertion that 'the cause of the Church and the cause of Truth are one'), this has not always been the case. R. G. Colling-

---

[1] Iris Murdoch, *The Sovereignty of Good* (1970), pp. 48, 95.
[2] A. J. Ayer, *Language, Truth and Logic*, 2nd edn (1946), p. 146.
[3] A. T. Kolnai, *Ethics, Value and Reality* (1977), p. 31.

wood, for instance, was no authoritarian, and he believed he could detect 'an irrationalist epidemic sweeping over at least a large part of Europe'. 'If the people who share a civilization are no longer on the whole convinced that the form of life which it tries to realize is worth realizing,' he wrote in 1940, 'nothing can save it. If European civilization is a civilization based on the belief that truth is the most precious thing in the world and that pursuing it is the whole duty of man, an irrationalist epidemic if it ran through Europe unchecked would in a relatively short time destroy everything that goes by the name of European civilization.'[4]

The classic rationalist critique of non-cognitivism has recently been supplemented by an interesting phenomenological objection to the theory. The objection is made by David Wiggins in his 1976 British Academy Lecture, 'Truth, Invention and the Meaning of Life'. Wiggins' phenomenological objection is not, however, independent of the rationalist argument mentioned above: rather, it draws attention to the subjective consequences of embracing, at the philosophical level, an irrationalist ethical theory of the non-cognitive type.

Wiggins sets out, in his lecture, to 'explore the possibility that the questions of truth and the meaning of life really are the central questions of moral philosophy.'[5] These questions are closely related, he thinks, in that our ability to find meaning in life depends upon a presumption of the truth-status of propositions which assert that such and such an activity is (intrinsically) worthwhile. This view is contrasted with that of the 'naïve non-cognitivist' (the same theorist who figures in section 1 above as the non-cognitivist *tout simple*), who holds that the only meaning individual lives can have is supplied by the investment of a 'free-floating commitment' in some of the activities of which those lives are composed. Thus, in a sample case cited by Wiggins, it is suggested that the life of a Sisyphus who is condemned to roll stones

---

[4] R. G. Collingwood, *An Essay on Metaphysics* (1940), pp. 139, 140.
[5] David Wiggins, 'Truth, Invention and the Meaning of Life', *Proceedings of the British Academy* (1976), p. 331.

interminably uphill without ever getting them to the top can derive meaning from Sisyphus's own attitude to his task of stone-rolling. If he feels that it is worthwhile, then it *is* worthwhile: he cannot be mistaken, because the value of the activity is *constituted* by the satisfaction the agent gains from it. Here, then, we get a new perspective upon the voluntarist tendency of non-cognitivism, which was noted in section 1. That 'free-floating commitment', to which the theory appeals for an account of the possibility of moral engagement in any human activity, is simply the spontaneous partisanship upon which non-cognitivists rely to make the world safe for morality – but seen, now, in its relation to the life of the individual as distinct from that of the community.

Wiggins objects that the idea of such a commitment cannot yield a satisfactory answer to our (legitimate) metaphysical question: what is the point in doing anything? For it is false that, in our capacity as *agents,* our sense of the value of what we are doing is independent of any objective considerations. It is false, for example, that that sense of value would be unaffected by the suspicion that our efforts were not going to have a successful outcome. And it is false that we conceive ourselves, as individuals, to possess ultimate authority on the value of our various activities. On the contrary, the human will 'picks and chooses, deliberates, weighs concerns. It craves objective reasons; and often it could not go forward unless it thought it had them.'[6]

The phenomenological argument of Wiggins' lecture might perhaps be paraphrased as follows. We saw earlier that non-cognitivism exhorts us to identify ourselves with our appetitive dispositions and to affirm them in our dealings with one another, unabashed by the alleged fact that these dispositions are 'subjective', i.e. not amenable to rational criticism. In this sense non-cognitivism aims to restore volition to a more respectable status in our conception of ourselves; it is a reaction against the idea of the will as an essentially threatening and anti-moral force. But there is a difficulty with this rehabilitation of the 'subjective', in so far as it involves

---

[6] Ibid., p. 341.

thinking of the latter as logically isolated from that part of our mental life which is regulated by external reality. The difficulty is that 'subjective' dispositions, thus represented, are liable to flag when too much attention is fixed upon them. The part they are expected to play is embarrassingly naïve – as if we were to be asked to relive the experience of some early childhood birthday party, where we were expected to gurgle enthusiastically over our presents, but under the benign scrutiny of a band of adult spectators, were awkwardly unable to mount the required show of glee (for even a child can grasp the fact that he is only a child, and that although the scrutiny of the adults is benign, there is also condescension in it). *[logical isolation]*

But this experience, it is now suggested, is equally familiar to the adults themselves; at any rate, in consumer societies. The goods are laid out on the counter – but the relation between *taking what one wants* and *achieving happiness* remains problematic. If value is constituted by our desires, simply as such, there can be no objectively valid reason why we should want one thing rather than another; what difference does it make, then, what we choose? And what is to prevent us from lapsing into an inert condition in which no choice seems worth making? That is the phenomenological objection to non-cognitivism from the 'inner' or 'participative viewpoint'. *[problematic relation]* *[desires?]* *[phenomenological objection]*

------- 3 -------

Wiggins' lecture is symptomatic of a deep-seated change of mood. During the 1970s, and especially the late 1970s, others too have become conscious of the destructive aspect of ethical irrationalism, and have begun to consider with renewed interest the possible application to moral life of such notions as *humility, sensitivity, submission to reality*. *[destructive aspect]*

This development has taken place in the context of a continuing debate within the philosophy of language – a debate prompted by the writings of Donald Davidson and (more immediately) of Michael Dummett. The subject of that *[philosophy of language]* debate has been the form which a theory of meaning for a language ought to take.

Dummett has suggested that our task in this connection is to identify the correct 'central notion'[1] for such a theory, namely, that notion, an account of whose application to each sentence of the theory's object-language (determined recursively on the basis of its application to the primitive semantic components of that language) would constitute a correct theoretical representation of what is known by someone who understands the language in question. This suggestion of Dummett's is motivated by uncertainty about the claim of *truth* to serve as the central notion in a theory of meaning, as Frege (the originator of the general conception of semantics with which Dummett operates) held that it could. Dummett himself, as we shall see in section 6 below, has sought to show there are grounds (of an epistemological kind) for ousting the notion of truth from this central role, and replacing it with that of verification, falsification, or some other (so far unspecified) concept; if these considerations were valid, we should be obliged to opt for a theory of meaning which was 'anti-realistic', i.e. did not represent language-mastery in terms of a grasp of the conditions under which particular sentences are true. We should thus be left with the formal framework, as it were, of a Fregean semantics, but not with the original content.

Others have responded to Dummett's challenge by defending the legitimacy of a truth-conditional, or 'realistic', theory of meaning in respect of those regions of discourse to which the challenge applies. In order to deflect anti-realist criticism, however, it has been necessary to question certain presuppositions upon which such criticism seems to rest. Drawing on the terminology supplied by Dummett's own discussion, we can say that this questioning has focused upon what is seen as an unduly restrictive conception of the kinds of sentence which can be 'barely true'[2] – whose truth (where

(margin notes: verification replaces truth; 'anti-realistic' theory of meaning; anti-realist criticism)

---

[1] See, for example, Michael Dummett, 'What is a Theory of Meaning? (II)', in Evans and McDowell (eds.), *Truth and Meaning: Essays in Semantics* (1976), p. 75.
[2] Cf. ibid., p. 89.

they are true) is not dependent upon the availability of a non-trivial answer to the question, 'What *makes* it true?'

A sentence which can be 'barely true', in this sense, is a sentence of whose truth we can be *non-inferentially* aware. Non-inferential awareness may also be referred to, in a Kantian spirit, as 'intuition'. *[non-inferential awareness]*

Realist resistance to a narrow conception of the possible objects of non-inferential awareness has begun to impinge upon moral philosophy. We are witnessing a paradoxical situation in which the attempt to propagate anti-realism, so to speak, from the edges of language to the centre – i.e. to argue from the illegitimacy of a realist semantics for certain limited regions of discourse to a global anti-realist position – has provoked a reaction which is tending to push realism forward again into an area from which it has been excluded in recent years. In fact, the current realist revival in ethics appears to have the potential to depose non-cognitivism from its former role as the dominant meta-ethical doctrine. *[narrow conception]* *[realist revival]*

To date, the most ambitious statement of the sort of moral realism I have in mind (namely, moral realism inspired by recent work in truth-conditional semantics) is the one offered by Mark Platts in the final chapter of his book, *Ways of Meaning* – a text to which I shall make a number of references in the early sections of this book, not because I wish to ascribe any special authority to it, but because it provides a useful starting-point for the discussion of various aspects of the proposed theory. Platts' contribution illustrates, among other things, the realist's reliance on a liberalized conception of the kinds of circumstance which can be immediately present to our awareness, or (to put it another way) which can be non-inferentially known to obtain; for he claims that 'We detect moral aspects [of a situation] in the same way we detect (nearly all) other aspects: by looking and seeing.'[3] The position defended, then, is a form of intuitionism: we are invited to postulate a realm of moral facts of which individuals can become directly aware, and which they can record in *[liberal conception]* *[looking & seeing]* *[intuitionism]*

---

[3] M. Platts, *Ways of Meaning: an Introduction to a Philosophy of Language* (1979), p. 247.

11

propositions whose assertibility-conditions are nothing less than <u>truth-conditions</u>. (Platts hastens to insist, however, that his theory does not involve us in talking about a 'distinctive faculty of ethical intuition'; that, it appears, would be a mere 'contribution to the unintelligible pseudo-psychology of the faculties of the mind'. I shall argue that it is unnecessary to protest so much: see section 12 below.)

truth-conditions

Significant changes must have been taking place in the philosophical climate, if there is now felt to be some serious prospect of acceptance for such a provocative view. I call it 'provocative' on the grounds that most people trained in analytical philosophy – not to mention the countless unhappy victims of empiricist 'common sense' who inhabit the wider world – operate with a distinctive conception of 'fact', or 'objectivity', which is incompatible with the one employed by Platts. These people will feel entitled to an explanation of the sense in which, as regards morality, there is anything *there* to be 'seen'. In the absence of such an explanation they will interpret the use of emphatic pronouncements about 'looking and seeing' as the mark of an underlying mysticism – like the mysticism of the early Wittgenstein, with his talk of 'seeing the world aright' (*T* 6.54). And they can hardly be blamed if they then proceed to point out that <u>mysticism, as much as subjectivism, is traditionally a means to the 'suicide of thought'</u>.

mysticism?

Objections of this kind deserve to be met. It is less than thirty years since P. H. Nowell-Smith could purport to show the bankruptcy of intuitionist ethics by remarking that, on that view, 'If I disagree with you' – sc. about a moral issue – 'you must charge me either with insincerity or with moral blindness.'[4] His thought was that, while the charge of insincerity was often plainly false, that of moral blindness was never anything but vacuous. Until recently this argument would have carried almost universal conviction; and anyone who wishes, today, to reintroduce 'moral blindness'[5] (and the rest of the visual idiom) into moral philosophy is indeed

---

[4] P. H. Nowell-Smith, *Ethics* (1954), p. 46.
[5] Cf. Platts, *Ways of Meaning*, p. 262.

under an obligation to explain why the familiar non-cognitivist critique of intuitionism is misplaced. It is not enough to commend the latter position as 'deeply attractive'.[6] We shall see later (sections 6-15 below) what can be done to supplement this aesthetic argument.

On the other hand, critics of moral realism must give due weight to the 'attractiveness' of that theory. Its appeal results, I suppose, from the bold and simple way in which it responds to the 'craving of the human will for objective reasons' – that craving which, because non-cognitivism could not satisfy it, made the latter theory untenable from the subjective standpoint. (Wiggins' argument, as reported in section 2 above.) The moral realist can respond to this demand for objective reasons by claiming that a moral fact, or circumstance, of the kind posited by his own theory *is* at the same time a (potential) objective reason[7] for doing something. For the world *qua* moral – that world which is the totality of moral facts[8] – is a world '*compulsively* present to the will':[9] moral discourse, on this view, is a region of discourse in which the

moral facts   _objective reason for doing something_   _moral discourse_

---

[6] Cf. ibid., p. 263.

[7] 'Reason' and 'rational' in this context should of course be understood in the non-hypothetical sense. The reasons craved by the will, according to Wiggins, are both objective and intrinsic – their absence from the non-cognitivist's universe reflects the absence from that universe of objective, intrinsic *values* (see section 1 above). _'reasons'_

[8] Cf. Wittgenstein, *T* 1.1: 'The world is the totality of facts, not of things.' This doctrine flows directly from the fountain-head of western metaphysics. Thus Charles H. Kahn writes in 'The Greek Verb "To Be" and the Concept of Being': 'The language of Greek ontology naturally lends itself to the view that the structure of reality is such as to be truly expressed in discourse. For the Greek concept of truth is precisely this: *ta onta legein hōs esti, ta mē onta hōs mē esti,* to say of the things that are (the case) that they are, and of the things that are not that they are not ... Being for [Plato and Aristotle] as for Parmenides means what is or can be truly known and truly said. *To on* is first and foremost the object of true knowledge and the basis or correlative of true speech ... The chief discrepancy between the Greek concept of Being and the modern notion of existence lies precisely here, for we normally assign existence not to facts or propositions or relations, but to discrete particulars: to creatures, persons, or things. (*Foundations of Language* (1966), pp. 253, 260, 261). _facts, not things_   _discourse_   _discrete particulars_

[9] Murdoch, *The Sovereignty of Good*, p. 39.

13

description of objectively existing circumstances *coalesces* with the rational justification, or explanation, of human actions. The same moral statement can perform both functions simultaneously. 'Why should it not just be a brute fact about moral facts,' asks Platts, 'that, without any further element entering [sc. any reference to a non-cognitive mental state of the prospective agent], their clear perception does provide sufficient grounding for action?'[10] And this, in effect, is his proposed remedy for the will's inhibition in the face of the excessive demands made upon it by non-cognitivism.

───── 4 ─────

The divergence between realist and non-cognitivist theories of ethics with regard to moral psychology is reflected in the fact that each type of theory selects for emphasis a different portion of our moral vocabulary. Realism promotes a concentration on concrete ascriptions of value, i.e. judgements in which we predicate of an object a concept of which the following things are true: (1) it denotes a property which it is *prima facie* good (or bad) for a thing to have; (2) its application is governed by impersonal criteria. (The classic source for this strategy is Philippa Foot's 1958 article, 'Moral Arguments',[1] where the example used is the notion of 'rudeness': unquestionably a value-term, but one which must be used in accordance with certain fixed criteria if it is to be used at all.)

Thus we find Wiggins, in the lecture mentioned earlier, picking out a class of *evaluative* moral propositions typified by 'x is brave', 'malicious', 'corrupt', etc. of which he will later assert that it is either false or senseless to deny that they involve reference to properties in a (real) world – as distinct from the class of *practical* moral judgements ('I must ψ', 'I ought to ψ', etc), which he admits may fall short of full

---

[10] Platts, *Ways of Meaning*, p. 258.

[1] Philippa Foot, 'Moral Arguments' (1958), in *Virtues and Vices* (1978).

truth-status;[2] while Platts, in a similar vein, regards moral concepts with a concrete descriptive content as 'the interesting, basic terms' of moral assessment – as distinct from abstract concepts such as 'good', which he considers to be logically derivative from lower-level evaluations.[3]

Non-cognitivists, by contrast, focus initially upon just these abstract moral categories of right, good, duty, and the like; and it is only *after* they have established their analysis of these notions in terms of some sort of non-assertoric speech-act that they turn their attention to expressions which are both normative and (palpably) descriptive. The non-cognitivist account of such expressions is that they involve a 'wedding'[4] of straightforward empirical description with some other kind of speech-act (commending, prescribing or whatever) which is held to be constitutive of value-judgement as such. In this way the proposition 'x is brave', for example (if uttered without irony – a complication to be discussed below, section 38), would be analysed into (1) a statement that x has a certain property or complex of properties, specified in evaluatively neutral terms, and (2) an expression of a favourable moral orientation towards that property on the part of the speaker. These two components of a moral judgement are supposed to be analytically distinct: 'It is true,' writes Hare, 'that there is no single evaluatively neutral word which . . . can be used to describe [courageous] actions without committing the describer to any evaluation; but we *could* have such a word.'[5] The importance of this claim of the logical separation of description and commendation resides, as stated (section 1), in the alleged opposition between our 'freedom' as regards what we prescribe or commend, and our relative unfreedom as regards what factual observations we make.

Moral realists, on the other hand – as one would expect, in

---

[2] Wiggins, 'Truth, Invention . . .', pp. 338, 372.
[3] Platts, *Ways of Meaning*, p. 246.
[4] C. L. Stevenson, *Ethics and Language* (1944), p. 210: 'Ethical definitions involve a wedding of descriptive and emotive meaning.'
[5] Hare, *Freedom and Reason*, p. 189.

15

view of their emphasis upon the qualitative part of moral discourse – treat the category of autonomy, or self-determination, with an indifference verging on hostility. The ideal moral agent of post-Kantian philosophy, tellingly depicted by Iris Murdoch as he intervenes in the mechanistic world of nature by an unconstrained movement of his 'free, independent, lonely'[6] will, does not accord with a doctrine which makes moral judgement consist essentially in the skilled use of a repertoire of highly specific value-concepts. We noted earlier that anyone who undertakes to use such concepts is obliged, on the realist view, to use them according to the prevailing rules. But the idea of morality as a medium of self-expression or self-assertion – implicit in the non-cognitivist thesis that it is up to me what I commend or prescribe – can only stand in the way of a delicate grasp of those rules, which *ex hypothesi* are not invented by the individual, and cannot be overturned by him. Therefore, that idea can only detract from our powers of apprehension of moral truth. So runs the realist argument.

Accordingly, critics of non-cognitivism tend on the whole to be unsympathetic towards any kind of high-profile behaviour. Thus Kolnai, defending his own variant of intuitionistic realism in an article called 'Moral Consensus', sneers at ' "moral rebellion" with its [obviously meretricious!] glamour of "originality" and "creativeness" ', and at the 'bitter resentment' and 'disappointed moralism' of those whose imagination has been captured by ideals.[7]

The current ascendancy of realism in ethics indicates, then, a turning away from the individualistic or anti-authoritarian values exhibited in non-cognitive theories. It indicates a rejection of the idea – more or less overtly present in all such theories – that moral judgements manifest our 'passions',

---

[6] Murdoch, *The Sovereignty of Good,* p. 80. 'Unconstrained': Murdoch sees no important *moral* distinction between those among Kant's successors who have followed him in maintaining a system of formal constraints upon moral judgement (as in prescriptivism) and those who have done away with all constraints whatsoever (as in existentialism).

[7] Kolnai, *Ethics, Value and Reality,* pp. 162, 156.

16

conceived in the Humean manner as 'original existences'[8] (that is, brute phenomena of consciousness, not subject to rational appraisal). For on the realist view, perception in ethics is logically prior to feeling: the morally blind man, according to Platts, 'does not feel *because* he does not see sufficiently.'[9]

perception precedes feeling

———— 5 ————

Our discussion of the realist reaction against non-cognitivism has so far been conducted mainly in terms of its consequences for our conception of ourselves as moral agents. It is time now to say something about the metaphysical and epistemological basis of that reaction. We can begin by listing some characteristic features of the type of metaphysical position with which non-cognitive theories of ethics are associated. I shall refer to this as the *empiricist* position: the term 'empiricist', loose as it is, will be sufficiently precise to point a contrast with the rival position which underpins contemporary moral realism.

moral agents

metaphysical epistemo- logical reaction

empiricist position

In the first place, empiricism embodies a specific view of language: it sees language as an *instrument* for the communication of thought. On this view, thought is conceived as logically prior to its expression in words; and the historical advent of language tends, accordingly, to be seen merely as a strikingly successful technical innovation which enabled individuals to tell one another what they were thinking,

language as instrument

thought is logically prior

---

[8] David Hume, *Treatise of Human Nature*, ed. Selby-Bigge/Nidditch (1978), p. 415, and context.
[9] Platts, *Ways of Meaning*, pp. 257-8, 262 (emphasis added). For the opposite view on the logical ordering of moral sentiment and moral perception, cf. Shakespeare, *King Lear*, IVi:

Heavens, deal so still!
Let the superfluous and lust-dieted man
That slaves your ordinance, that will not see
Because he does not feel, feel your power quickly:
So distribution should undo excess,
And each man have enough.

whereas they had previously been unable to do so. Hobbes puts the point as follows: 'But the most noble and profitable invention of all other, was that of SPEECH, consisting of *names* or *appellations,* and their connexion; whereby men register their thoughts; recall them when they are past; and also declare them to one another for mutual utility and conversation.'[1]

instrumental conception

This instrumental conception reflects an attempt to understand natural language on the model of a scientific calculus or symbolism – that is, an artificial language designed for optimum performance of some function within a particular field of theoretical activity. One important result of this way of thinking is a tendency to suppose that the meanings of words in humane use – like those of the terms employed in a calculus – are fixed by their definitions in such a way as to exclude any possibility of rational disagreement about their correct application. At any rate, it is thought that in so far as the natural use of words fails to measure up to the ideal of semantic rigour represented by the calculus, natural language is unsuited to serve as a means of acquiring knowledge. To quote again from Hobbes:

fixed definitions

> Seeing then that truth consisteth in the right ordering of names in our affirmations, a man that seeketh precise truth had need to remember what every name he uses stands for, and to place it accordingly, or else he will find himself entangled in words, as a bird in lime twigs, the more he struggles the more belimed. And therefore in geometry, which is the only science that it hath hitherto pleased God to bestow on mankind, men begin at settling the significations of their words.[2]

It is essential to the empiricist idea of language as a calculus that as soon as our definitions have been stated, what we can correctly say is *out of our hands;* we can define our terms in

---

[1] Thomas Hobbes, *Leviathan* (1651), I iv; ed. C. B. Macpherson (1968), p. 100.
[2] Ibid., p. 105.

any way we like, but once we have done so we have, so to speak, signed away our freedom as regards the assignment of truth-values to sentences (sc. in the light of experience). There is an analogy here with a remark of Dummett's: 'We naturally think that, face to face with a mathematical proof, we have no alternative but to accept the proof if we are to remain faithful to the understanding we already had of the expressions contained in it.'[3] Empiricism implies that, given our initial definitions of natural-language expressions, the configuration of objects in the world will determine the truth-value of propositions *independently of any mediation by us,* i.e. by the human subjects who use the expressions in question. We are thus pictured as having 'no alternative', when confronted by certain facts, but to label certain sentences as true and others as false. (My use of the normative word 'fact' in this context is intended to echo Dummett's use of the normative word 'proof'.)

Next, empiricism involves a belief that all our evidence for the truth or falsity of propositions is derived from our senses. More precisely, it involves a belief that sensory experience provides the ultimate rational grounds for any rationally grounded belief which is not analytic, i.e. not a mere matter of definition. But if sensory experience is to serve as the rational foundation of our beliefs – and hence of our theories – about the world, then it must itself be thought of as possessing a determinate character prior to the construction or deployment of any theory. Thus, following Hume, empiricists have posited a class of primitive phenomena of consciousness – a class, namely, of qualitatively determinate 'impressions', 'sense-data' or 'percepts' – which they have supposed to constitute a source of information from which we *infer* how things stand: we affirm those propositions which *follow* from our sense-impressions.[4] 'Though one is not normally conscious of making any inferences when one ventures on such a simple perceptual judgement as "This is an ashtray" or "That

---

[3] Michael Dummett, 'Wittgenstein's Philosophy of Mathematics' (1959), in *Truth and Other Enigmas* (1978), p. 173.
[4] Cf. Wittgenstein, *PI* I §485.

independent of mediation

no alternative

sensory experience

is a pencil", ' writes A. J. Ayer, 'there is a sense in which they do embody inferences. But then these inferences must have some foundation. There must, in Bertrand Russell's terminology, be "hard data" on which they are based. And Hume's impressions are simply these hard data, called by another name.'[5]

'hard data'

Finally, the empiricist has a distinctive view about the kind of information our senses can give us (cf. my reference in section 1 to the contentiousness of Hare's notion of 'fact'). The peculiarity of his view is that he acknowledges as real, or objective, only those entities which are denoted by the terminology of the experimental sciences, or by other (more familiar) terminology which is reducible to that of the experimental sciences. Because he holds that the 'fabric of the world'[6] is composed of these entities and these alone, he cannot allow that there is anything else which might impinge on our senses; consequently, he cannot admit the idea of an immediate experience which is the experience of a non-scientific subject-matter, such as Moore's notion of goodness as a non-natural but directly intuited property. J. L. Mackie has spoken, in this context, of an 'argument from queerness' which the non-cognitivist moral philosopher can use: 'If there were objective values, they would be entities or qualities or relations of a very strange sort, utterly different from anything else in the universe. Correspondingly, if we were aware of them, it would have to be by some special faculty of moral perception or intuition, utterly different from our ordinary ways of knowing everything else.'[7] The argument is, of course, circular in that it assumes our 'ordinary way of knowing' to be the way recognized by the non-cognitivist, viz. the recording of canonical interpretations of our sense-impressions in a language acceptable to natural science.

experimental sciences

I referred above to the 'impressions' of the empiricist tradition as 'primitive phenomena of consciousness'. It will be remembered that non-cognitivism, the tendency in moral

---

[5] A. J. Ayer, *Hume* (1980), p. 40.
[6] Cf. J. L. Mackie, *Ethics: Inventing Right and Wrong* (1977), p. 15.
[7] Ibid., p. 38.

philosophy which is associated with that tradition, also bases itself upon the idea of a 'primitive phenomenon of consciousness': that of the 'passion' as an 'original existence'. Both 'sense-impressions' and 'passions' are supposed to force themselves upon us unbidden; but when we seek to put the contents of our consciousness into words, a different kind of linguistic act is generated respectively by each. The difference can be expressed by saying that the empiricist distinguishes an active and a passive mode of judgement. Thus in our capacity as describers of the world, we passively read off what we say from the facts (as displayed by our senses) according to a set of rules (the definitions we have given to our words):[8] while in our capacity as judges of value, we are active in the sense that we are responding, emotionally, to those facts, and perhaps making a bid to exert control over the emotional dispositions of others.

In the twentieth century, the opposition set up by empiricism between these two modes of judgement has been reformulated in terms of an alleged distinction between the 'descriptive' and the 'expressive' functions of language itself. This distinction gives rise to the idea that there are two contrasting kinds of meaning that words can have: on one hand 'descriptive' or 'cognitive' meaning; on the other, 'evaluative' or 'emotive' meaning. The cognitive meaning of a word is conceived, on Fregean lines, as consisting in its systematic individual contribution to the truth-conditions of sentences in which it occurs; while emotive meaning is, perhaps, conceived as attaching to words in virtue of their systematic contribution to the aptitude of a sentence for expressing or evoking dispositions of the will, and thus for influencing the behaviour of those addressed.

This opposition is represented as an absolute one: the evaluative meaning of a word is not held to play any part in determining the truth-conditions of sentences containing it. This is what makes it possible for Hare to assert (cf. section 4 above) that the evaluative meaning of (say) the term 'courageous' could be, as it were, drained off from it without

---

[8] Cf. Wittgenstein, *PI* I §292.

prejudice to the extension of the concept – or, in other words, that we could in principle have a concept 'courageous' which was predicated of exactly the same range of actions, persons, etc. as currently, but without our actually having any positive moral attitude towards 'courageous' actions, etc. as such.

dualism about meaning

The same dualism about meaning underlies the empiricist view that there is no such thing as an objectively valid inference from descriptive premisses to a practical conclusion. This reflects the idea which we have seen to be characteristic of non-cognitive theories of ethics, namely, that the content of our moral attitudes is not subject to any logical or rational constraints.

no constraints

It is really the segregation of 'reason' and 'sentiment', or 'reason' and 'passion', in the faculty psychology of the eighteenth century[9] which has been perpetuated in the 'fact/value distinction' of modern analytical philosophy. As in the eighteenth century, so in the twentieth, non-cognitive theorists of ethics have identified judgements of value not by the occurrence in them of any specific vocabulary, but simply by their possession of the abstract property of being 'action-guiding': a property which non-cognitivists deny, *a priori*, to statements about the objective world. The reason for that denial is to be found in these theorists' distinctive conception of the world's 'fabric', as noted above: the conception, that is, according to which the only objectively real entities, qualities or relations are those referred to in natural-scientific discourse, or in other kinds of discourse reducible thereto. This idea of the objective world – that of which human knowledge aspires to be an adequate representation – as something morally or spiritually dead (or, as John McDowell has put it, 'motivationally inert'),[10] is widely

fact/value distinction

action-guiding

---

[9] Cf. Hume, *Treatise*, p. 457: 'Since morals . . . have an influence on the actions and affections, it follows, that they cannot be deriv'd from reason; and that because reason alone . . . can never have any such influence. Morals excite passions, and produce or prevent actions. Reason of itself is utterly impotent in this particular. The rules of morality, therefore, are not conclusions of our reason.'

[10] John McDowell, 'Are Moral Requirements Hypothetical Imperatives?' in *PASS* (1978), p. 19.

accepted as the central achievement of the European Enlightenment: at once an intellectual coming-of-age with respect to natural science, and a painful loss of the former conviction of moral meaning or unity in nature.[11]

It is also the doctrine of the early Wittgenstein, who writes in the *Tractatus* that the meaning or value of the world must lie 'outside the world' (*T* 6.41). The facts of which that world is the totality (cf. *T* 1.1) are *natural-scientific* facts. Thus, when all possible scientific questions have been answered, there are no questions left (*T* 6.52) – for scientific questions are the only ones which can be framed in language at all. The author of the *Tractatus* differs from non-cognitivists such as Stevenson and Hare in that he regards value as 'transcendental' (*T* 6.421), while they regard it as subjective (in the sense previously indicated); but he does, at any rate, concur with them in not recognizing moral entities as part of the 'fabric of the world'.

--------- 6 ---------

We must now consider the rival metaphysical position associated with moral realism. The whole contrast between this and the non-cognitive theories is encapsulated in the realist's rejection of the 'fact/value distinction' on which empiricist thinkers have insisted. We have already seen the evidence of this rejection in the realist's idea of a 'moral fact', i.e. the idea of a circumstance recorded by an indicative sentence which may be used simultaneously to report on the world and to supply a non-hypothetical rational justification for doing something (section 3 above).

Correspondingly, moral realism involves a rejection of the empiricist's twofold classification of the functions of language (description versus expression), and of the associated distinction between cognitive and emotive meaning. It treats the 'action-guiding force' of any judgement which can be held (on phenomenological grounds) to possess such force as a

---

[11] Cf. Charles Taylor, *Hegel* (1975), ch. 1 passim.

function of the *cognitive* meaning of that judgement – or, ultimately, of its primitive semantic components. For this theory of ethics is inspired by a philosophy of language whose initial assumption is that 'in rendering linguistic comprehension intelligible a central, ineliminable role will be played by a notion of the *strict and literal meaning of a sentence*.'[1] As applied to moral discourse, that assumption yields the idea that to be competent in such discourse is to have a grasp of the literal assertion-conditions of moral sentences; and this is construed by the realist as a grasp of their (literal) *truth*-conditions.

literal meaning [margin annotation]

truth-conditions [margin annotation]

I commented earlier (sections 3 and 5) on the 'queerness' of this idea from the point of view of analytical philosophy and of liberal-individualist 'common sense'. I mentioned, too, Dummett's epistemological challenge to those who talk of 'realities' which, from that point of view, are non-standard: we learn nothing from such talk, Dummett has claimed, unless it can be fleshed out with some account of our *mode of access* to the relevant class of true judgements. 'Even the most thorough-going realist,' he writes, 'must grant that we could hardly be said to grasp what it is for a statement to be true if we had no conception whatever of how it might be known to be true; there would, in such a case, be no substance to our conception of its truth-condition.' And Dummett goes on to say that it must be possible to specify *non-trivially* the appropriate method of verification for any class of statements whose meaning is to be conceived in realist terms. Even if we have to appeal for this purpose to some notion of superhuman powers of apprehension, these, he argues, 'must always bear a recognizable relation to the powers which we in fact possess; they must be analogous to, or an extension of, our actual powers.'[2]

In what follows, I shall confine my attention to one particular account which the moral realist can give of his position: an account designed to meet the legitimate demand, implicit in the sentences just quoted from Dummett, for an

[1] Cf. Platts, *Ways of Meaning*, p. 2.
[2] Dummett in Evans and McDowell (eds), p. 100.

assurance that that position is not mystical or anti-scientific in character (cf. section 3 above). In order to escape the charge of being anti-scientific, a realist theory of ethics would have to meet the following requirements: (1) that it render our mastery of moral language intelligible without suggesting that, in gaining that mastery, we are taught to do anything more than suit our linguistic responses to the circumstances which variously impinge on our awareness; (2) that it be consistent with the view that physics, at its own level, can supply a unified and explanatorily adequate description of reality.

The position I shall consider is a form of moral realism derived from the later philosophy of Wittgenstein. Such a view is well-qualified to meet the requirements just mentioned; for it is a *naturalistic* realism, in the non-technical sense that it represents moral discourse – like other human institutions – as embedded in the world of (physical) nature. I shall try to construct an idealized version of this position as I understand it, so that my discussion will have as its object a philosophical theory rather than a specific philosopher or group of philosophers.

What Wittgenstein offers us, in the *Philosophical Investigations* and elsewhere in his later work, is a homogeneous or 'seamless' conception of language. It is a conception free from invidious comparisons between different regions of discourse, or (relatedly) between different aspects of mental activity. Just as the early Wittgenstein considers all *propositions* to be of equal value (*T* 6.4), so the later Wittgenstein – who has, however, abandoned his previous normative notion of what counts as a proposition – regards all *language-games* as being of 'equal value' in the transcendental sense of the *Tractatus*. On this view, the only legitimate role for the idea of 'reality' is that in which it is coordinated with (or, as Wittgenstein might have said – cf. *PI* I §136 – 'belongs with') the metaphysically neutral idea of 'talking about something'.[3]

---

[3] There is a parallel here with the following words from Wittgenstein's 'Lecture on Ethics' of 1929 (*Philosophical Review* (1965), p. 11): 'I am tempted to say that the right expression in language for the miracle of the

(Thus *OC* §66: 'I make assertions about reality.') It follows that 'reference to an objective reality' cannot intelligibly be set up as a target which some propositions – or rather, some utterances couched in the indicative mood – may hit, while others fall short. If something has the grammatical form of a proposition, then it *is* a proposition: philosophical considerations cannot discredit the way in which we classify linguistic entities for other, non-philosophical, purposes. (This is, of course, merely an instance of the principle that 'philosophy may in no way interfere with the actual use of language' (*PI* I §124); more specifically, however, cf. *PI* I §373: 'Grammar tells what kind of object anything is.')

The only way, then, in which an indicative statement can fail to describe reality is by *not being true* – i.e. by virtue of reality not being as the statement declares it to be. Thus Wittgenstein writes of the temptation to 'say that our way of speaking does not describe the facts as they really are. As if, for example the proposition "he has pains" could be false in some other way than by that man's *not* having pains. As if the form of expression were saying something false even when the proposition *faute de mieux* asserted something true.' (*PI* I §402).

The moral realist who bases himself on Wittgenstein's vision of language will presumably think of the non-cognitivist as one who finds fault with the indicative *form* of a moral judgement, even when it is a judgement to which he himself assents. He will take just this view, for instance, of the position defended by Mackie: for Mackie's doctrine – while conceding that it is not a waste of time to seek a reflective equilibrium within our moral outlook – nevertheless '[takes] the form of an error theory, admitting that a belief in objective values is built into ordinary moral thought and language, but holding that this ingrained belief is false.'[4]

---

existence of the world, though it is not any proposition *in* language, is the existence of language itself . . .'

[4] Mackie, *Ethics,* pp. 105-7, 48-9.

Thus Wittgenstein's view of language confirms us – provisionally, at least[1] – in the pre-reflective habit of treating as 'descriptive', or fact-stating, all sentences which qualify by grammatical standards as propositions. Instead of confining the descriptive function to those parts of language that deal with a natural-scientific subject-matter, it allows that function to pervade all regions of discourse irrespective of content.

propositions

pervasive functions

What, then, becomes of the other function of language recognized by empiricism – the 'expressive' function which corresponds to the 'value' term of the 'fact/value distinction'?

The answer is that on the view we are now considering, this function also comes to pervade language in its entirety. Linguistic meaning as such takes on the character identified by the empiricist as 'emotive' or 'expressive'. In other words, 'fact' and 'value' (in the metaphysical sense of those words) *coalesce* – and assertoric discourse is now seen to accommodate both impartially. Remaining for the moment with the terminology of empiricism, we can say that 'value' is thus reabsorbed into the 'real world' from which the non-cognitive theories expelled it.

fact and value coalesce

value is 'reabsorbed'

But can it seriously be maintained that in reporting on the objective features of our world – for example, on rock formations or aerodynamics or the digestive system of the earthworm – we are doing anything that could properly be characterized in terms of emotional expression?

This thesis can be, and has been, maintained *at the same level of abstraction* as the thesis that moral (and other evaluative) judgements are distinctively emotive, or otherwise non-cognitive, in character. For, like the 'fact/value distinction', it is integral to a specific metaphysical position: one which is best understood precisely in terms of its differences from the empiricist position outlined in section 5 above.

same level of abstraction

We can consider this different metaphysics first of all in its

---

[1] 'Provisionally': an alternative interpretation of the contrast between description and evaluation will be introduced in section 17 below.

linguistic aspect. Here it entails (a) a repudiation of the idea of speech as an instrument for the communication of thought, and (b) a turning away from the 'calculus' model of natural language.[2] It sees the use of signs, rather, as an organic outgrowth of human culture. It condemns as incoherent the empiricist tendency to think of word-meaning *in general* as a function of an explicit agreement among prospective speakers, made before speech begins: for, as the theory points out, it is only where language of a pre-technical, or expressive, kind already exists that individuals can confer to create a technical, semantically rigid language.[3] In this picture, ordinary speech is conceived, not on a model suggested by natural science or technology, but on one suggested by art. The expression of thought in language is likened to its expression in any other artistic medium: until it is embodied in the medium, it is without determinate content. Or, to state the same point in a philosophical idiom that is especially congenial to it: a thought is a 'spiritual' entity in the sense that its essence is not specific, but individual, so that it is not merely accidental but essential to such an entity that it should achieve a concrete realization.[4]

---

[2] For Wittgenstein's explicit rejection of this model, see *BB* p. 25.

Remember that in general we don't use language according to strict rules – it hasn't been taught us by means of strict rules, either. *We*, in our discussions on the other hand, constantly compare language with a calculus proceeding according to exact rules.

This is a very one-sided way of looking at language. In practice we very rarely use language as such a calculus. For not only do we not think of the rules of usage – of definitions, etc. – while using language, but when we are asked to give such rules, in most cases we aren't able to do so. We are unable clearly to circumscribe the concepts we use; not because we don't know their real definition, but because there is no real "definition" to them. To suppose that there *must* be would be like supposing that whenever children play with a ball they play a game according to strict rules.

When we talk of language as a symbolism used in an exact calculus, that which is in our mind can be found in the sciences and in' mathematics. Our ordinary use of language conforms to this standard of exactness only in rare cases . . .

[3] Cf. R. G. Collingwood, *The Principles of Art* (1938), p. 225.

28

The expressive theorist, then, denies the logical priority of thought over the language in which it is made manifest. It is for this reason that he cannot accept the instrumental conception of language, which posits a relation between two logically distinct entities: thought (which is in our minds) and language (by means of which we make our thoughts accessible to one another). *[expressivist theory]* *[no instrumental conception of language]*

The expressivist view of language did not originate with Wittgenstein, though he may be said to have reinvented it for himself in the process of transition from his earlier to his later philosophy. As far as the modern world is concerned (I pass over the ancient: an expressivist doctrine is developed, for instance, by Lucretius),[5] it seems to have originated in the eighteenth century with Vico and Herder, two theorists of culture whose work may be seen as a reaction against the scientism of the Enlightenment, and as an initial contribution to the thought of the Romantic movement. Hegel took as the foundation of his system the idea – owed ultimately to these two thinkers – that universal mind is both historically and conceptually prior to individual mind, and that the collective mind of a community is expressed in its peculiar social institutions, apart from which it has no reality.

Marx and Engels (in *The German Ideology*) reaffirm the view that thought is logically inseparable from its physical manifestation in language, and that language itself arises only in the context of a collective life:

> From the start the 'spirit' is afflicted with the curse of being 'burdened' with matter, which here makes its appearance in the form of agitated layers of air, sounds, in short, of language. Language is as old as consciousness, language *is* practical consciousness that exists also for other men, and for that reason alone it really exists for me personally as well; language, like consciousness, *[language as consciousness]*

---

[4] Cf. M. B. Foster, *The Political Philosophies of Plato and Hegel* (1935), pp. 26-7; also Taylor, p. 16: on the view we are considering, 'the realization of a form clarifies or makes determinate what that form is'.

[5] Lucretius, *De Rerum Natura*, V 1028ff.

only arises from the need, the necessity, of intercourse with other men. . . . Consciousness is, therefore, from the very beginning a social product, and remains so as long as men exist at all.[6]

Essential to their position, however, is a materialist conception of the shared way of life in which language is embedded. Marx's '8th Thesis on Feuerbach' states that 'All social life is essentially *practical*. All mysteries which lead theory to mysticism find their rational solution in human practice and in the rational comprehension of this practice.'[7]

language as social institution

'acting'

Wittgenstein, too, sees language as a social institution[8] which is grounded, like other institutions, in the shared way of life of a community. For him, 'It is our *acting* which lies at the bottom of the language-game' (*OC* §204): we shall see in more detail below (sections 14-15) what is meant by this. One remark of Wittgenstein's which deserves immediate comment, however, concerns the process of language-*acquisition*: 'The child learns to believe a host of things,' he says; 'i.e. it learns to act according to these beliefs' (*OC* §144). This account gets its point through opposition to the rival account criticized in the opening pages of *PI*, which – in keeping with the empiricist view that meaning is, or ought to be, fully determined prior to use – represents language-learning as a two-stage process: first we are taught the names of objects, then a selection of facts about those objects. Wittgenstein rejects all this, advancing instead the idea that a process of training

training

(not unlike the manipulative training we use upon animals) turns the child little by little into the sort of creature to whom we *ascribe* (a) beliefs, (b) a grasp of the meanings of

beliefs and meanings

individual words. There is no determinate moment when it becomes correct to credit him with either of these things; yet, sooner or later, our attitude towards the child becomes

---

[6] Marx and Engels, *The German Ideology*, ed. C. J. Arthur (1974), pp. 50-1.
[7] Ibid., p. 122.
[8] Cf. *RFM* VI§32: 'A game, a language, a rule, is an institution.'

an 'attitude towards a soul' (cf. *PI* II p. 178). Meanwhile, from the child's point of view, 'light dawns gradually' (cf. *OC* §141) over the propositional content of the total language-game into which he is being initiated; and the goal of that initiation is a practical one, namely, that he should be able to participate in the practice of talking to other people.

This practical training is not something which could in principle be replaced by theoretical instruction in the use of language. Wittgenstein writes (*Z* §432): 'I describe the language-game "Bring something red" to someone who can himself already play it. Others I might at most teach it.' The following remark of John McDowell's might be taken as a gloss upon this: 'A theory of sense [i.e. cognitive meaning] can reasonably be required to play a part in a systematic description of what is involved in understanding the language of which it is a theory; that is quite different from its being called upon to serve as a possible means to the acquisition of a command of its object-language.'[9]

—— 8 ——

In the context of an expressivist theory of language which maintains (a) that thought is necessarily embodied in a linguistic medium, (b) that language is necessarily embedded in a shared form of life, we can arrive at a better understanding of the property of *semantic depth* which is ascribed to moral concepts by Mark Platts.

This property, according to Platts, is displayed in the fact that 'experience can enrich our concept of what, say, courage is; our concept can meanwhile remain the same.'[1] We start, in other words, with a minimal, schematic understanding of the meaning of a moral term, such as might be captured in a

---

[9] John McDowell, 'Truth-conditions, Bivalence and Verificationism', in Evans and McDowell (eds), p. 56.

[1] Platts, *Ways of Meaning*, p. 262.

dictionary definition;[2] then, by exploring those aspects of life which moral terms pick out, we can *enrich* our understanding of those terms without it being the case that we ever come to mean something *different* by 'courage' (for example) from what we meant at an earlier stage of the exploratory process. The significance of the alleged 'semantic depth' of moral concepts is that it explains how the truth-condition of a moral sentence may transcend a speaker's recognitional abilities even if he knows the meanings of the relevant moral words – a possibility on which Platts considers himself bound to insist, given his own realist approach to the theory of meaning in general.[3]

Moral discourse certainly represents a clear case in which the 'calculus' model of language is inapplicable. Learning the meaning of a moral word is, as Platts correctly implies, not a matter of sudden and total enlightenment (like the sudden apprehension of a mathematical rule: cf. Wittgenstein, *PI* I §151 and context, 'Now I understand!') This is an area which conforms, rather, to Wittgenstein's description of how we gain sound judgement as to the genuineness of expressions of feeling (*PI* II p. 227): 'Can one learn this knowledge? Yes; some can. Not, however, by taking a course in it, but through "experience" . . . What one acquires here is not a technique; one learns correct judgements. There are also rules, but they do not form a system, and only experienced people can apply them right.'

We saw in section 7 above, that, on Wittgenstein's account of language-acquisition, 'learning correct judgements' involves learning a particular mode of *behaviour*. The use of moral concepts by individual speakers (as they progressively

---

[2] Platts' account is flawed here, in terms of the Wittgensteinian position outlined in section 7 above, by his apparently driving a wedge between possession of this 'austere', *theoretical*, grasp upon a concept, and possession of a *practical* grasp upon the conditions of its application. But this does not, I think, prejudice the general interpretation which I shall offer.

[3] Ibid., p. 245. For more on the idea of recognition-transcendent moral truth, and on ways in which the realist can deal with scepticism in that connection, see sections 18-19 below.

acquire competence in that area of language) is grounded in an diversified capacity increasingly diversified capacity for participation in social practices, i.e. practices mediated by language or other symbolic systems. But the induction of an individual into a communal form of life is a gradual process: until it is gradual process complete, there will be some 'correct judgements' which escape him, and hence some moral facts which transcend his awareness.

In order to convince ourselves that, despite all the imperfections of his sensitivity to the various manifestations of courage, it can still be true to say of an individual that he knows what the word 'courage' means, we can refer to the notion of a 'scale of forms', borrowed from Plato and scale of 'forms' Aristotle and perpetuated within the idealist tradition. Collingwood explains the application of this idea in his account of the proper method of defining a philospchical concept. Such definition takes the form of a process in the course of which our thinking about a certain subject-matter becomes 'clearer and more complete'. We think of the chosen concept, in the first instance, as 'specifying itself in a form so rudimentary that anything less would fail to embody the concept at all'; then we proceed to 'modify this minimum definition by adding new determinations, each implied in what went before, but each introducing into it qualitative changes as well as additions and complications. Finally, a phase will be reached in which the definition contains, explicitly stated, all that can be found in the concept; the adequate concepts definition is now adequate to the thing defined and the process is as complete as we can make it.'[4]

process of definition

However, as Collingwood has previously remarked, each term in a scale of semantic forms 'sums up the whole scale to that point. Wherever we stand in the scale, we stand at a culmination . . . because the specific form at which we stand is the generic concept itself, so far as our thought yet conceives it.'[5]

The bearing of this upon Platts' idea of semantic depth

---

[4] R. G. Collingwood, *An Essay on Philosophical Method* (1933), pp. 100-1.
[5] Ibid., p. 89.

should be clear. The pursuit of moral understanding, success in which is reflected in an ever more subtle apprehension of the meaning of moral words, seems (on Platts' account) to resemble the project of philosophical definition by ascent through a 'scale of forms'. As we make additions to our repertoire of 'correct judgements' in connection with a given moral concept, we acquire the *intuitive* basis for our next step up the scale of forms of *reflective* specification of the content of that concept.

Failing such additions to our experience, the last specification we gave will remain adequate, since it will make explicit 'all that can be found in the concept' – sc. all that can be found *by us,* on the basis of the total array of judgements we have had occasion to make, using that concept.

Moreover, at any given moment in the life-history of the individual, his moral understanding will be complete in the sense that it will be a *culmination* – what he understands at that moment will sum up the whole evolution of his grasp upon moral concepts up to that point. This is the reflection in language of the fact that an individual's induction into the form of life of his community also partakes of the character of a scale of forms, each phase of which is a culmination: at each moment the individual will be a person who is intellectually complete as far as he goes. He will be a competent participant in various rule-governed practices, and will therefore possess an identity as a rational (social) being, even though other such practices exist in which he has *not* learnt to participate – perhaps because they have never impinged upon him.

The same can be said about the historical development of whole cultures. Social practices may gain in complexity over time, but this does not mean that earlier, and simpler, phases of the developmental scale were flawed by the absence of subtle features that did not arise until later. Thus Wittgenstein writes (Z §372): 'One imagines the feeble-minded under the aspect of the degenerate, the essentially incomplete, as it were in tatters. And so under that of disorder instead of a more primitive order (which would be a far more fruitful way of looking at them).' This echoes a passage at *BB* p. 19:

34

'The contempt for what seems the less general case in logic springs from the idea that it is incomplete. It is in fact confusing to talk of cardinal arithmetic as something special as opposed to something more general. Cardinal arithmetic bears no mark of incompleteness; nor does an arithmetic which is cardinal and finite.'

The sense in which, according to Platts, we possess from the very outset of moral experience a grasp of the meaning of moral concepts which is adequate as far as it goes, parallels the sense in which the more rudimentary phases in a scale of semantic or other developmental forms are adequate, as far as *they* variously go, to the concept they instantiate. They are not rendered absolutely inadequate by the fact of their relative inadequacy when compared with later phases of the scale.

Is there a moment when we can say we have achieved a *fully* adequate specification of a philosophical concept – or, in terms of Platts' account, a fully adequate understanding of a moral word? Platts thinks not: 'We must rest content with the thought that at death *approximate* understanding is all that we can hope for.' I believe we shall come nearer the truth if we distinguish two interpretations of the question at issue here, which is: can we ever get to the top of a scale of semantic forms? In that case I think the correct answer will be that, relative to the form of life in which we participate, we can in principle reach the top of the scale; but that, in an absolute sense, we cannot do so – for our form of life will undergo further historical development in future, so that the semantic depth of, for example, the concept of courage (as employed in our community) will be enhanced in ways that go beyond the experience of any existing speaker.

If this is right, then we can, after all, admit the possibility of achieving full understanding of the meaning of moral words, since this will be a concomitant of achieving full competence in the use of moral language. Individuals who succeeded in doing this would be in a position analogous to that of the philosopher himself, as described by Collingwood:

The philosopher, in constructing a system, has his place

35

in a scale whose structure is such that every term in it sums up the whole scale to that point; however far up the scale he goes, he never comes to an absolute end of the series, because by reaching this point he already comes in sight of new problems; but he is always at a relative end, in the sense that, wherever he stands, he must know where he stands and sum up his progress hitherto, on pain of making no progress henceforth.[6]

The philosopher here is said to be 'at a relative end' not just in that he has constructed a system *of some sort*, but in that he has constructed a system which 'arises by objective necessity out of his situation in the history of thought and the problem with which he is confronted':[7] his work gives philosophical expression to the experience of participating in a particular form of life at a particular historical moment, just as the understanding possessed by a fully competent user of moral language expresses that experience in a different dimension.

───── 9 ─────

In section 6 we noted that Wittgenstein's later philosophy embodies a 'homogeneous' conception of language.

The homogeneity of language is not, of course, asserted at the phenomenal level (the level at which we 'describe language-games', cf. *PI* I §486), for there are manifestly 'countless different kinds of use of what we call "symbols", "words", "sentences"' (*PI* I §23). It is asserted at the metaphysical level – the level at which empiricism drives a wedge between factual and evaluative meaning. Wittgenstein's view of language implicitly denies any metaphysical role to the idea of 'reality'; it denies that we can draw any intelligible distinction between those parts of assertoric discourse which do, and those which do not, genuinely *describe* reality. This is an instance of the principle that 'if the

---

[6] Ibid., p. 191.
[7] Ibid., p. 192.

words "language", "experience", "world", have a use, it must be as humble a one as that of the words "table", "lamp", "door" ' (*PI* I §97): the 'humility' in question here consists in an absence of metaphysical pretension.

As with 'reality', so with 'knowledge'. On the present view, knowledge can no more be *elucidated* in terms of rationally justified belief than truth can be elucidated in terms of correspondence with reality. It is not that the postulated conceptual connection is spurious: the link between the idea of knowledge and that of cogent evidence is real enough. The point is, rather, that all we can hope to gain by focusing attention on that link is a sharpened awareness of the grammar of our language; what we cannot hope to gain is a substantial metaphysical insight of the kind the empiricist was looking for in this area.

The reason why such an insight is not forthcoming coincides with the reason why none is forthcoming from the 'correspondence theory of truth'. It resides in our lack of access to any distinction between those of our beliefs which are *actually true,* and those which are merely *held true by us.* No such distinction can survive our conscious recognition that some human authority has to *decide* the claim of any proposition to be regarded as true – and, accordingly, that the objective validity of an assertion or an argument is always at the same time something of which human beings (those human beings who *call* it 'objectively valid') are subjectively persuaded. This kind of subjective conviction may be either direct or indirect; it is indirect when, as constantly happens, we accept an opinion from a source that we believe to be trustworthy.

We saw in section 5 above that, for the empiricist, the making of a perceptual judgement such as 'That's a pencil' necessarily involves an inference from 'hard data' supplied by our senses. Wittgenstein, by contrast, rejects the idea of a system of rules connecting particular sensory inputs with particular forms of words which register them correctly (cf. *PI* I §§292; 485). He thus reiterates, in effect, the standard objection to foundational theories of knowledge. That objection takes the form of a dilemma. On one hand, if we are to

37

think of perceptual judgement as involving a matching-up of sentences with sensory inputs, we must think of each of these sensory inputs as having a determinate individual character; but, since the latter cannot be specified except in language, we must acknowledge (as stated above) that human speakers are the final arbiters of what that character actually is, i.e. of what evidence their senses are presenting to them. The canonical description of sensory input thus falls within the scope of Wittgenstein's considerations on rule-following (cf. section 14 below), which would make the correctness of a perceptual judgement a function of human linguistic practice and not of fidelity to the supposed 'hard data' of individual awareness. On the other hand, if we are to think of reality as impinging on us in the guise of an as yet unconceptualized sensory manifold, we shall be unable to make sense of the idea of *matching up* sentences with objective circumstances: unable, therefore, to make sense of the empiricist notion of 'inference' from sensory data to propositional conclusions.

Michael Williams sums up the difficulty as follows:

> In so far as the content of immediate experience can be expressed, the sort of awareness we have in our apprehension of the given is just another type of perceptual judgement and hence no longer [in] contact with anything which is *merely given*. But if the content of immediate experience turns out to be ineffable or non-propositional, then the appeal to the given loses any appearance of fulfilling an explanatory role in the theory of knowledge: specifically, it cannot explicate the idea that knowledge rests upon a perceptual foundation.[1]

The alternative to a theory which makes sensory evidence the ultimate rational basis of knowledge is to renounce altogether (in face of its seeming incoherence) the idea that such a basis is needed – to hold, in other words, that knowledge can 'stand without foundations'.[2] This does not,

---

[1] Michael Williams, *Groundless Belief* (1977), p. 30.
[2] Wiggins, 'Truth, Invention . . .', p. 377 n. 2.

of course, involve rejecting the very idea of the rational justification of beliefs and actions; what it does imply, however, is that the process of justification is not regulated by the concept of an absolute or rationally irrebuttable end-point (e.g. in physical description, conformity to sensory evidence; in ethics, conduciveness to maximum utility), but instead is relative to a context and to the expectations of an audience.

In the normal course of events, demands for justification – whether theoretical or practical – tend to elicit the sort of response which the questioner will find relevant and plausible: otherwise, as Wittgenstein would point out, the language-game of justification would not exist. But if such demands are pressed beyond a certain point (perversely – as, for example, by a child or a metaphysician), the supply will run out and the questioner will be brushed aside with: 'This is simply what I do' (*PI* I §217; cf. *OC* §148, *Z* §309, etc.). And this response is not a symptom of pig-headedness, but an essential feature of the use of language – which, as we have seen, is represented by Wittgenstein as an activity interwoven with the total system of behaviour of a community. (That the 'dogmatism of ordinary language', as we may call it, is not indicative of pig-headedness is a fact whose importance can easily be overlooked: see sections 22 and 48 below.)

The practice of talking about an objective world rests, according to Wittgenstein, not upon an alleged rational foundation in our sensory experience but upon certain material facts – facts about the 'natural history' of language-users (cf. *PI* I §25; *OC* §617). Thus, for example, it is our possession of a common perceptual structure which underlies the use of colour-predicates: our agreement with respect to attributions of colour is what makes objective discourse about colours *possible*, even though that agreement itself is not what we are talking about when we talk about the colour of an object (*Z* §430). Indeed, logic itself 'belongs to the natural history of man' (*RFM* VI §49): propositions of logic, though they do not *assert* the existence of an agreement among speakers, depend none the less on the *fact* of such agreement.

It is in this sense that David Pears can correctly ascribe to Wittgenstein the idea that 'objectivism, in its only tenable form, collapses into anthropocentrism.'[3]

Thus Wittgenstein's conception of language incorporates a non-foundational epistemology which displays the notions of objectivity (sound judgement) and rationality (valid reasoning) as grounded in *consensus* – theoretical in the first instance, but ultimately practical. The passage about logic, from which I quoted above, continues: 'The agreement of humans that is a presupposition of logic is not an agreement in *opinions,* much less in opinions on questions of logic.' It is an agreement, we are told elsewhere (*PI* I §241), in 'form of life'. And this is the idea to which Wiggins appeals when he writes of 'a shared form of life which is constitutive of rationality itself, can yield proofs [in practical ethics] which are not compulsions but procedures that guide our conceptions, and can still explain our sense that sometimes we have no alternative but to infer this from that.'[4]

The negative side of this insight has been made familiar to us recently in connection with the project of 'radical interpretation' – the interpretation of an unknown language from first principles in the light of empirical (behavioural) evidence. Thus Donald Davidson[5] has condemned as incoherent the suggestion that different linguistic communities might operate with different, and mutually incommensurable, 'conceptual schemes'. The policy of assuming general agreement in propositional attitudes (notably, beliefs and desires) between himself and his subjects is 'not an option' for the interpreter, Davidson argues, 'but a condition of his having a workable theory'; and although the assumption of agreement will doubtless be modified later on, when sufficient progress has been made with the task of interpretation, still 'it is meaningless to suggest that we might fall into massive error by endorsing it.'

---

[3] David Pears, *Wittgenstein* (1971), p. 171.
[4] Wiggins, 'Truth, Invention . . .', p. 369.
[5] Donald Davidson, 'On the Very Idea of a Conceptual Scheme', *Proceedings of the American Philosophical Association* (1973), esp. pp. 18-20.

Davidson concludes, not that all human speakers share a single conceptual scheme, but that the idea of such a scheme lacks application: for 'if we cannot intelligibly say that schemes are different, neither can we intelligibly say that they are one.' The most that can be said about the 'world-view' or 'conceptual scheme' to which we are transcendentally related (related, that is, in the sense intended by the 'incommensurability' theorists to whom Davidson's critique is addressed) is that departure from that world-view 'would not mean that we saw something different, but just that we ceased to see.'[6]

——— 10 ———

We must now consider the bearing of these ideas on the particular philosophical development with which we are concerned: the reaction against non-cognitive theories of ethics. That reaction, as stated earlier, has taken place against the background of a shift in the dominant philosophical assumptions about language. I have tried to characterize this shift as a rediscovery of some of the central themes from the 'expressivist' tradition, and have proposed an exploration of these themes as they appear in the work of the later Wittgenstein – perhaps the most important exponent of that tradition in our own times.[1]

The non-foundational view of knowledge suggested by Wittgenstein's work is especially relevant to a possible resurgence of realist views in moral philosophy. For, just as Wittgenstein rejects any theory which seeks to assign a different metaphysical status to the different kinds of indicative sentences we use, so he rejects any attempt to draw metaphysical boundaries between different parts of our total system of beliefs – boundaries which would separate off a

---

[6] Cf. Bernard Williams, 'Wittgenstein and Idealism', in *Moral Luck* (1981), p. 160.

---

[1] Another contender for this title would be Heidegger, whose work I am not, however, competent to discuss.

privileged class of beliefs, deemed to possess an ultimate rational foundation, from an inferior class not supposed to be thus grounded. His position can be seen as the antithesis of the one taken up by Mackie: 'Intersubjectivity is not objectivity.'[2] This doctrine of Mackie's must be questioned by anyone who accepts Wittgenstein's vision of language – not because Wittgenstein holds that objectivity *means* intersubjectivity (we saw in the previous section that he does not, and we shall see this in its direct application to moral judgement at sections 35–6 below), but because he holds that, materially speaking, there is nothing else for it to *be*. The possibility of discourse about an objective world is determined by the fact of intersubjective agreement; and conversely, where such agreement exists, the particular discourse grounded in it can properly be called 'objective', regardless of its subject-matter.

This homogeneous conception of the relation between language and the world can be understood, by comparison with the empiricist view, either as a levelling-up of evaluative discourse *vis-à-vis* scientific discourse, or as a levelling-down of the latter relative to the former. It tells us that there is just one standard of assertibility which applies to all assertoric uses of language – namely, *truth* (the word whose use is interwoven with that of the word 'proposition', cf. *PI* I §225): not a double standard of (transcendent) truth on one hand and (consensually warranted) assertibility on the other. We are not debarred, on this view, from saying (as we have presumably always said) that the propositions of natural science possess truth-status; but we are shown that there is nothing in the notion of truth, correctly understood, which would prevent us in principle from assigning the same status to the propositions of ethics. In this sense ethics is promoted to the metaphysical status enjoyed already by the sciences. But, on the other hand, this conception of language also tells

---

[2] Mackie, *Ethics*, p. 22: 'Subjective agreement would give intersubjective values, but intersubjectivity is not objectivity.' For the Wittgensteinian position, cf. John McDowell, 'Virtue and Reason', *The Monist* (July 1979), p. 339.

us that the assertibility of sentences belonging to natural science consists (on a philosophical view) in nothing more than what the empiricist would have been willing to concede to sentences belonging to morals or politics or aesthetics: namely, conformity to the consensual standards of sound judgement. In this sense natural science is demoted to the metaphysical status formerly allotted to ethics.

The same levelling process occurs in respect of *rationality* as in respect of *assertibility*. Wittgenstein rejects any *a priori* division of the subject-matter of our thought such that, on one side, we get a region where the going consensual norms of argument cannot be rejected by the individual on pain of irrationality; on the other, a region where the acceptance of the going norms is optional, except in so far as social pressures make it mandatory. Such a division would be motivated by the idea that the rational norms operating in the second region of discourse were only contingently valid – in other words, that their validity rested merely on an inter-subjective uniformity in habits of thought, as against the supposedly absolute validity of the norms in the first region. Instead, Wittgenstein's view of language allows us to point out that it is in fact just as feasible to banish oneself from rational discourse about *moral* questions by rejecting the going canons of evidence, as it is from rational discourse about (say) the physical environment. 'There may be the strictest rules of evidence even where an evaluative conclusion is concerned,' writes Philippa Foot. 'The only recourse of the man who refused to accept the things which counted in favour of a moral proposition as giving him a reason to do certain things or to take up a particular attitude, would be to leave the moral discussion and abjure altogether the use of moral terms.'[3]

Moral reasoning, then, can be restored to parity with scientific reasoning on the strength of its answerability to similarly public canons of evidence. But parity can also be restored by arguing, so to speak, in the opposite direction. Consider, for instance, the following passage from *Language*,

---

[3] Foot, *Virtues and Vices*, p. 105.

Truth and Logic, in which Ayer seeks to show that what we call 'moral argument' is really empirical argument set against a background of shared evaluative attitudes and assumptions:

> When someone disagrees with us about the moral value of a certain action or type of action, we do admittedly resort to argument in order to win him over to our way of thinking. But we do not attempt to show by our arguments that he had the 'wrong' ethical feeling towards a situation whose nature he has correctly apprehended. What we attempt to show is that he is mistaken about the facts of the case . . . We do this in the hope that we have only to get our opponent to agree with us about the nature of the empirical facts for him to adopt the same moral attitude towards them as we do. And as the people with whom we argue have generally received the same moral education as ourselves, and live in the same social order, our expectation is usually justified.[4]

Ayer's account represents moral argument as a procedure whereby one party brings evidence for his conclusion – relevant considerations – in the confidence that the other party, having received much the same kind of education and training and thus having assimilated much the same idea of what counts as a telling argument, will be persuaded of the truth of that conclusion. And this confidence, he suggests, will normally be well-founded.

But this is just the picture drawn by Wittgenstein in connection with *every* manifestation of the activity we call 'reasoning'. A phenomenological description of such activity will never reveal anything more than the attempt to secure agreement by advancing relevant arguments: arguments, that is, whose relevance or cogency is publicly acknowledged among the debating parties because their debate takes place against a background of shared assumptions, and (ultimately) of shared social practice. (They 'belong to a community

---

[4] Ayer, *Language, Truth and Logic,* pp. 146-7.

bound together by science and education' (*OC* §298).) Thus scientific, and even mathematical, rationality turn out to consist in nothing more than conformity to the consensual norms of valid reasoning which happen to apply within the appropriate field.

—— 11 ——

Wittgenstein writes at *RFM* VI §23: 'Not empiricism and yet realism in philosophy, that is the hardest thing.' The difficulty is presumably this: we wish to purge our critical concepts (such as 'truth', 'rationality', 'validity') of the absolutist or transcendent connotations attaching to them in the context of a foundational epistemology; but we do not wish, in the process, to find ourselves abolishing those concepts altogether. What is difficult is to pursue the twofold aim of showing, on one hand, that it does not make sense to look for a source of authority external to human practice which would *certify* as true (e.g.) those propositions that we *call* true; while, on the other hand, resisting the proffered alternative to our former, metaphysically contaminated use of those concepts – an alternative which would consist simply in jettisoning the concepts in question and replacing them by others. (Thus it might be argued that we should replace 'true' by 'assertible', and 'rational' by 'in keeping with the prevailing intellectual norms'.)

Wittgenstein evidently feels there is something paradoxical about the programme indicated by the words, 'not empiricism and yet realism'. The appearance of paradox is dispelled, however, when we come to consider that programme in its application to ethics. For in ethics, and in evaluative discourse generally, any move towards realism – that is, towards the view that the assertibility-conditions of evaluative sentences are *truth*-conditions – is *ipso facto* a move away from the empiricist position, which involves a denial that moral judgement is answerable to truth.

In relation to ethics, the suggested programme is not 'hard', but obvious and natural. We renounce empiricism by subscribing to an expressivist theory of language (section 7 above), a non-foundational theory of knowledge (section 9), and a non-transcendent theory of rationality (section 10); and this change of perspective, far from discrediting the critical concepts, allows them to penetrate again into the various regions of discourse from which empiricism has banished them. In particular, the proposed reinterpretation of those concepts makes it possible again to take a rationalist view of morals and politics, without having to revert to a pre-scientific attitude of mind in order to do so.

———— 12 ————

In section 3 I referred to Mark Platts' assertion that moral aspects of a situation are detected intuitively, by 'looking and seeing'. I also noted, however, that Platts explicitly refuses to postulate a 'distinctive faculty' of ethical intuition – a move which has traditionally been prompted by the desire to offer an *explanation* of our capacity for moral judgement, but which satisfies that desire only in a trivial sense.

Non-cognitive theorists of ethics will concur with this refusal. But they will then look to Platts for a response to their own general pattern of argument against ethical intuitionism – the pattern exemplified by Nowell-Smith's objection to the idea of 'moral blindness'. The force of that objection, they will claim, is in no way diminished by Platts' disavowal of faculty psychology.

We are now in a position to see how Platts might have responded to this demand. His use of the visual idiom in ethics could have been made both intelligible and challenging to the non-cognitivist by linking it with a non-foundational theory of knowledge of the kind imputed to Wittgenstein in the foregoing sections.

Platts himself points the way towards such an account when he argues that the relation between moral and non-moral facts is to be understood by analogy with the relation 'between there being a certain arrangement of black dots on a white card and there being a face there pictured to be seen'.

'There is only a face there to be seen,' he continues, 'because the dot arrangement is as it is; the dot arrangement *fixes* (subject, perhaps, to existing conventions of pictorial representation) whether or not there is a face there to be seen. Still we do not *see* the face by *attending* to that dot-arrangement, where that arrangement is characterized in terms free of picture and face-vocabulary . . . Thus we do not *infer* that the face is there from judgements in this non-pictorial, non-facial vocabulary about the arrangement of the black dots.'[1] In the same way, he suggests, we garner moral information directly from the scene that meets our eyes when we turn them in a particular direction: we do not make moral inferences from information of a non-moral kind, despite the fact that ethics as much as any other region of discourse conforms to the general principle that 'for things to be truly describable as we describe them, they need only be (physically) as they are.'[2]

There is a precedent in Wittgenstein's writings for an ethical intuitionism along these lines. The precedent is to be found in what we might call Wittgenstein's 'physicalism of communication': the insight that what is going on in another person's mind is typically made manifest to us – directly, without the mediation of any inference – in the disposition of that person's body. For language is a special case of expressive gesture; it is gesture systematized and subjected to the constraints of a particular form. (This way of thinking is, of course, characteristic of the 'expressivist theory of meaning' discussed in section 7 above.)

With respect to the non-verbal manifestation of emotion, Wittgenstein's remarks about the appraisal of emotional sincerity (cf. section 8 above) give some indication of his views. More explicit, though, is the following (Z §225): '"We *see* emotion." – As opposed to what? We do not see facial contortions and make inferences from them (like a doctor framing a diagnosis) to joy, grief, boredom. We describe a face immediately as sad, radiant, bored, even when we are unable to give any other description of the features . . .' The

---

[1] Platts, *Ways of Meaning,* p. 244.
[2] Cf. James Hopkins, 'Wittgenstein and Physicalism', *PAS* (1974-5), p. 142.

idea expressed here – namely, that the states of consciousness of other persons are sometimes directly present to our awareness – gets its significance by opposition to the idea that emotion is essentially something concealed, so to speak, inside the mind; something which can be ascribed to another person only hypothetically, on the basis of external clues.

Wittgenstein's rejection of this idea in relation to 'raw' emotional states is paralleled by his rejection of it in relation to those mental contents which are mediated by language. These also, on his account, are *manifested in* rather than *evidenced by* the events which constitute our criteria for making an attribution of the relevant state of consciousness. 'If I give anyone an order,' he writes (*PI* I §503), 'I feel it to be *quite enough* to give him signs. And I should never say: this is only words, and I have got to get behind the words. Equally, when I have asked someone something and he gives me an answer (i.e. a sign), I am content – that was what I expected – and I don't raise the objection: but that's a mere answer.' Just as a person's grief or joy, then, can (in a favourable case) be directly perceived in his physical bearing, so can his *meaning me to do so and so* be directly perceived in his physical production of the appropriate sign. In either case it is true to say that 'nothing is concealed' (*PI* I §435) – or, at any rate, that 'what is hidden . . . is of no interest to us' (*PI* I §126). And this continuity is precisely what we should expect to find, given a conception of language in general as an elaboration of our natural repertoire of expressive behaviour.

In the following passage (*Z* §223), it is as though Wittgenstein were assuming the role of referee in the debate between intuitionists and non-cognitivists as to the legitimacy or otherwise of talking about 'moral perception':

"If you only shake free from your physiological prejudices, you will find nothing queer about the fact that the glance of the eye can be seen too." For I also say that I see the look that you cast at someone. And if someone wanted to correct me and say that I don't really *see* it, I should take that for pure stupidity.

On the other hand I have not *made any admissions* by

48

using that manner of speaking, and I should contradict anyone who told me I saw the glance 'just the way' I see the shape and colour of the eye.

For 'naîve language', that is to say our naïve, normal way of expressing ourselves, does not contain any theory of seeing – does not show you a *theory* but only a *concept* of seeing.

Platts, if I understand him correctly, could have clarified his position by explicitly identifying himself with the modest form of intuitionism suggested here. He could have pointed out that an ethical theory which was intuitionistic in this sense would be so simply in virtue of the fact that it did not disregard the license given to us by our 'naïve language' to talk about 'seeing moral aspects of a situation'. This manner of speaking would not involve any ontological 'admissions' which need alarm the non-cognitivist in his capacity as spokesman for the claims of natural science to supply, within its own terms of reference, a total description of the objective world (cf. section 6 above). The non-cognitivist would, indeed, have reason to be alarmed if our talk of 'moral perception' were meant to imply the existence of a realm of *supernatural* entities – the supposed objects of an intuitive 'faculty' which, while not itself physical, was conceived as a species of the same genus as the various physical 'faculties'. For any such idea of parity between physical and non-physical senses would suggest that the natural-scientific description of reality was essentially flawed – inadequate to the task allotted to it – on account of its failure to encompass the various features which those further 'senses' record. But we can now see that it is open to the ethical intuitionist to disclaim that suggestion, for he can explain the relation between moral and physical perception in a different way.

He can also offer a metaphysically inoffensive explanation of what is involved in possessing the 'faculty of moral intuition' – an explanation, that is, which would leave him uncommitted to anything at all in the way of faculty *psychology*. For he need not concede that possession of a *sui generis* 'moral sense', a 'distinctive faculty of ethical intuition', amounts to anything more than possession of the specific range of discursive skills which enable us to report on moral features of the world: the counterpart, in terms of moral judgement, of those skills which enable us correctly to describe a certain configuration of black dots on a white ground as the image of a human face. Moral intuition will then be *sui generis* in so far as the moral description of reality is *sui generis* – i.e. not analysable in terms of some other, non-moral, system of concepts; and the philosophical point of labelling oneself a moral intuitionist will lie, not in any consequences which that view might have for a supposed transcendental psychology, but simply in the implication that moral judgements are to be regarded as non-inferential – that the moral assessment of a situation is not best understood, for example, as the outcome of a weighing-up of the consequences of possible actions in terms of their effects upon human mental states. On the proposed view, it will not be possible in the case of a true proposition of ethics to give a non-trivial answer to the question: '*In virtue of what* is this proposition true?' (cf. section 3 above).

According to this understanding of the intuitionist position, the conception of a *moral fact* or *circumstance* takes its place among those 'problematic conceptions' – problematic, that is (in the view of some) from the standpoint of realist semantics – whose acquisition, in the words of John McDowell, 'is acquisition of competence with the relevant part of a language'. Exercising such a conception, writes McDowell, 'is nothing but exercising the relevant linguistic competence, in speech of one's own or in understanding the speech of others. Puzzlement over how the relevant sort of circumstance can figure in a person's thoughts, if not by way of imagery, is misplaced. The possibility of its figuring in his thoughts is secured . . . by the possibility of its figuring *in his speech*.'[3]

---

[3] John McDowell, 'On "The Reality of the Past"', in Hookway and Pettit (eds.), *Action and Interpretation* (1978), p. 141. I am not sure to what extent the view outlined in the present section brings me into conflict with McDowell's own claim that 'failure to see what a circumstance means, in

These considerations provide a basis for the defence of our proposed intuitionistic moral realism against the type of objection exemplified by Nowell-Smith's argument (cf. section 3 above). We shall see below (sections 14ff.) how far they actually go towards meeting such objections.

———— 13 ————

If Platts had been willing to identify himself more completely with the expressivist conception of language, he could also have arrived at a rational account of what he is condemned to regard as a 'brute fact about moral facts':[1] viz. that their clear perception can provide sufficient grounds for action.

We saw in section 7 that, according to Wittgenstein, 'it is our *acting* which lies at the bottom of the language-game.' The categories employed in natural languages, then, articulate distinctions which are of interest to us in deciding how to act. The presence in our language of any given predicate displays the fact that, on some occasions, we see fit to distinguish between cases – to *treat cases differently* – in a way reflecting the distribution of the property denoted by that predicate. And the degree of ease, or difficulty, with which we can imagine a language lacking the relevant predicate mirrors our capacity, or incapacity, to imagine what it would be like not to care about the distribution of the corresponding property (though imaginative skills of this sort can, of course, be deliberately cultivated).[2]

This emphasis on the shaping of human perceptions by human interests is precisely what makes Wittgenstein's

---

the [morally] loaded sense, is of course compatible with competence, *by all ordinary tests,* with the language used to describe the circumstances; that brings out how loaded the [relevant] notion of meaning . . . is.' ('Are Moral Requirements Hypothetical Imperatives?', p. 22 (emphasis added).)

---

[1] Platts, *Ways of Meaning,* p. 258; cf. also section 3 above.
[2] Many passages in Wittgenstein's later writings seem to affirm the value of such skills; e.g. *PI* II p. 230; *Z* §378.

philosophy 'not empiricist' (cf. section 11 above). For the ideal towards which empiricist thought aspires is a description of reality purged of all elements which reflect the specific concerns of human beings: a description, in other words, couched exclusively in concepts which would not be 'human-relative'.[3] This ideal seems, perversely, to be sponsored by Platts, who believes that his theoretical purposes demand a conception of factual belief as being free from all appetitive elements.[4]

Now the idea that our linguistic categories articulate our practical concerns applies, *a fortiori*, to *moral* categories. These can be seen as registering distinctions which are of *unconditional* practical interest to us in virtue of our concern to live a life deserving of praise and not of contempt. Nothing, short of indifference to that aim, can make moral considerations irrelevant; and we naturally think of them, further, as overriding other kinds of consideration, since there seems to be some incoherence involved in setting aside the constraints imposed on one's conduct by the design one seeks to impress upon one's whole life. This is not, of course, to say that our interest cannot in practice be deflected from moral considerations, temporarily or indeed permanently; but that in so far as such considerations act upon us at all, they do so in a way which is not contingent upon transient circum-

---

[3] Cf. section 47 below.

[4] Platts, *Ways of Meaning*, p. 257. It is interesting to notice that although Platts is inclined to doubt whether there are any mental states which are purely appetitive – since 'all desires appear to involve elements of belief' – the converse doubt does not appear to have struck him. For a characteristically graphic dismissal of the idea of belief uncontaminated by desire, cf. F. Nietzsche, *The Gay Science*, §57: 'You sober people who feel well armed against passion and fantasies and would like to turn your emptiness into a matter of pride and an ornament: you call yourselves realists and hint that the world really is the way it appears to you . . . [But] you are still burdened with those estimates of things that have their origin in the passions and loves of former centuries. Your sobriety still contains a secret and inextinguishable drunkenness. Your love of "reality", for example – oh, that is a primeval "love" . . .'

Cf. also Wittgenstein, *PI* I §473: 'The belief that fire will burn me is of the same kind as the fear that it will burn me.'

stances or projects. Moral judgements, as Stuart Hampshire has written, 'are . . . judgements of unconditional necessity, in the sense that they imply that what must be done is not necessary because it is a means to some independently valued end, but because the action is a necessary part of a way of life and ideal of conduct.'[5]

I have suggested that an expressivist conception of meaning on Wittgensteinian lines supplies an appropriate basis for the realist treatment of moral discourse, and in particular for Platts' claim that there are *features of reality* which can provide sufficient (i.e. non-hypothetical) grounds for action. It supplies that basis in the sense that it allows us to recognize the existence of *propositions* which record the incidence of properties possessing an unconditional practical interest for us. This is all we need for moral realism, taking into account our earlier reflection that the use of the word 'proposition' is interwoven with that of the word 'true', and the latter in turn with that of 'reality'. But if we see moral realism as resting on such a basis, we shall no longer think of the unconditionally action-guiding character of moral perception as a *brute fact*. The reason why it has that character will be found in the line of thought set out above: moral concepts, like the general run of concepts in natural language, exhibit a scheme of practical concerns; they differ from other concepts in that they alone exhibit the *unconditional* concerns arising out of our vision of an intrinsically admirable life. It is because the concerns displayed in moral thinking have this distinctive type of content that moral perceptions, as Platts observes but cannot explain, can provide sufficient – *unconditional* – reasons for action.

The social anthropologist Mary Douglas gives a pleasing example of practical necessity residing in the nature of a situation, as specified in the language of the community concerned. In any culture worthy of the name, she argues, we find various provisions for dealing with ambiguous or anomalous events. 'For example, when a monstrous birth

---

[5] Stuart Hampshire, 'Morality and Pessimism', in Hampshire (ed.), *Public and Private Morality* (1978), p. 13.

occurs, the defining lines between humans and animals may be threatened. If a monstrous birth can be labelled an event of a peculiar kind the categories can be restored. So the Nuer treat monstrous births as baby hippopotamuses, accidentally born to humans and, with this labelling, the appropriate action is clear. They gently lay them in the river where they belong.'[6] The Nuer might say that, when a woman had the misfortune to give birth to a baby hippopotamus, this fact could be directly perceived (who, indeed, could overlook it?); and that anyone who perceived it would be provided, *eo ipso*, with a sufficient reason to take the infant and place it in the river. (If he were subsequently asked to justify his action, he could point out that the baby was a hippopotamus; and this would be a logically complete answer.) But the disposition of the Nuer to describe the case in this way is evidently connected with a broader conception of what is morally or spiritually fitting; and this in turn would be fully intelligible only in the context of their total form of life. And the same thing is true of our own moral perceptions.[7]

14

Returning now to the development of our proposed moral realist position, it will be helpful to reconsider what was meant in section 9 by the statement that according to Wittgenstein's conception of language, objective discourse 'rests upon', or 'is grounded in', a consensus within the speech community – an agreement initially in judgements, but ultimately in actions. The full significance of this claim emerges from Wittgenstein's account of following a rule (*PI* I §§139–242, and associated remarks elsewhere).

It now seems to be widely agreed that the right way to read that account is as a reappraisal of the sense in which rules can

[6] Mary Douglas, *Purity and Danger: an Analysis of the Concepts of Pollution and Taboo* (1966), p. 39.
[7] The relativistic difficulties which suggest themselves at this point will be discussed in section 36 below.

properly be regarded as normative, or 'action-guiding'. Wittgenstein rejects a common conception of the way in which logical or grammatical rules *compel* us, and substitutes an alternative conception of his own. The position rejected by him is one inspired by the view of language which I outlined in section 5, and to which I attached the label 'empiricist'. According to that view, once we give definitions of our words (i.e. rules governing their future use), that use is determined *in a way which owes nothing to the future behaviour or decisions of human beings*. We have the idea, Wittgenstein suggests, that in the rule-governed development of a series 'the steps are *really* already taken, even before [we] take them in writing or orally or in thought' (*PI* I §188). And so we think that as from the moment when we lay down a certain rule for ourselves, failure to conform to the rule consists essentially in deviation from a path prescribed for us by an authority independent of ourselves – the authority of logic.

Wittgenstein recommends a different understanding of logical compulsion. On his account, *we say* that an error has been made in developing a series when a step is taken which we perceive as a deviation from the way the series is developed *by us*. But 'we' are a body of people who have all been subjected, as children, to a basically similar process of training in the use of our native language. And this training is, at any rate in the initial stages, manipulative in character: it essentially involves the exercise of certain powers of control over the learner.[1] To the extent that it eventually ceases to be manipulative, this happens because the learner comes in the course of his training to internalize the goal set before him by his trainers, viz. acquisition of a knack (or complex of knacks) of producing the same behavioural responses as other people in given circumstances.[2] But what is both historically and

---

[1] Cf. *BB* p. 77: 'I am using the word "trained" in a way strictly analogous to that in which we talk of an animal being trained to do certain things. It is done by means of example, reward, punishment and suchlike.'

[2] Cf. Aristotle, *Politics*, II viii: 'It is from habit, and only from habit, that law derives the validity which secures obedience' (trs. Ernest Barker (1946), p. 73).

logically prior to this sort of co-operative learning process is an operation in which coercion has the central place. It is in virtue of our having been subjected to this original, coercive type of training that we can be said to belong to a community which is bound together by a common education. And it is because such training is able to instil uniform patterns of behaviour in different individuals that one specific response to (say) the command 'Add 2!' is *recognized* as constituting obedience to that command – while any lapse (or any anarchic foray) into a variant response will be rejected as 'wrong'. (Thus I, who claim to be competent in simple arithmetic, do not hesitate to say that if a person is asked to add 2 to 3 and gives the answer '6', he has got the sum wrong.) The rejection which operates here turns out, when we examine it in its most primitive form, to be a physical thing: 'I do it, he does it after me; and I influence him by expressions of agreement, rejection, expectation, encouragement. *I let him go his way, or hold him back . . .*' (*PI* I §208; emphasis added. Notice also the prominence of examples involving physical interaction at *PI* I §172, where Wittgenstein is discussing the 'experience of being guided'.)

Elsewhere Wittgenstein reiterates his view that the uniformity of practice which makes objective discourse possible is sustained, ultimately, by material coercion. Thus the laws of inference compel us, he writes (*RFM* I §116), in the same sense as other laws in human society: if we deviate from the usual way of drawing inferences, we shall find ourselves in conflict with society, and also with other aspects of our own practice. So the laws of inference – and the same applies to all norms of meaningful behaviour, of which the use of language is an instance – are social laws, enforced by human agency. If I flout them, certain material penalties will be imposed upon me; and this is, indeed, an element in the meaning of that bullying tone which Wittgenstein so often introduces into his discussions of the finitude of justification (e.g. *Z* §309, '*This* is how we think. *This* is how we act. *This* is how we talk about it.')

The implication is that sanctions will be brought to bear upon anyone who seeks to think, act or talk in a deviant way.

These sanctions may consist in acts of physical violence, as when a child is smacked for doing something 'naughty'; but of course there are other, less direct approaches which are used in cases of greater social complexity. Thus if someone takes himself to be pursuing a particular artistic or scientific discipline, but produces results which fail to meet our standard of good results for that discipline, we say he is no good at what he is doing and we give a material expression to our adverse judgement – for example, by not buying the objects he produces, or by not appointing him to a university lecturing post.

But if, as Wittgenstein maintains, the compulsion exerted by logical laws is grounded in the coercion exerted by a linguistic community upon its individual members, it follows that in respect of the community *as a whole*, the idea of logical compulsion will lack application. For Wittgenstein's account implies that where there is no material agency to coerce, there is no rule to compel; and there is, *ex hypothesi*, no one outside the *total* speech community who could exercise the necessary coercion. No one, that is to say, penalizes the total community if it adopts a different social practice in place of its current one. It is in this sense that 'any logic good enough for a primitive means of communication needs no apology from us' (*OC* §475).[3]

In relation to the community itself, then, as distinct from its constituent members, linguistic rules are not prescriptive but descriptive. They are abstract representations of what is actually done by speakers: representations, in other words, of particular aspects of the use of language. As such, they are *read off from* the various collective practices which constitute

---

[3] Of course, a change in social practice may incur certain *natural* penalties, sc. if it is not ecologically viable; in that case it would presumably not qualify as 'good enough for a primitive means of communication', since *any* means of communication is dependent on the existence of a sustainable form of life. But natural (ecological) sanctions are not imposed by any (empirical) *agency*, and so they do not represent an objection to the claim that the practice of a community is not subject to the same sort of constraints as the practice of its individual members.

linguistic behaviour; they do not *govern* those practices *qua* collective. The moral significance of this insight will be considered below (sections 27ff.).

———— 15 ————

Highly reminiscent of Wittgenstein's account of the role of coercion in language-teaching is a notion employed by W. v. O. Quine in *Word and Object:* that of the 'pull toward objectivity'.[1]

Quine's suggestion is that this 'pull' is brought to bear upon each individual by those from whom he acquires his native language. In this picture, what we have to learn in order to gain competence in the use of any given predicate (Quine's chosen examples are 'red' and 'square') is a kind of *discipline* or conformism. If we are to communicate with others, we have to 'regiment' our linguistic responses to sensory stimulation in such a way that we come, for instance, to describe a surface as 'square' when it really is square – even though the images projected upon our respective retinas will vary in shape according to our position in relation to the surface. Predicates can be classified, along these lines, as more or less objective in proportion as their correct use involves a more or less complete emancipation from what Quine calls the 'subjectively simplest rule of association'. ('Square', for example, is more objective than 'red' because 'all the assembled retinas are irradiated by substantially the same red light, whereas no two of them receive geometrically similar projections of the square.')

Let us consider the implications of this view. In the first place, there is the idea that exposure to the 'pull toward objectivity' is a *socializing* process – i.e. that our method of turning out our children as competent participants in objective discussion is by getting them to see things in essentially the same way as ourselves. A competent speaker is one in whom the 'myriad corrective cues' which steer us towards

---

[1] W. v. O. Quine, *Word and Object* (1960), pp. 5-8.

acceptable speech operate automatically, so that that individual no longer needs supervision to help him produce appropriate verbal behaviour in response to the impact of events on his awareness.

Secondly, there is the idea that in making any kind of objective judgement our aim must be to position ourselves on the spot (or 'standpoint') towards which the 'pull toward objectivity' seeks to pull us. That is to say, the attempt to judge objectively is here *equated* with the attempt to occupy that standpoint. Consequently, the standpoint in question turns out to be identical with that of the 'ideal observer' sometimes invoked by moral philosophers: to arrive, intellectually, at the destination marked out for us by the 'pull toward objectivity' is precisely to achieve the status of an ideal observer of reality, whether in respect of morals or of any other subject-matter. But this is not because *experience has shown* that that particular standpoint is the one which offers the best view of reality: rather, it is because reality is *defined* as that which one apprehends when one looks at the world from the standpoint in question. Reality is what is observed by the ideal observer – the person of sound judgement.

Finally, it seems clear that to be in a position to exert the 'pull toward objectivity' is necessarily to be in a position of *authority* over those upon whom it is exerted. (Wittgenstein asks at *OC* §493: 'So is this it: I must recognize certain authorities in order to make judgements at all?' This is very much to the present point, if we take it as being of the essence of a 'judgement' that it be answerable to truth.) There can be no weightier opinion on perceptual questions than that of a person who is acknowledged as having *normal* vision, hearing, etc.; and similarly, if there really existed an 'ideal spectator' of the moral life of human beings, the most significant feature of our relation with that person would be that we always had to accept his judgement. If we disagreed with him, it would be we who were wrong and he who was right; and this would be a matter not of fact, but of logic (or 'grammar', as Wittgenstein would put it). This relationship would be not unlike the one which actually obtains between parents and small children. But, of course, parents are not the only bearers of such authority: it is also held, to take a domestic example, by the professional practitioners of an academic discipline in relation to their students. Universities have the task, or privilege, of exercising the 'pull toward objectivity' at this more rarefied level of thought, for they are (collectively) the arbiters of value in academic research: it is their job to pass judgement as to what would be agreed upon by impartial investigators. They are therefore also the arbiters of 'partiality', just as it has often been noted that television newsrooms are in a certain sense the arbiters, for the audiences they serve, of political 'moderation' and 'extremism'.

Iris Murdoch writes in her book *The Fire and the Sun:* 'Plato's connection of the good with the real . . . is the centre of his thought and one of the most fruitful ideas in philosophy . . . We do not have to believe in God to make sense of the motto of Oxford University, displayed upon an open book, *Dominus illuminatio mea.*'[2] On the basis of the foregoing considerations about objectivity, we can agree that the motto lends itself to a secular reading – but we can suggest an alternative reading which would stand alongside the one proposed by Murdoch. '*The Lord* is my light', my source of truth: however, a 'lord' is primarily a holder of temporal power; it is only within religious discourse that the word takes on a spiritual dimension. *Dominus illuminatio mea* draws attention to the link between truth, or objectivity, and material control ('domination', if one wanted to make a polemical use of etymology; but the point is not just a polemical one).[3]

Reflection on these matters prompts the inevitable question: who says what is to count as an 'objective' view of the world? Who determines the spot where the 'ideal observer' is to stand?

[2] Iris Murdoch, *The Fire and the Sun* (1976), p. 45.
[3] A piquant symbol of this thought is to be found in the Ashmolean Museum, Oxford, where we see the motto of the University attractively painted on some wooden truncheons once carried by the (now disbanded) University police force.

The answer to this question seems to be that that spot is determined by the community of speakers in the same, stipulative way in which, for example, they identify certain sorts of evidence as compelling. (*PI* I §483: 'A good ground is one that looks *like this*.') This does not, of course, mean that we are to imagine the relevant 'decisions' being made around a conference table. What it means is that certain canons of thought are upheld by a *shared way of proceeding* – for which, as we saw in section 9 above, there is on Wittgenstein's view no such thing as an absolute rational justification. (*PI* I §482, 'this ground comes up to a particular standard of good grounds . . . but the standard has no grounds!')

We noted in the preceding section that the norms implicit in a community's linguistic and other social practices are 'upheld', in a quite material sense, by the sanctions which the community can bring to bear upon deviant individuals. The 'pull toward objectivity', then, must also be at bottom a material 'pull': the young child does not consent to the process by which he is transformed into a person able to make judgements about reality from the standpoint of the ideal observer.

However, as participants in objective discourse (as opposed to philosophers theorizing about such discourse), we must think of the community's authority over our judgement not as material, but as intellectual authority. For our aim in talking about the objective world is not to say something acceptable to the powers that be, but to say something *true*;[4] and in pursuit of that aim we must recognize certain persons as possessing, not temporal power over the institutions within which discussion takes place (though they *may* in fact possess this), but sound judgement in respect of the relevant subject-matter. We must do this, because if we held that no one could legitimately correct anyone else's judgement in respect of that subject-matter, we could not think of what we (or anyone else) said about it as being answerable to truth; which, it will be remembered, was precisely the position of the non-cognitivists as regards our talk about morals.

---

[4] This is to be read as a proposition of logic, not of sociology.

It is this relationship of intellectual authority between teacher and learner which explains Wittgenstein's admonition (*OC* §206) to the person who questions something which, for us, counts as a certainty: 'I can't give you any grounds, but if you learn more, you too will think the same.' 'If you *learn* more': not 'if I shine bright lights into your eyes'. The latter, indeed, might also be true; yet it would not, as the other does, display the special status of the speaker – his status as a subscriber to that 'totality of judgements' which has to be made plausible to anyone destined to participate in the going form of life. This status is what makes it correct for the speaker to identify the process by which the other person comes to 'think the same' as a process of *learning,* i.e. of advancing in *knowledge.* Apart from that status, there would be no normative significance to the fact that one person came to share the views of another.

—— 16 ——

These considerations suggest that according to the Wittgensteinian view of language which we are proposing to ourselves as a possible basis for moral realism, a given class of judgements is to be regarded as *objective* (or *answerable to truth*) just in case we regard our discourse about the relevant subject-matter as being regulated by a 'pull toward objectivity' in the sense indicated above. The linkage of these ideas holds good, *a fortiori,* for moral judgements, since we are operating now (as I have already pointed out) with a metaphysically homogeneous conception of language. Moral judgements, on this view, are answerable to truth because moral discourse, like almost every other kind of assertoric discourse,[1] is subject to the Quinean 'pull': in order to use moral predicates correctly, we have to emancipate ourselves from certain subjectively natural principles of association, and achieve a perspective on the world which is accessible alike to

---

[1] '*Almost* every other kind': I here introduce a qualification which will be explained in section 17 below.

ourselves and to others. Our proposed theory of ethics, in short, is a realist theory in that it asserts the existence of *intellectual authority-relations* in the realm of morals, whereas non-cognitivism denies these.

I should like, at this point, to refer again to the essay by Stuart Hampshire from which I quoted in section 13. In that essay Hampshire speaks of morality (or, strictly, of the array of moral *prohibitions* that we acknowledge) as constituting 'a kind of grammar of conduct, showing the elements out of which any full respectworthy conduct, as one conceives it, must be built'.[2] The idea of a 'grammar of conduct' seems to express a recognition that because moral *discourse* is (necessarily, *qua* discourse) rule-governed, therefore our *conduct* – in so far as we seek to represent that conduct as morally appropriate – is also subject to the constitutive rules of a particular symbolic system, namely 'morality'.

The concept of *representation* plays an essential role here. We can think of our conduct as regulated by quasi-grammatical rules only to the extent that that conduct is described, or conceptualized, in terms of a set of publicly acknowledged moral categories. It is our use of moral concepts to describe our own, and one another's, behaviour which endows that behaviour with moral meaning, and thus brings it within the scope of the going moral 'grammar'. This is, of course, an aspect of the familiar idea that the rules do not apply to you unless you join in the game (cf. my reference to Philippa Foot in section 10 above). The norms governing our thinking about what we should or should not do, and for what sorts of reasons, are also norms governing our actions – *on condition* that we aspire to act rationally, in terms of the morality current in our community.

Now the view of linguistic rules which we have been considering in the foregoing sections – the insight, namely, that obedience to a rule consists in conformity to a practice – is strongly reminiscent of the Hegelian concept of *Sittlichkeit*, or 'concrete ethics'. *Sittlich* obligation enjoins the individual to maintain, or recreate, an already existing social practice

---

[2] Hampshire, *Public and Private Morality*, p. 13.

which, because of his personal contribution to the common task of maintaining it, is also the objective expression of his own identity. Such obligation emanates from an 'ethical order with a stable content independently necessary and subsistent in exaltation above subjective opinion and caprice' – an order whose 'moments are the ethical powers which regulate the life of individuals.'[3] Thus the content of *Sittlichkeit* in any society is determined by that of the norms which shape the public life of the society in question.

Hegel also employs a negative concept of moral obligation, that of *Moralität*, with which he took Kant to have identified moral obligation in general. *Moralität*, by contrast with *Sittlichkeit*, requires us to bring about that which *ought* to be, but *is* not (yet). Because it is a form of obligation to which the individual is subject not in virtue of belonging to a particular community, but simply in his capacity as a rational agent considered in the abstract, the paradigmatic status assigned to it by Kant made the Kantian theory incapable, in Hegel's view, of supplying a content for morals; for the latter can be determined only by reference to the way of life of some concretely existing society.

The idea of an *obligation to sustain the institutions which embody a shared way of life* seems to characterize to perfection the way in which, according to Wittgenstein, we are governed by the rules of our language. The fact of participation in language-games imposes on the individual a system of *sittlich* obligations: injunctions to 'do the same' as regards the manner of responding, verbally, to the changing configuration of things in the world. For 'the use of the word "rule" and the use of the word "same" are interwoven' (*PI* I §225). By engaging in speech (which, let us assume, implies the intention to communicate with others), the individual commits himself to perpetuate the institutions which go to make up the total linguistic practice of his community. 'To obey a rule, to make a report, to give an order, to play a game of chess, are *customs* (uses, institutions)' (*PI* I §199).

If this is right, then Hampshire's description of morality as

---

[3] *Hegel's Philosophy of Right*, trs. T. M. Knox (1952), §§144-5.

a 'grammar of conduct' can be read by subscribers to our Wittgensteinian moral realism as a reassertion of the *sittlich* character of moral obligation. They can see Hampshire's 'grammar' in this light because they see grammar in all its manifestations as a system of constraints imposed upon individual behaviour by the behaviour of the collective: constraints which operate through the *rejection* of deviant usage by mainstream participants in the practice of following a given grammatical rule. But a rule whose observance is a matter of *conformity with a public practice* will govern our actions in precisely the same way as the kind of obligations which, in Hegelian terms, make up the content of *Sittlichkeit*.

Conversely, what Hampshire's formulation adds to the Hegelian picture is the thought that moral obligation is *sittlich* because it is a species of the genus of rule-governed behaviour. The *sittlich* character of morality thus becomes intelligible as an instance of the *sittlich* character of meaningful systems in general. Our specifically moral obligations turn out, in other words, to be part of a complex of obligations binding us, as members of a community, to sustain the institutions which provide a structure for our collective life.

———— 17 ————

Objectivity, we have supposed, is a function of what Quine calls a 'pull' toward habits of judgement which are consistent with the adoption of a publicly accessible perspective on the world. Objective discourse is discourse in which, as a matter of logic, we cannot participate unless we are prepared to acknowledge certain intellectual authorities (cf. Wittgenstein, *OC* §493, quoted in section 15).

However, both the strength of the 'pull toward objectivity' and its mode of operation differ from one region of discourse to another. The constraints imposed on our judgement by intellectual authority vary according to the subject-matter under consideration. What counts, in practice, as 'doing the same' will depend upon context (cf. *PI* I §70 on the meaning of 'exactly like this'); and so, correspondingly, will the type of guidance exercised by the community over individual speakers who may aspire to follow the relevant rules.

A moral realist who bases himself on Wittgenstein's conception of language should agree that there are some 'language-games' within which it is not essential to secure a high degree of uniformity in the way people respond to a given situation. Some linguistic practices are, indeed, premissed upon our interest in the *variety* of individual responses (cf. *RFM* VI §24: '"So you took that for correct then, did you? The rest of us did it like *this*."') Others, by contrast, involve a training process which is not complete until all personal idiosyncrasies have been eliminated. For instance, the goal of a child's training in the use of the word 'table' is that he should come to apply it in such a way that, ordinarily speaking, he *never* disagrees with other people about the truth of 'That's a table' (accompanied by pointing). Learning to apply such predicates is an experience almost as hostile to individualism as learning to count – a technique in which we are trained 'with endless practice, with merciless exactitude' (*RFM* I §4).

As an example of the first type of language-game, we might take the use of the predicate 'fun'. In this game – that is, in talking about whether or not such and such an activity, etc. is fun – complete agreement is not only *absent,* but the pursuit of it would actually run counter to the spirit of the game. Thus if you tell me, for example, that it is great fun to ride on the big dipper, and I then undertake to prove to you that you are mistaken and that in fact it is not really fun at all, you will be right to infer that (for whatever reason) I have failed to make myself at home with the concept of 'fun'. Grasping that concept does not call for a high degree of emancipation from the 'subjectively simplest rule of association'; the language-game with 'fun' is a clear case of the kind of game which ends with one person's relishing what another does not (cf. *PI* II p. 228).

Those areas of discourse which cater to our interest in individual peculiarities – whether of taste, temperament or commitment – are marked out by the fact that they do not assign to the quest for consensus that 'ultimate kind of significance'[1] which it possesses, notably, in natural science (rationalistically conceived). We might say that in the application of certain predicates there is a partial – or, in extreme cases like 'fun', near-total – analogue of 'first-person privilege' *vis-à-vis* the ascription of sensations. And this privilege seems to exist even though the statements concerned are in the *third* person. Thus, 'It's great fun to ride on the big dipper' is a third-person statement, but in relation to it, the 'pull toward objectivity' hardly acts upon me at all. Within the limits of intelligibility,[2] I have the last word on what is fun – and not 'fun for me' either, but 'fun' *tout court*. There is no such thing as an authoritative verdict as to whether it is fun to ride on the big dipper: and a person who did not understand this phenomenon – who did not, in other words, grasp that his judgement was not in all respects answerable to intellectual authority – would not be a fully competent user of the sort of natural language with which we are familiar. If it is possible to ask in connection with *mathematics,* as Wittgenstein does: 'Contradiction. Why just this *one* bogy?' (*RFM* IV §56), that question is all the more appropriate in connection with the language of values.

Our Wittgensteinian moral realist can admit, more specifically, that *moral* discourse is an area where the reach of intellectual authority is relatively short. Even here, it is far from negligible (if it were negligible, there would be no basis for a rationalist critique of non-cognitivism); but it is short by comparison with the scope allowed to intellectual authority in the natural sciences, where very mild deviations from consensus (except, presumably, at the frontiers of our knowledge) are liable to result, by common consent, in forfeiture of one's right to participate in the game.[3] The natural way to express the contrast between the two cases would be to say

---

[1] Cf. Bernard Williams, 'Consistency and Realism' (1966), in *Problems of the Self* (1973), p. 205.

[2] Cf. G. E. M. Anscombe's remarks in *Intention* (1957), §37, on the intelligibility of 'I want a saucer of mud'.

[3] The historical decay of intellectual authority in relation to ethics will be considered in section 21 below.

that moral discourse, or the use of moral predicates, is more *subjective* than the use of natural-scientific predicates.

But what becomes, now, of the moral *realist* position we were in the process of constructing? Surely it is the role of the *non-cognitive* theorist to insist on the subjectivity of evaluative discourse, and that of the realist to counter with an insistence that after all, such discourse has no worse a claim to be called objective than the discourse of natural science?

The answer is that our version of moral realism is realistic *in a purely metaphysical sense*. It is a conception of our thinking about morals which is defined by its opposition to the empiricist conception, whose own defining characteristic, as we saw earlier (section 5), was a *metaphysical* distinction between 'fact' and 'value'. Our moral realism merely denies that distinction at the level at which the non-cognitive theorist of ethics asserts it. This does not involve any commitment to denying that there are *phenomenological* distinctions between different language-games, in terms of the extent to which each is regulated by a 'pull toward objectivity'. It does not prevent us from recognizing that different departments of our thinking exhibit varying degrees of objectivity.

The kind of realism we are considering maintains, then, that there is no valid metaphysical reason to equate the 'evaluative' with the 'subjective', as non-cognitivism effectively does. It does not, however, rule out the possibility that evaluative judgements might have a *non*-metaphysical way of failing to be objective. It can thus accommodate, not indeed an absolute 'fact/value *distinction*', but a 'fact/value *continuum*' based on the more or less extensive role played by intellectual authority-relations within different regions of discourse. The role of intellectual authority within any given region of discourse will then be a phenomenological question; i.e. the right way to determine it will be by 'describing language-games'.

18

Mark Platts writes in *Ways of Meaning:*

> Competence in understanding the sayings of others, and of themselves, implies in realistic semantics that speakers can have knowledge of the truth-conditions of sentences that transcend at least their present capacities for determining whether those sentences are true or false. This general consequence of realistic semantics must be accepted in the area of moral vocabulary by anyone wishing to treat such vocabulary realistically. A speaker can know, have a grasp of, the truth-conditions of a moral sentence even if those truth-conditions are beyond his (present) recognitional abilities.[1]

Does our proposed Wittgensteinian type of realism conform to this requirement as regards moral discourse? Does it, that is to say, allow us to make sense of the idea of a *recognition-transcendent moral fact?*

This question needs to be dealt with in two stages, since it contains an ambiguity which is reflected in Platts' reference (in the passage quoted) first to 'speakers', then to 'a speaker'. I shall consider the question in one of its senses in the present section, and in its other sense in section 19 below.

The first sense of the question answers to the mention of 'a speaker' in the singular. In this sense it means: can our proposed realism accommodate the idea of a moral fact, or circumstance, which transcends the awareness of the individual? It is possible for me, as an individual user of moral language, to have a grasp of the truth-condition of a moral sentence even though, in some cases, it will be beyond my powers to tell whether or not that condition obtains?

We saw in section 8 that Platts himself tacitly points us in

---

[1] Platts, *Ways of Meaning,* p. 245. Cf. also McDowell in Evans and McDowell (eds.), p. 48: McDowell takes the 'defining thesis' of realism to be 'that the truth-condition of a sentence may obtain, or not, independently of our capacity to tell that it obtains, or that it does not.'

the direction of a philosophical concept – that of the 'scale of forms' – which can be invoked in support of an affirmative answer. Our Wittgensteinian conception of language, being an expressivist conception, represents the individual's acquisition of linguistic competence as an aspect of his progressive induction into the shared way of life of his community. Learning to talk is equated here with learning to participate in a way of life; and the capacity to do this is one which can be possessed in varying degrees. Those who possess it in less than the maximum degree, however, (such as children) should not on that account be considered devoid of identity as rational beings: their relation to social practice (as compared with that of adults) is best understood not under the aspect of disorder, but of a more primitive order (cf. Z §372).

As applied to the moral dimension of our thought and practice, this idea yields an account of moral concepts which would credit those concepts, in Platts' words, with 'a kind of semantic depth'. There is, of course, no reason to suppose that moral concepts are the only ones displaying this property, but they do at any rate exemplify it particularly clearly in virtue of the non-technical character of moral language and of the correspondingly gradual and intuitive process of mastering it.

The phenomenon of 'semantic depth' suggests a naturalistic explanation of the fact that moral circumstances can transcend individual awareness. It accounts for this fact by pointing out that, while a speaker may master the use of a moral word adequately for the purposes of participation in a certain limited range of language-games involving that word, yet the same word may also figure in various other language-games into which he has not so far been initiated. Accordingly, some of the more elusive features of its use may be lost upon him. And I, as an individual speaker, acknowledge this possibility in relation to myself when I concede that there may be a correct answer to a particular moral question even though it is not obvious, here and now, to me. For what I thereby concede is that my competence with the existing moral vocabulary may not be total – or, to switch from the linguistic to the perceptual idiom, that my own powers of moral

70

intuition may in some respects fall short of those possessed by the 'ideal observer' of moral reality as my community conceives him. To recognize that there may be moral truths which transcend one's awareness is to submit one's moral judgement to further correction by the 'pull toward objectivity': it is an act of submission to intellectual authority in the sphere of morals. (The alternative would be to nominate *oneself* as the ideal observer of moral reality, with the consequence that in doubtful cases one would assert intellectual authority over others, but would never concede any authority to them in return: a situation which perhaps scarcely ever arises in practice as far as individual judgement is concerned, but which is perfectly familiar to us, as I suggested in section 15, in connection with opinion-forming *institutions*.)

Our proposed realism explains, then, how the truth-conditions of moral sentences may transcend the recognitional abilities of the individual, even if he understands the meanings of their constituent moral words. It explains this fact by reference to the possible shortcomings of individual perception *vis-à-vis* the prevailing consensual norms of judgement.

A precedent for the suggested account is supplied by Hume's defence of the objectivity of literary criticism in his essay 'Of the Standard of Taste'[2] of 1757; though Hume himself does not seek to extend his conclusions to morals, for these, he says, are 'in continual flux and revolution'. His concern is to refute a radically non-cognitivist view of *aesthetic* value, according to which the taste of all individuals would be 'on an equal footing'. Concentrating, as contemporary moral realists have done (cf. section 4 above), on the concrete aspects of evaluation in his chosen field ('elegance, propriety, simplicity, spirit in writing . . .'), he argues that although individuals may disagree in picking out instances of the various value-properties they claim to be able to detect, this kind of disagreement is not necessarily ultimate. For

---

[2] David Hume, 'Of the Standard of Taste' (1757), in Alasdair MacIntyre (ed.), *Hume's Ethical Writings* (1965). All the passages cited occur between pp. 275 and 293.

there is a standard of correctness to which we can appeal: the opinion of the *qualified judge,* who is a person possessing delicate and unprejudiced powers of perception. (Hume recognizes the risk that disagreement may arise, in turn, about the qualifications of the judges, but he is confident that 'some men in general, however difficult to be particularly pitched upon, will be acknowledged by universal sentiment to have a preference above others.')

The position maintained in the essay on taste is not supposed to involve any withdrawal from the ontology of the *Treatise:* even colour is still 'merely a phantasm of the senses', projected by the human mind upon a colourless world. However, Hume now shows a heightened awareness of the part played by language in constituting our evaluative sensibilities: 'That people, who invented the word *charity,* and used it in a good sense, inculcated more clearly and much more efficaciously, the precept, *be charitable,* than any pretended legislator or prophet, who should insert such a *maxim* in his writings.' This change of emphasis allows him to account for the objectivity of one specific class of value-properties – those relevant to literary appreciation – in a way which comes equally naturally to the modern philosopher, though the latter will formulate the same account in linguistic terms: the 'true and decisive standard', to which aesthetic judgement must conform on pain of error, will then appear as a standard of competence with aesthetic language. Something is beautiful, or elegant, or insipid, on this view, just in case it would be described as such by a person who knows how to use those words properly – a person with a command of the relevant critical vocabulary.

This, as I have tried to show, is precisely the view indicated in connection with *moral* evaluation by a Wittgensteinian conception of language. Such a view would therefore admit the idea of recognition-transcendent moral truth at least in the minimal sense that it would not place the moral judgement of all individuals 'on an equal footing'. And that feature alone is enough to differentiate it from the non-cognitivist position as outlined in section 1, which does not even admit the logical possibility of ignorance or error of a genuinely ethical kind.

19

The second sense of the question posed in section 18 answers to Platts' mention of 'speakers' in the plural. In this sense, the question means: can our proposed realism accommodate the idea of a moral circumstance which would transcend the awareness of the entire community of speakers? Can it provide the basis for an understanding of moral discourse which is realistic in that stronger sense in which realism implies the possibility of *universal* ignorance or error? Does it, in other words, enable us to make sense of the idea that there might be intelligible moral sentences in our language such that no one could tell whether or not their truth-conditions actually obtained?

There seems to be no *general* difficulty for Wittgenstein's conception of language in the concept of a fact which is, in the present strong sense, recognition-transcendent. That concept, too, has its place in the language-game. We can think of Wittgenstein's position here as comparable to that of Kant, for whom the phenomenal realm as such transcends the totality of propositions that we believe, as of now, to be true. Kant's view, as it has been expressed in a recent study, is that 'we are far from the full truth about the world of appearances; that is what we should have if science were completed – completed in accordance with the principles that govern human thought.'[1] Although the phenomenal world is constructed by our own mental activity – by the imposition on a sensory manifold of the forms of intuition and the categories of understanding – yet 'it contains objects whose existence does not depend on our having the appropriate sense-data and which can therefore, in another and more ordinary sense, be said to be independent of us. It contains such objects just because that is the way we construct it.'[2]

Wittgenstein's philosophy might also be said to incorporate the idea of a 'phenomenal world', of which it is the governing

---

[1] Ralph C. S. Walker, *Kant* (1978), p. 130.
[2] Ibid., p. 109.

purpose of our thought to achieve a progressively more adequate theoretical understanding. This is the 'world', or 'reality', which is the extra-linguistic counterpart of the assertoric portion of our language: it is defined, as I explained in section 6, as *that which we make assertions about*. There is accordingly a sense in which it is 'constructed' by human thought, like the phenomenal world of Kant. Wittgenstein, however – unlike Kant – points us towards a naturalistic account of the mind's constructive activity. I have suggested that the world, for him, is simply the extra-linguistic object to which (as a matter of logical, or grammatical, necessity) we refer when we use language for making assertions. The commitment to 'bring words back from their metaphysical to their everyday use' (*PI* I §116; cf. also *PI* I §97) makes it impossible for the philosopher to go beyond this meta-physically neutral notion – just as, in the *Tractatus*, 'We cannot say in logic, "The world has this in it, and this, but not that" ' (*T* 5.61). However, we have also seen that Wittgenstein thinks of the use of language as an aspect of the *behaviour* of human communities: it is our acting which 'lies at the bottom' of our speech and thought (*OC* §204; cf. *PI* I §546, 'words are also deeds'). And so it is within the matrix of our shared physical activity that there arises – in the course of cultural history, so to speak – a practice of communication by means of signs possessing objective reference. The real world is what we talk about; and speech is a human activity.

It was stated above that, according to Kant, the pheno-menal world – although constructed by our own thought – nevertheless contains objects which are inaccessible to our awareness; and that it does so 'because that is the way we construct it.' We have just been considering how the theme of the mind-dependence of reality is preserved, yet transmuted into a naturalized form, in the thought of Wittgenstein. It remains to observe that this is also true of the Kantian idea that the phenomenal world – the world as we construct it in empirical thought – contains recognition-transcendent objects. 'Thought can as it were *fly*,' writes Wittgenstein (*Z* §273), 'it doesn't have to walk.' Just as we can represent infinity in mathematics by using a suitable calculus, so in the descriptive parts of our language we can represent to ourselves states of affairs which have never been, and perhaps never will be, present to our awareness.

We saw in section 6 above that such claims have been subjected to criticism in a verificationist spirit: criticism, that is, centring on the claim that if linguistic competence is imparted to us by a training which consists solely in getting the learner to produce appropriate verbal responses to the circumstances confronting him, then there will be certain sentences in our language, an understanding of whose meaning cannot legitimately be represented in terms of a grasp of their truth-conditions. For any legitimate realistic theory of meaning in respect of a specified region of discourse would need (according to this view) to include an account of our *means of knowing* whether or not a sentence of the relevant class is true; and there will be some classes of sentence for which such an account cannot be given – for example, because we have no method of deciding their truth-value.

As previously stated, no one who subscribes to a realist conception of meaning of the kind suggested by Wittgenstein's philosophy will raise any objection to the naturalistic considerations about language-learning on which this criticism rests. Such a theorist will point, however, to the creative possibilities conferred upon language by its *systematic* character, which enables us to compose and understand new sentences on the basis of competence with a finite semantic and syntactic repertoire. This feature of language manifests itself in the necessity under which the theorist of meaning is placed of taking as his object of study a *system of communication* rather than a *collection of discrete sentences*. Thus a theory of sense can be characterized as one which 'works systematically across a language, generating a specification of the content of propositional acts potentially performed in the utterance of any sentence, by way of its structure and properties assigned to its components'.[3]

The sentences which our competence with a language – a linguistic *system* – enables us to produce will include some

---

[3] McDowell in Evans and McDowell (eds.), p. 46.

whose truth-conditions transcend our powers of recognition. Because we possess language, we have the means to 'construct possible worlds, some of which, later on, thought will find real or action will make real.'[4] In the theoretical and in the practical case alike, it is our capacity for the creative manipulation of linguistic resources that allows us to represent to ourselves, and communicate to one another, the idea of those states of affairs about whose possible recognition-transcendent obtaining we are speculating – or whose possible realization we are contemplating.

Can our understanding of sentences belonging to this speculative, or imaginative, category be represented by the theorist of meaning as consisting in an understanding of their truth-conditions – with which, *ex hypothesi*, we have never been confronted, and perhaps never shall be? John McDowell has argued that it can, on the grounds that if it is right to think of our mastery of any part of assertoric discourse as the outcome of a process of familiarization with the truth-conditions of sentences, then the systematic nature of language makes it right, also, to think of our understanding of the sentences used in speculative discussion as consisting in a grasp of the truth-conditions of *those* sentences. For they, too, are put together according to familiar syntactic principles out of a familiar stock of words: and the familiarity of the words consists, by common consent, in our knowing what contribution is made by each to determining the assertion-conditions (which are, of course, *truth*-conditions, if this line of argument is valid) of sentences in which they occur.

Thus all that is needed, according to McDowell, in order to render a theory of sense (cognitive meaning) acceptable to someone who insists that our competence with language *as a system* be portrayed by such a theory as 'not independent of sensitivity to evidence', is 'that its representation of understanding be appropriately related to evidence in respect of each simple sentence-constituent and each mode of combination.' That, McDowell continues,

---

[4] Collingwood, *The Principles of Art*, p. 286.

would be secured, ideally, by direct consideration of the evidential prompting of some sentences containing each. The systematic nature of the theory would involve its consequently representing the understanding of other sentences . . . as consisting – as with all sentences – in knowledge of truth-conditions, even though there might be no possibility, with those other sentences, of such direct consideration of evidential prompting. Even in the absence of such direct consideration, the theorist could claim, wholly on the basis of the acceptability, else-where, of his theory, that speakers' (potential) uses of those other sentences were potentially sensitive to appropriate evidence.[5]

Within our proposed Wittgensteinian realism, then, the fact that recognition-transcendent circumstances can figure in our thoughts is explained, in so far as it admits of 'explanation', by the fact that they can figure in our language.[6] This is the force of my earlier statement that Wittgenstein's philosophy sustains, in its own different idiom, the Kantian idea that we construct the phenomenal world in such a way that not everything contained in it is accessible to our awareness.

What we have now to consider is whether we can in fact be said to construct a world containing *moral* circumstances which transcend the awareness, not just of individuals, but of the entire linguistic community. We have to investigate whether the proposed form of realism holds good for morals; and we have to do this by asking whether recognition-transcendent moral facts, in the strong sense with which we are concerned in the present section, can figure in our discourse. Do we know 'what it would be like' for *everyone* to be wrong about a question of morality? This is no longer a question of the technical possibility of constructing certain kinds of sentence out of the available vocabulary and syntax: it is a question of whether the resulting sentences have a *use* – whether we can 'do anything with them'.

---

[5] McDowell in Evans and McDowell (eds.), p. 63.
[6] Cf. section 12 above.

By way of comparison, take the phenomenon of specula-
tion about some problem at the frontiers of a natural science:
for example, about the physical properties of a distant star.
We certainly suppose that there is a fact of the matter here,
even though there may be no reason to believe that any
inhabitant of this planet will ever be able to find it out.
(Astrophysics is a subject-matter that can be conceived
realistically in the light of the general constraint upon realism
laid down by Dummett, and to which I referred in section 6
above. For we do have what Dummett would acknowledge as
a conception of how our astrophysical hypothesis might be
verified – namely, by going there and looking, so to speak –
even though the trip happens not to be feasible: this would be
an instance of the appeal to superhuman powers which,
however, bore a recognizable relation to our own actual
powers of material-object perception.) The example suggested can be seen as an updated version of Kant's thought
that to say there may be men in the moon 'only means that in
the possible advance of experience we may encounter them.'[7]
Our assumption of the possibility of universal error or
ignorance about the physical properties of the star is,
likewise, a belief that in the 'possible advance' of astrophysical methods we may change our current theory in that regard,
or find ourselves for the first time in a position to devise a
theory at all.

In what sense, if any, do we find an analogue of this case in
moral thinking? 'Perhaps it is really better for students not to
sleep with their tutors after all . . .' – Does this mean that in
the 'possible advance of experience' we may *discover* it to be
better? Would that be a matter for discovery in the same way
that people make discoveries in physics?

The difference between the natural-scientific case and the
moral case can perhaps be understood in the following way.
The idea of a circumstance which may obtain beyond the
awareness of the entire community is bound up with that of a
possible experience which would prompt a *more or less*

---

[7] Immanuel Kant, *Critique of Pure Reason*, A493/B521, trs. N. Kemp
Smith (1929).

uniform and immediate response among competent speakers, in terms of their becoming disposed to make a change in their assignment of truth-values to particular sentences, or to assign a truth-value to a sentence about which they were previously agnostic. In the astrophysical example, we can imagine being confronted by fresh evidence to which all competent speakers would respond in this sort of way ('Jones's findings have refuted the conjecture of Smith'). It may simply be a phenomenological fact about a given area of discourse that speakers are, typically if not invariably, *certain* what they must say in the face of some new experience. And natural-scientific discourse seems to be a case in point. Dummett has written that 'it is part of the meaning of "observation" that the deliverances of observation – assertions which report the results of observation – are more or less immediate.'[8] I am suggesting that the reason it makes sense to suppose we might all be wrong about a question of astrophysics is that *observation,* whose deliverances are 'more or less immediate', might at some time or other *show* that we were.

This is not what it is like for a community to change its mind about a moral issue – or, normatively, to attain to a deeper moral insight. The reason indicated by the considerations just offered is that changes in collective moral outlook – as in individual moral outlook – tend on the whole to happen slowly, by contrast with the immediacy of changes in what we all believe about the physical world. (If this appears contentious, I should like to stress that I am not referring to 'paradigm changes', or to any other high-level phenomena of scientific inquiry. What I have in mind is the familiar fact that with regard to a question such as 'Has the milk gone off?', a certain experience will lead anyone who understands the question to revise his theory from one moment to the next.)

In connection with moral judgement, we do not have the idea of *fresh evidence* which, when it came to light, would prompt a uniform and immediate reassignment of truth-

---

[8] Michael Dummett, 'Platonism', in *Truth and Other Enigmas* (1978), p. 203. Cf. also W. v. O. Quine, *Word and Object,* pp. 40ff.

values to sentences on the part of competent speakers. That idea 'belongs to' our concept of the physical world, but not to our (possible) concept of the moral world. This is a corollary of the fact that moral concepts do not have 'fixed limits'. (Wittgenstein, Z §374: 'Concepts with fixed limits would demand a uniformity of behaviour. But where I am *certain*, someone else is uncertain. And that is a fact of nature.') The consensus which underlies the use of moral concepts is not normally so rigid as to give us the feeling, which we get, for example, in arithmetic, that the practical implications of the rules governing that use are fully determinate (cf. *PI* I §188, ' "The steps are *really* already taken . . ." ').

There is certainly a role in moral thinking for the concept of fresh evidence (fresh considerations which can be brought to bear upon a moral question), but that concept does not have the same status here as in our thinking about the physical world: for in ethics there is room for a certain amount of *decision-making* as regards what judgements it is appropriate to make in the face of what experience (cf. *OC* §362, 'doesn't it come out here that knowledge is related to a decision?'). The rules which govern our use of moral words have to be applied, not only 'without guidance' in the transcendent sense (cf. *PI* I §292) – i.e. without guidance from any authority external to human practice – but also 'without guidance' in the immanent, or material, sense, sc. because intellectual authority is not so extensive in morals as to determine every detail of the practice which counts as obeying the rule. Thus it is a 'fact of nature' that fresh considerations introduced into moral debate or deliberation often leave us uncertain what conclusion to draw, so that in the end we may have to 'act and not consider' (cf. *RFM* IV §56): 'For at this level the expression of the rule [e.g. the relevant rule of moral argument] is explained by the value, not the value by the rule' (Z §301).

(This is related to the point made in section 17 above about language-games within which intellectual authority is limited because they cater to our interest in individual differences; but it is not the *same* point, because the indeterminacy of the practice which constitutes obedience to a rule is not always due to any lack of a sense of urgency about achieving consensus. It may happen, as we shall see in more detail later, that the practice *cannot* be rendered determinate because of conflict within the linguistic community: as F. de Saussure observes, 'Language furnishes the best proof that a law accepted by a community is a thing that is tolerated and not a rule to which all freely consent.'[9])

What makes us doubt the intelligibility of the idea that we might all be wrong about a moral question is that we do not know where to look for the background consensus that would supply the relevant canons of judgement. We can all be wrong about a question in physics, because there is agreement among competent users of natural-scientific language in their (potential) verbal responses to new experiences bearing upon that question. But this kind of agreement is absent in morals.

Thus moral circumstances seem not to qualify, in terms of our proposed Wittgensteinian realism, as capable of transcending the awareness of the entire community. But the distinction between moral judgements and material-object statements in respect of recognition-transcendence (in this strong, collective sense) can be maintained without recourse to metaphysics: it can be maintained as a phenomenological distinction; i.e. a difference in the 'physiognomy' of moral and physical discourse respectively. In this way we can conclude that moral facts have a non-metaphysical way of failing to be, in the collective sense, recognition-transcendent, just as we found in section 17 above that moral judgements have a non-metaphysical way of failing (sometimes) to be objective.

These reflections show that to reject the non-cognitivist view of ethics at the metaphysical level (to exchange it, that is, for the sort of position we have been developing) is not *ipso facto* to discount the phenomenological differences between moral and natural-scientific discourse which so impressed the non-cognitivists, and which they inflated to metaphysical proportions. It is no accident, for example, that the (strictly

---

[9] F. de Saussure, *Course in General Linguistics*, trs. Wade Baskin (1974), p. 71.

immanent) 'description of the moral language-game' should throw up references to 'decision-making' – the very activity which Hare takes to be characteristic of moral judgement in virtue of its special *metaphysical* status.

———— 20 ————

The argument of sections 14-15 showed it to be a consequence of our proposed conception of language that the objectivity of moral discourse, in so far as it is objective, is grounded in a system of material relationships which constitute the basis of intellectual authority with respect to moral questions. But to call these relations 'material' is to say that they are embodied in concretely existing civil institutions such as the family, the nation-state, schools, universities, professional bodies; and also, of course, in those quasi-institutions which, though not formally constituted, nevertheless count among the facts that determine the possible physiognomy of the moral language-game for any given community (cf. Wittgenstein, OC §617, 'doesn't it seem obvious that the possibility of a language-game is conditioned by certain facts?') Such quasi-institutions would include, for example, structural relations of power between different social groups, and the associated systematic differences in status.

It is this institutional aspect which confers on intellectual authority-relations their essential permanence and stability: essential, because if that stability were lacking then the *sittlich* relation discussed in section 16 above would be inconceivable. For it would not then make sense to talk of 'doing the same': there would be no fixed point to which one could turn for an authoritative verdict as to what that meant in practice.

David Wiggins' reference to a 'shared way of life which is constitutive of rationality itself' (cf. section 9 above) appears to invoke the idea we are now exploring: namely, that rationality in general – and hence, *a fortiori*, moral rationality – rests upon a shared practice which is *embodied* in institutions. The 'moral world' posited by our realist theory of ethics is in a sense identical with this array of institutions, for it cannot exist in a disembodied state, any more than the individual members of the community in question can exist apart from their individual bodies.

(The line of thought which rules out the idea of a disembodied mind is roughly as follows: to have a mind is to be able to think; but there is no thought without language;[1] therefore, to have a mind is to be able to use language; but language is a spatio-temporal phenomenon (Wittgenstein, *PI* I §108; cf. also Marx and Engels, cited in section 7 above) and, as such, is essentially an attribute of embodied creatures, for they alone can emit sounds, push pen across paper, etc.)

'The human body,' writes Wittgenstein (*PI* II p. 178), 'is the best picture of the human soul.' This remark lends itself to a satisfying non-metaphorical interpretation in the light of the expressivist thesis that we find out what is going on in people's minds by paying attention to what they do with their bodies (cf. section 12 above): by 'seeing relations between a person and bits of the world, not prying into a hidden place [sc. the mind, conceived as a repository of thoughts] whose contents could be just as they are even if there were no world.'[2] This is the sense in which, as we saw in section 12, 'nothing is [in principle] concealed' as regards the states of consciousness of other persons.[3]

---

[1] I am here ignoring complications such as the dog who believes his master is at the door (Wittgenstein, *PI* II p. 174). I do not think these affect the main expressivist position on the relation of thought to language in any fundamental way.

[2] John McDowell, 'On the Sense and Reference of a Proper Name', in Platts (ed.), *Reference, Truth and Reality* (1980), p. 154.

[3] Cf. Oscar Wilde: 'It is only shallow people who do not judge by appearances. The true mystery of the world is the visible, not the invisible' (*The Picture of Dorian Gray*, ch. 2).

The reverse side of this coin is presumably the 'conquest of appearances' celebrated by Henry James (e.g. in the second part of *The Golden Bowl*) – an achievement which constitutes the *virtù* of certain of his characters and the aspiration of others. The achieved state brings with it the power to grant to one's fellow men and women in relation to oneself just so much of a hermeneutic foothold as one wishes, and no more – i.e. to ensure that no one else ever has a better idea than you do of what is going on in your mind. (*Complete* success in this project would perhaps be a misfortune rather than a blessing.)

Similarly, it is implicit in our Wittgensteinian type of realism (about morals or anything else) that 'the social body,' as we might put it, 'is the best picture of the social soul.' Thus the actual moral institutions of a community exhibit the moral spirit of that community in the same way in which, for Wittgenstein, body exhibits mind. There is no mystification involved in this suggestion – no spectre, for example, of state-worship arising from the hypostasization of a transcendent 'national destiny': for the mind-body relation, whether at the macrocosmic or at the microcosmic level, is to be understood as one of *immanence* (or 'supervenience'). What is exhibited in an embodied form has objective (public) existence; what remains in principle unexhibited, and so inaccessible, 'drops out of consideration as irrelevant' (*PI* I §293). Institutions, then, may be seen as the objective expression of the spirit of the community that operates them; and it was under this aspect that they appeared (in section 16 above) as the focus of *sittlich* obligation.

This talk of 'objective spirit' confronts us once again with the Hegelian tradition, from which we have already borrowed the idea of *Sittlichkeit* itself. Nor should the confrontation come as a surprise, for recent gestures towards a Wittgensteinian moral realism do in fact bear a striking resemblance to the kind of ethical theory advanced by the idealist philosophers of late nineteenth-century Oxford. The most important theme which contemporary moral realism appears to derive (albeit tacitly) from idealist philosophy is that of the *expressive relation* presumed to obtain between the individual and the institutions which regulate his moral life. I will try to illustrate this claim by comparing the position of F. H. Bradley in his essay of 1876, 'My Station and its Duties',[4] with that of Wiggins in his 1976 lecture.

We can begin by noticing that Bradley rejects the false dilemma which would compel us to choose between an absolute (ahistorical) morality, and a morality which is 'relative, and hence no morality at all'. He asserts that 'a

---

[4] F. H. Bradley, 'My Station and its Duties', in *Ethical Studies*, 2nd edn (1927), pp. 160ff.

morality which was *not* relative would be futile . . . At any given period to know more than he did, man must have been more than he was; for a human being is nothing if he is not the son of his time; and he must realize himself as that, or he will not do it at all . . . Morality is "relative", but is none the less real. At every stage there is the solid fact of a world so far moralized. There is an objective morality in the accomplished will of the past and present . . .'[5]

The moral world, according to Bradley, 'is a whole, and has two sides. There is an outer side, systems and institutions, from the family to the nation; this we may call the body of the moral world. And there must also be a soul, or else the body goes to pieces: everyone knows that institutions without the spirit of them are dead . . . you cannot have the moral world unless it is willed . . . [and] to be willed it must be willed by persons.'[6] As at the individual level, so at the level of collective existence, there cannot be mind without body; but conversely, the customs and institutions in which a common way of life finds its material expression are sustained only by the *sittlich* identification of individuals with the relevant practices. The 'inner side' of morality is neither more nor less than 'the outer universal . . . presented by me inwardly to myself as the universal which is my true being.'[7] Thus it is only as a member of some community that I exist as a moral being, a subject of rights and duties: a person to whom the unconditional demands of morality apply. Bradley is here asserting with reference to the foundations of ethics what T. H. Green was later to reaffirm with reference to political obligation: 'To ask why I am to submit to the power of the state, is to ask why I am to allow my life to be regulated by that complex of institutions *without which I literally should not have a life to call my own*, nor should be able to ask for a justification of what I am called on to do.'[8]

---

[5] Ibid., pp. 189-90.
[6] Ibid., p. 177.
[7] Ibid., p. 179.
[8] T. H. Green, *Lectures on the Principles of Political Obligation* (1895), p. 122 (emphasis added).

The inner side of morality is 'the outer universal presented by me inwardly to myself.' Here, as in section 16 (where morality appeared as an example of a symbolic system, so that what was true of symbolic systems in general was true of morality in particular), we find that moral discourse illustrates certain general considerations about language which have been advanced within the expressivist tradition. Just as it is only as a member of a linguistic community that I exist as a rational being,[9] so it is only as a participant in the public institutions of moral language that I exist as a bearer of moral rationality, and am subjected to the constraints imposed thereby.

We must bear in mind, however, that the alleged role of the community in endowing the individual with identity (sc. as a social rather than a merely biological being) requires that the outer, or public, side of the moral world should present itself to the individual as his own 'true being'. It presupposes, in Hegel's words, that 'each has only the certainty . . . of finding in the actual world nothing but himself.'[10] But these words refer to a postulated condition of society in which the expressive relation between public and private existence is unflawed: a condition in which the values expressed in public institutions coincide with those around which individual members of the community choose to construct their personal lives. A community which met this demand would be one that offered its citizens a life of freedom, not in the empiricist sense in which freedom means emancipation from control, but in the rationalist sense derived from Rousseau's famous thesis: 'Obedience to a law which we prescribe to ourselves is liberty.'[11]

---

[9] For the idea of personality as constituted by the reflection of shared values in the individual mind, cf. also Collingwood, *The Principles of Art*, p. 292: 'The self is expressed in the world, the world consisting of language whose meaning is that emotional experience which constitutes the self, and the self consisting of emotions which are known only as expressed in the language which is the world.'

[10] G. W. F. Hegel, *Phenomenology of Spirit*, trs. A. V. Miller (1977), §351.

[11] J.-J. Rousseau, *The Social Contract*, trs. G. D. H. Cole (1913), Book I, ch. 8. Cf. also Charles Taylor, *Hegel and Modern Society* (1979), p. 90.

I suggest that what we have recently begun to see in moral philosophy is an attempt to reformulate some of these ideas from the point of view of the philosophy of language. The concept of 'objective spirit' has been reintroduced, with a linguistic gloss. The following passage from Wiggins is especially significant here:

> I shall argue that . . . the non-cognitive account [of the meaning of life] depends for its plausibility upon abandoning at the level of theory that inner perspective which it commends as the only possible perspective upon life's meaning. This is a kind of incoherence; and one which casts some doubt upon the whole distinction of the inside and the outside viewpoints. I believe that once we break down the supposed distinction of the inner or participative and the outer, supposedly objective viewpoints, there is a way forward. At no point will this lead back to the intuitive certainty which we began by envying as enjoyed in an earlier age.[12]

Wiggins, then, calls for a reintegration of our conception of ourselves as thinking and acting subjects (the 'inner viewpoint') with our conception of ourselves as natural objects, and hence as capable of being understood in scientific terms (the 'outer viewpoint'). And this is connected with another

---

It may be objected that according to this criterion, prescriptivism – contrary to the way in which we have so far mapped out the terrain of moral philosophy – will count as a *rationalist* theory *par excellence*. But that line of thought is closed off by a passage in the *Philosophy of Right* where Hegel – in an argument whose substance is recapitulated by the Wittgensteinian rule-following considerations – derives a contradiction from the idea of the *individual* as his own moral legislator: 'Conscience is . . . subject to the judgement of its truth or falsity, and when it appeals only to itself for a decision, it is directly at variance with what it wishes to be, namely the rule for a mode of conduct which is rational, absolutely valid and universal.' (§137Z) (Cf. §258Z, 'Rationality, taken generally and in the abstract, consists in the thorough-going unity of the universal and the single.') If this is accepted, it will follow that the 'law which we prescribe to ourselves' cannot be a merely personal or 'private' law.

12 Wiggins, 'Truth, Invention . . .', p. 340.

demand, which emerges from his discussion of how one might construct a recursive theory of meaning for moral language: the demand that, in constructing such a theory, the semantic theorist be 'ready to put his mind where his mouth is at least once for each sentence *s* of the object-language, in a statement of assertion conditions for *s* in which he himself uses either *s* or a faithful translation of *s*.'[13]

The theorist's goal, as Wiggins sees it, is to be able to pair any given sentence of his object-language (in this case, the language of morals), on the basis of its simple semantic constituents and syntactic structure as perceived by himself, with an assertion-condition (e.g. a truth-condition) for that sentence. The pairing will be recorded by a theorem of the recursive theory of meaning, and will be stated (in the meta-language, i.e. the language in which the theory as a whole is stated) by a theorem of the form: '*s* is assertible if and only if *p*' (where *s* replaces a designation of a sentence in the object-language, and *p* replaces a sentence in the meta-language). The force of Wiggins' remark about 'putting one's mind where one's mouth is' is that in order to be able to assert the theorems of his own theory, the theorist must be ready to *use* (*in propria voce*), on the right-hand side of those theorems, expressions with the same sense as those *mentioned* on the left-hand side. He must be able to participate ingenuously – that is, without irony or sentimentality – in the practice of using moral language.

The moral philosopher who cannot, or will not, 'put his mind where his mouth is' with regard to morals finds himself in a contradictory position. For the attempt to theorize a mode of thinking in which one does not participate cannot be a contribution to the project of self-understanding, in which philosophy essentially consists. (Cf. Wiggins: '[Meta-ethics] is still the best way for us to understand ourselves better.'[14]

There is an analogy between the structure of designation and use in truth-conditional semantics – for instance, in a

---

13 Ibid., p. 355.
14 Ibid., p. 351.

truth-conditional theory of meaning for moral language – and the idea of a moral world with an 'inside' and an 'outside', which we found in Bradley. Use and mention – the use of an expression on the right-hand side of a homophonic truth-theorem or semantic axiom, and its designation on the left-hand side – correspond respectively to the 'soul' and the 'body' of those practices which, according to Bradley's (and our own) form of realism, are constitutive of moral rationality. When I participate in the moral language-game, as I must if I am to allow moral language into the meta-language in which I carry out my interpretative task, I breathe life into the institutions of moral language-use; prior to the work of interpretation, I merely survey them from outside, treating them as natural (objective) phenomena.[15] The moral sentences designated in my truth-theorems are no more than the 'body', the material aspect, of the system of linguistic practices in virtue of which there is a moral world; the 'spirit' is that practical orientation of *mine* – a subjective orientation – which permits me to use expressions with the same sense as the designated ones, in order to *give* the sense of the latter.

It will be remembered that, in Bradley's view, 'institutions without the spirit of them are dead.' In the same way, concepts of unconditional value – whether in morals or politics or aesthetics – are available for our (non-ironic) use only in so far as we can 'find ourselves' in the specific repertoire of social practices which happen, historically, to 'lie at the bottom' of evaluative discourse within the community to which we belong. They can be said to be available to us only in so far as an expressive relation can be said to exist between those practices and ourselves. Thus it is only where such a relation exists that we shall have access to the concepts of non-instrumental value which we need, in the

---

[15] Cf. Wittgenstein, *PI* I §432: 'Every sign by itself seems dead. *What* gives it life? In use it is *alive*. Is life breathed into it there? Or is the *use* its life?'

The Romantic connotations of this idea should be obvious. Cf. S. T. Coleridge, 'Dejection: an Ode' (1802):

I cannot hope from outward forms to win
The passion and the life, whose fountains are within.

light of the phenomenological considerations of section 2 above, if we are to find a meaning in life.

The Wittgensteinian view that linguistic rules are institutions reiterates, although with a changed emphasis, an idea inherited from the Romantic movement by Hegel and his successors: it is the other side of the thought that institutions display objective mind, and as such have a semantic value. There is a single tradition of thought which encompasses, on one hand, Bradley's declaration that 'man is a social being; he is real only because he is social, and can realize himself only because it is as social that he realizes himself';[16] and on the other, Wiggins' view that moral meaning – the meaning of life – shares the essentially social character which, on the basis of the private language argument, we must ascribe to meaning in general.

Non-cognitivism in moral philosophy was described in section 1 as an anti-authoritarian tendency, since it represents morality as a sphere within which no intellectual authority exists. Every adult, according to Hare, has the conviction that he is 'free to form his own moral opinions'; any 'pull toward objectivity' in that sphere will therefore be perceived as illegitimate.

But if, as Wittgenstein suggests, it is necessary to recognize certain authorities in order to make (objective) judgements at all (cf. section 15), then it would seem that there must be a direct connection between this anti-authoritarian aspect of non-cognitivism – this intellectual anarchism in respect of morals – and the difficulties to which the theory has been held to lead as regards the 'inner viewpoint'. For it is the non-cognitivist's refusal to recognize the possibility of legitimate moral authority which places objective judgements of value beyond his logical reach; and unless we can think of moral judgements as objective – unless we can conceive as an

---

[16] Bradley, *Ethical Studies*, p. 174.

impersonal fact the unconditional worthwhileness of doing certain things – we shall not be able to find a meaning in life, according to the considerations of section 2.

This is, on the face of it, a serious objection to non-cognitivism, and one which should prompt us to ask how that theory ever came to win general acceptance. I believe that what was said in the foregoing section sheds light on this question.

We have seen that it is integral to the expressivist conception of language to maintain that the individual speaker cannot 'put his mind where his mouth is' – cannot animate with meaning the 'outward forms' of indicative sentences – unless he can 'find himself' in certain extant public habits of thought. He cannot, for example, think of himself as seeking to make *true* moral judgements, nor (consequently) as seeking to apprehend moral *reality*, unless there exists within his social environment a shared practice of talking about moral questions, such that he can regard that practice as an expression of the values by which he defines his identity as a rational being. If no such practice is accessible to him, he will be in the position of 'not recognizing any authorities': not accepting any of the institutions which underlie moral discourse as *expressing himself*.[1] In these circumstances, any 'pull toward objectivity' whose operation he may detect within moral discourse will indeed be perceived by him as an alien, coercive force to which he will be unable, in good conscience, to submit. And if there is no authority which he can acknowledge in his own moral thinking, there will be nothing which he can call 'sound judgement' in questions of morality. For there will be, in his own estimation, no 'skilled judge' to whom he can defer.

But this means that as far as the individual is concerned, the question of the meaningfulness of life can present itself as a *historical* question. It is open to the individual to ask whether an expressive relation does really exist between himself (*qua*

---

[1] But this is not a theory based on the idea of 'self-expression' in the kindergarten sense – an idea which, as we saw in section 4, is viewed with some contempt by moral realists. See below, sections 29-38.

thinking subject, i.e. identified in terms of his values and beliefs) and the moral or political institutions under which he lives: whether, in other words, there is a habit of moral thought in his community with which he can enjoy a *sittlich* identification. This question is 'historical' in the sense that one can answer it only by inspecting the actual social arrangements which inform one's life. In so far as such an inspection reveals those arrangements as devoid of expressive significance, it reveals also the impossibility of giving allegiance to any self-styled moral authority which may currently exist. And in so far as it reveals that impossibility, it reveals the absence of one of the preconditions of objective moral discourse, which – according to Wiggins' line of argument – is in turn a precondition of any meaningful human existence.

Non-cognitivism as a tendency in moral philosophy has arisen out of historical conditions which cause large numbers of people to suffer from a sense of meaninglessness, because they cannot find in society any institutions which they can sincerely acknowledge as the seat of legitimate intellectual authority in questions of value. Institutions which formerly served as the focus of *sittlich* identification – the material basis of recognized moral authority – no longer exist, or are in the process of being abolished, in the competitive and individualistic society with which non-cognitivism is coordinated. This thought is too familiar to need further elaboration here. Marx and Engels express it as follows: 'Constant revolutionizing of production, uninterrupted disturbance of all social conditions, everlasting uncertainty and agitation distinguish the bourgeois epoch from all earlier ones. All fixed, fast-frozen relations, with their train of ancient and venerable prejudices and opinions, are swept away, all new-formed ones become antiquated before they can ossify. All that is solid melts into air, all that is holy is profaned . . .'[2]. This is an accurate description of the sort of society within which all that can be said to someone with a

---

[2] Marx and Engels, 'Manifesto of the Communist Party', in Karl Marx, *The Revolutions of 1848: Political Writings*, Vol. I, ed. David Fernbach (1973), p. 70.

moral problem is: 'Well, God help you.'[3] The sense of meaninglessness experienced by many people in such a society results, in the end, not from 'bewitchment' by a false meta-ethical theory, but from the material conditions of which – as regards the absence of intellectual authority in morals – that theory is a faithful representation.

Of course, to say that there is no recognized moral authority in our intellectual universe is not to say that there is no moral authority, *tout court*. The background 'consensus' which, according to non-cognitivism, creates a semblance of rational discussion about morals and politics (cf. section 10 above) – a seemingly contingent consensus of shared attitudes, which are supposed to be 'original existences', like the Humean 'passions' – is in reality not contingent at all, but manufactured by the various influences which turn us into social beings. The young child is 'continually tampered with', as Bradley observes:[4] by watching television, and later by reading newspapers and magazines, he 'learns to believe a host of things' (cf. Wittgenstein, OC §144). But as long as these moral and political steering agencies are not explicitly acknowledged as such (sc. because it is assumed that what we learn to believe are 'facts' in the empiricist sense, innocent of interpretation or evaluation), they are not even logically possible candidates for *conscious* adoption as paradigms of sound judgement about moral and political reality.

The economic order of which Marx and Engels wrote has now evolved to the point where, as Charles Taylor mildly remarks, 'the value of unlimited growth cannot but come into question';[5] where its endemic 'agitation' has reached a pitch that almost defies us to think sanely about the future; and where the concept of the autonomous individual on which non-cognitivism is founded has been kicked upstairs into the realms of mythology. Such a situation understandably gives

[3] Cf. Rush Rhees's account of a conversation with Wittgenstein in 1942, in which Wittgenstein discusses what a moral dilemma is like for 'the man who does not have an ethics' (*Philosophical Review* (1965), p. 22).

[4] Bradley, *Ethical Studies*, p. 171.

[5] Taylor, *Hegel and Modern Society*, p. 128.

rise to mounting anxiety about the prospects of the particular way of life which is mirrored in non-cognitive theories of ethics. And it is equally understandable that that anxiety should find expression (*inter alia*) in a reaction against non-cognitivism itself, towards a different conception of morality which would reinstate the vanished element of *Sittlichkeit*.

—— 22 ——

But there is a certain moral (and political) ambiguity to this reaction. It can be interpreted either in a favourable or in an unfavourable sense. I believe that the present renewal of interest in a realist approach to ethics owes something to each of the impulses which I will now try, in turn, to characterize.

On the side of charity, the following points can be made. First, disenchantment with non-cognitivism might be taken to reflect disenchantment with the essentially anti-social view of human nature which informs that theory. Anyone with a sense of the dangers inherent in such a view, and in the subjectivist conception of value that goes with it, will presumably see the development of an alternative conception as essential to the task of thinking effectively about those dangers. Moral realism of the kind we have been discussing provides a possible alternative in the idea of value as something expressed, holistically, by a sustainable form of life.

Next, rejection of the kind of ethical theory associated with empiricism involves a salutary reappraisal of the currently dominant technical notion of rationality. That is to say, it encourages us to query the identification of rationality as such with an ability to find the objectively right means to a subjectively determined end, and to embrace instead the less restrictive idea of rationality as constituted by a system of social practices possessing expressive significance for those who participate in them. This change at the level of theory permits us to do something which could not be done within the terms of reference of liberal individualism. It permits us to assess as rational or otherwise, in terms of certain publicly acknowledged values, those individual desires whose satisfaction is represented as the *raison d'être* of our whole way of life; and consequently to say (where appropriate) that the institutions which minister to those desires, and in which the prevailing way of life is embodied, are irrational – i.e. that they fail to express ourselves *qua* thinking beings. Here, too, moral realism presents itself as a rationalistic and progressive tendency, since it provides a better theoretical framework for the criticism of our actual social arrangements.

The realist tendency is also rationalistic in so far as it reflects an urge to demystify intellectual authority in morals: to replace the non-cognitivists' *denial* of authority, behind which the real agencies of moral guidance can lurk un-acknowledged (cf. section 21 above), with a conscious *recognition* of its existence and nature (cf. sections 14-15 above). Once we have brought to conscious awareness the role of intellectual authority in objective discourse, our subsequent participation in any practice of talking about objective reality will be contingent on our acknowledging the legitimacy of the particular mode of intellectual authority by which that practice is governed (see below, sections 27-31).

Finally, the resurgence of moral realism would be a healthy development in that it would discredit the sinister mythology of male and female 'principles' embodied in the 'reason/ sentiment' opposition. The expulsion of intrinsic value from the 'real world' – which, as we saw in section 5 above, is a distinguishing mark of non-cognitivist theories – is an idea which both sustains and feeds upon a real division of functions within society. It belongs with a way of life which restricts the exercise of the emotions to the private, or domestic, sphere and defines the 'real world', by contrast, as the theatre of those activities which call for dispassionately descriptive or technical habits of thought. And this way of life, since it allots the public and private spheres to men and women respectively, inevitably determines 'sentiment' (and therefore moral sensitivity, which is held to be a manifest-ation of that faculty) as a characteristically feminine attribute, while (instrumental) 'reason' is determined as characteristically masculine. ('Women are really much nicer than men:/No wonder we like them,' as Kingsley Amis once put it.)[1]

Empiricism, we might say, relegates the (non-instrumental) values of moral and aesthetic appreciation to the peripheral position of the (non-productive) bourgeois wife: it represents our discourse about those values as a trimming round the edge of the serviceable, fact-stating fabric of language proper. Thus there is no need to ask, as regards C. L. Stevenson's 'wedding of descriptive and emotive meaning', which of the parties is wearing the long white dress (cf. section 4 note 3 above).[2]

But if it is right to see non-cognitivist ethics as incorporating a metaphysics of commuter-land, then it will also be right to see moral realism as the (prefigurative) representation of a different kind of social order: one in which humane (i.e. non-technical, qualitative) values would be reabsorbed – not just theoretically, but materially – into the 'real world'. A conception of language which was free from any metaphysical fact/value distinction would be the fitting expression of a form of life within which no one was expected to *specialize* in maintaining a sense of what is humanly acceptable.

In a variety of ways, therefore, the reaction against non-cognitivism seems to reveal a growing awareness of the irrationalities which have left their mark on empiricist moral

[1] Kingsley Amis, 'Something Nasty in the Bookshop', in *The New Poetry*, ed. A. Alvarez (1962), p. 110.

[2] In a recent work of medical sociology we read that, 'according to Talcott Parsons . . . fathers (and men generally) play "instrumental" roles in society, meaning they serve technical, executive and judicial functions. Mothers were "expressive" – emotional, supportive and nurturing' (Barbara Ehrenreich and Deirdre English, *For Her Own Good: 150 Years of the Experts' Advice to Women* (1979), p. 223).

Parsons' doctrine seems to be the outcome of a process whereby (a) a conceptual opposition comes into being through the unwitting projection on to mental (or linguistic) functioning of a contingent feature of social organization; then (b) the opposition thus generated is clawed back into the service of a (too easy!) piece of explicit theorizing about sexual differences.

philosophy. To take this view of the retreat from empiricism is to place a sympathetic construction upon it.

However, any reaction against the liberal tradition in morals or politics runs the risk of rejecting what is still of value in that tradition; in particular, the habit of respect for originality, non-conformity and conscientious dissent. The demystification of intellectual authority, which I have applauded as a means by which we can free ourselves from covert moral control, can also tip over into a kind of *celebration* of such authority, and of its energetic use against eccentric or subversive elements. A moral realism of that description would be well suited to form part of the ideology of a society which was 'authoritarian' in the ordinary and unphilosophical sense.

Our own proposed realist position – especially in its application to morals – undoubtedly involves, in some sense, a reaffirmation of the Romantic values associated with expressivist ideas about language and society: values such as those of community, historical continuity, and harmony with nature. These are, of course, all excellent things. Yet it is ironic that the spasm of protective emotion normally reserved for those traditional cultures whose products we consume in our leisure hours or on our holidays (folk music, local crafts, quaint elderly persons dressed in black, etc.) – that this same emotion should now be brought to bear upon the very life-style which, through its entrenched utilitarianism, has reduced those older ones to their present marginal status.

It is not always easy to say quite what degree of historical specificity is supposed to attach to the 'shared form of life' commended to us by certain moral philosophers as a focus of *sittlich* identification. The unclarity I have in mind is illustrated by these lines from the essay by Stuart Hampshire which I cite in sections 13 and 16:

> One may on reflection find a particular set of prohibitions and injunctions, and a particular way of life protected by them, acceptable and respectworthy, partly because this specifically conceived way of life, with its accompanying prohibitions, has in history appeared

natural, and on the whole still feels natural, both to oneself and to others. If there are no overriding reasons for rejecting this way of life, or for rejecting some distinguishing features of it, its felt and proven naturalness is one reason among others for accepting it.[3]

The question arises of what exactly is supposed to feel 'natural' here. Is it the cycle of birth, copulation and death, plus a few attendant rituals of the kind that make the whole world kin? Or is it the velvet upholstery into which the philosopher subsides at the end of the day? Hampshire's subsequent references to the 'natural order' (as a proper object of moral respect) suggest that the first reading may be truer to his intention. But between the first reading and the second there are indefinitely many gradations. A moment's reflection will show that considerable skill is needed in order to distinguish accurately, within the totality of one's social experience, between those elements which are relatively specific to one's own time and place and those which are relatively universal; and this means that any merely *intuitive* appeal to the 'felt and proven naturalness' of 'our form of life' may reasonably be suspected of flattering that point of view which is, indeed, a second nature to all rich people – a point of view from which it appears, for instance, that these cushions (which *feel* so delightfully natural) form part of something called the 'natural order', which cannot be violated without a kind of blasphemy. (Here, as elsewhere, we are apt to suppose that 'there has been history, but there is no longer any [history].')[4]

It would not be surprising, in the foreseeable future, to find expressivist concepts being put to increasingly disingenuous uses. We are all familiar with the idea that economic stagnation calls into question the customary defence of world capitalism in utilitarian terms – in terms, that is, of its power to satisfy our rationally unmotivated 'passions' for consumer-durables: how refreshing, then, to discover that the bourgeois

---

[3] Hampshire, *Public and Private Morality*, p. 21.
[4] Cf. Marx, *The Poverty of Philosophy* (1955), p. 105.

'way of life' has a value for us which cannot be measured by the frequency with which we buy a new car, but instead resides in the fact that that way of life is the objective manifestation of our very identity, so that the individual who attacks it 'sets his weapon against his own heart'.[5]

Nor would it be surprising if the idea of a 'shared form of life which is constitutive of rationality itself' were to assume growing philosophical importance against a background of international political crisis. In this connection, 'our way of life' definitely does not mean the way of life characteristic of men, women and children around the planet. Thus Margaret Thatcher recently spoke as follows in the House of Commons, urging British co-operation in the setting-up of a US-controlled 'rapid deployment force' for use in the Gulf region and elsewhere: 'I find it very alarming indeed that the Liberal Party, too, seems to be retreating from our first duty of defending our freedom as a Western Alliance . . . There would be no freedom, *no Western way of life,* unless we were prepared to defend it.'[6] This kind of rhetoric could certainly derive useful support from a revival of the doctrine of 'objective spirit' as interpreted, for example, by Bradley, who drew from his own version of that doctrine the conclusion that 'Death seems a little thing to those who go for her [their country] to their common and nameless grave.'[7]

23

The *de facto* connection of expressivist views about language with conservative social attitudes is not a new phenomenon. It begins, apparently, with Vico himself, to whom Isaiah

---

[5] Bradley, *Ethical Studies*, p. 172.

[6] *The Guardian* (3 March 1981) (emphasis added). Such pronouncements contain an implicit reference to the so-called 'Carter doctrine', which states that 'An attempt by any outside force to gain control of the Persian Gulf region will be regarded as an assault on the vital interests of the United States. It will be repelled by use of any means necessary, including military force' (*The Economist* (26 January 1980), p. 33).

[7] Bradley, *Ethical Studies*, p. 184.

Berlin attributes an 'anti-democratic bias' and an 'admiration for devout, authoritarian, semi-primitive societies'.[1] The connection becomes especially striking, however, towards the end of the nineteenth century, under the impact of advances in historical method and of the advent of philosophical sociology. These developments contributed to the general acceptance of the idea of morality as a social product. But they also suggested a possible substitute for the traditional (pre-Enlightenment) sense of moral security, which had rested on the (now increasingly fugitive) notion of natural law. The substitute which they suggested was the thought of a different kind of 'security' grounded in the sheer immovable bulk of society itself. The historicist habit of thought, in other words, dealt a further blow to belief in a metaphysical foundation for morality; but at the same time, its spokesmen promoted the view that morality could stand without any such foundation.

We saw in section 20 above that for Bradley 'morality is "relative", but is none the less real': it is a product of the historical experience of a particular community, but the demands it makes upon individual members of that community provide those individuals with the only idea of moral obligation which they, as 'sons of their time', can have. As new members are initiated into community life, they are confronted with the 'solid fact of a world so far moralized' – with the might, that is, of the institutions which form the material basis of moral authority; and they (or rather *we* – for it is our own situation that is being described) must learn that

---

[1] Isaiah Berlin, *Vico and Herder: Two Studies in the History of Ideas* (1976), p. xx. Similar attitudes on the part of Wittgenstein are well attested (see, for example, J. C. Nyiri, 'Wittgenstein's New Traditionalism', in *Acta Philosophica Fennica, Vol. 28 Nos. 1-3: Essays on Wittgenstein in Honour of G. H. von Wright* (1976), p. 503ff.), though he was also capable of using the word 'bourgeois' in a pejorative sense (cf. *CV* p. 17, 'Ramsey was a bourgeois thinker'). I find the evidence for Wittgenstein's own cultural conservatism entirely convincing, but must stress that I would not accept such evidence as telling against my proposed reading of his philosophy of language – a reading which I believe is adequately supported by his published work.

individual defiance of moral requirements can do nothing to shake the institutions themselves: 'despite our faults the moral world stands fast.'[2] Bradley would have concurred with the following remarks by the social anthropologist L. Lévy-Bruhl, which are intended to persuade the concerned public of the early 1900s that the 'scientific' investigation of morality will not, as his critics have claimed, bring about a general moral collapse:

> The foundation of morality . . . is inseparable from the very structure of each society. The morality of a social group, like its language and its institutions, is born with it, develops and evolves with it, and disappears only with it . . . The most anxious consciences can therefore be calm. The relative and provisional character of all morality, thus understood [sc. as analogous to the provisional character of language] – and it is in this sense alone that the science of morals entails it – does not compromise the stability of existing morality.[3]

It is still possible, in our own day, to find evidence of a *de facto* link between 'non-foundationalism' with respect to a particular type of thought, and conservatism with respect to the relevant subject-matter. I will mention two instances. The first, which has already been touched on in section 1, is Hare's response to the problem of 'fanaticism': the 'logical possibility of people becoming fanatics without self-contradiction', i.e. electing to prescribe universally a very eccentric set of moral principles. Hare thinks that we can deal with such people by challenging them to *try* to put their principles into practice in their own lives. The 'sting' attaching to this challenge is that even if, as Hare maintains, the individual is logically free to want *anything* (neutrally described)[4] and to issue *any* universal prescription, regardless of content, still he will not always be free to act upon his

---

[2] Bradley, *Ethical Studies*, p. 182.
[3] L. Lévy-Bruhl, *La morale et la science des moeurs* (1953), pp. xxiv, xxvii.
[4] Cf. Hare, *Freedom and Reason*, p. 110.

chosen principles, because if they are too pernicious, the rest of 'us' will prevent him. So there is, after all, a practical limit to the individualism of Hare's moral world – a limit imposed by the militant commitment of ordinary people to their own intersubjective, or consensual, morality. (This is Hare's rendering of the 'partisan' or 'voluntarist' theme which I have described as the crux of the non-cognitivist theory of ethics.)

The proposed treatment of 'fanaticism' is memorable for its presumption that the existing moral consensus will successfully withstand any attempted subversion. Hare's message, at this point, echoes that of Lévy-Bruhl: the non-cognitive status of morality in general does not compromise the stability of the morality we actually have.

The other case I wish to mention is drawn from a different area of philosophy. W. v. O. Quine, defending a modified natural-scientific empiricism in which 'the unit of empirical significance is [not the individual statement, but] the whole of science',[5] claims that 'the considerations which guide [a man] in warping his scientific heritage to fit his continuing sensory promptings are, *where rational, pragmatic.*'[6] Where we find ourselves unable to continue with our inherited, or otherwise established, total theory of nature in the face of fresh sensory evidence, we are (once again) *logically* free to adopt any strategy which will make that theory consistent with the 'recalcitrant experience': 'Any statement can be held true come what may, if we make drastic enough adjustments elsewhere in the system . . . Conversely, by the same token, no statement is immune to revision.'[7] In the event, however, our choice of strategy will be determined (Quine thinks) by a certain 'natural tendency to disturb the total system as little as possible'. 'Conservatism figures in such choices',[8] as does the quest for simplicity. Nor is there anything wrong with conservatism, for though it is 'the counsel of laziness', it is also 'the strategy of discovery'.[9] Conscious methodology will

---

[5] W. v. O. Quine, *From a Logical Point of View*, 2nd edn (1961), p. 42.
[6] Ibid., p. 46; emphasis added.
[7] Ibid., p. 43.
[8] Ibid., pp. 44, 46.
[9] Quine, *Word and Object*, p. 20.

prefer simplicity to conservatism where the two principles conflict, but 'conservatism is nevertheless the preponderant force'; and no wonder, adds Quine disarmingly, since 'it can still operate when stamina and imagination fail.'

Analogously, Quine holds that the question of what our scientific theories are about (i.e. what objects the theorems of those theories refer to) is one which cannot receive an absolute answer; it can be asked only in relation to some 'background language' in which the answer is to be stated. ('When we ask, "Does 'rabbit' really refer to rabbits?" someone can counter with the question: "Refer to rabbits in what sense of 'rabbits'?" thus launching a regress; and we need the background language to regress into.')[10] So it does not make sense to ask, in absolute terms, what the objects of a theory are: all we can do is to ask for a reinterpretation of the theory itself in terms of another theory which we happen to understand better. Eventually, however, we shall come to rest (on pain of giving up the inquiry as hopeless) with one or another paraphrase of the original theory, couched now in a language whose ontology is, for us, 'primitively adopted and ultimately inscrutable'.[11] And although no particular choice of background language is logically imposed upon us (cf. Wittgenstein, *OC* §475, quoted in section 14 above), still our *actual* choice will not be made at random: 'in practice we end the regress of background languages, in discussions of reference, by acquiescing in our mother tongue and taking its words at face value.'[12] The role of 'acquiescence' here corresponds to that of 'conservatism' in Quine's wider account of theory-building: a policy which, while not irresistible in principle, will turn out (most of the time) to be prohibitively difficult to depart from in practice.

---

[10] W. v. O. Quine, *Ontological Relativity* (1969), p. 48.

[11] Ibid., p. 51.

[12] Ibid., p. 49. It is interesting to notice that this sentence would not read so attractively if the idiomatic expression happened to be 'father tongue' instead of 'mother tongue'.

24

Before proceeding to a detailed examination of the way in which our proposed moral realism – drawing, as it does, upon expressivist ideas about language – can be misrepresented in the interests of conservative ideology, we should notice that that realism does, in fact, force upon us a certain line of thought which might fairly be described as 'conservative'. It does this in virtue of its emphasis upon *continuity*.

The point may be explained as follows. As we saw earlier (sections 7, 9, 10, 14), Wittgenstein holds that language, *qua* medium of communication, operates on the basis of an 'agreement in judgements', which is necessarily also an agreement in form of life (*PI* I §241-2). But the shared practice which Wittgenstein sees as the material basis of communication has not only a synchronic, but a diachronic aspect. It is implicit in his vision of language that if we are to be able to talk to one another, there must be a practice which persists over time, and with which language is interwoven.

We are already in a position to see what this continuity involves, in terms of the 'outer side' (as Bradley would put it) of language-use. The goal of linguistic training, it has been suggested, is to draw the individual into an established *Sittlichkeit* (cf. section 16 above) – to initiate him into a community of persons bound together by their allegiance to the rules of a single symbolic system (or 'language-game', in the holistic sense). To give allegiance to a linguistic rule is to acknowledge an obligation to 'do the same'. However, as we noted in section 20, the practices which constitute obedience to such rules possess a determinate content only in virtue of the institutional character of rules in general: we cannot meaningfully speak of following a rule, except where there exists a (temporally enduring) seat of authority from which we can find out what would count as a correct application of a rule in a particular context.

We must now consider this fact – the fact that language cannot function without some degree of material continuity –

from what Bradley would call its 'inner side': that is to say, we must ask what it means for the individual.

In the first place, it means that human personality is acquired by *imitating other human beings*.[1] The kind of imitation in question here is, by its very nature, uncritical, since it is identified as the means by which we learn to talk – and until we can talk, we are not reckoned as creatures who can *think* at all, critically or otherwise. It will help to bring this view into focus if we contrast it with the liberal ideal of the intellectual self-reliance of the individual: an ideal expressed, for example, in Mill's statement that 'if the grounds of an opinion are not conclusive to [a] person's own reason, his reason cannot be strengthened, but is likely to be weakened, by his adopting it.'[2] This is directly at odds with the Wittgensteinian position we are developing: according to that position, the 'strengthening' of individual reason to the point where critical thought begins to emerge is effected precisely by implanting in the learner a system of beliefs for which no grounds are offered. The language-game is access-ible to the learner only on condition that he 'trust something' (*OC* §509): in the course of his initiation he will often be confronted by the kind of dogmatism discussed in section 15 above, a dogmatism grounded in the *status* of his teacher as a competent exponent of existing practice. (The key text cited was *OC* §206, 'if you learn more, you too will think the same'; but cf. also *OC* §310, 'A pupil and a teacher. The pupil will not let anything be explained to him, for he continually interrupts with doubts, for instance as to the existence of

---

[1] Cf. T. Adorno, *Minima Moralia* (1944), trs. E. F. N. Jephcott (1974), p. 154: 'Genuineness [i.e. the 'authenticity' extolled by Kierkegaard and subsequent existentialist thinkers] is nothing other than a defiant and obstinate insistence on the monadological form which social oppression imposes on man. Anything that does not wish to wither should rather take on itself the stigma of the inauthentic. For it lives on the mimetic heritage. The human is indissolubly linked with imitation: a human being only becomes human at all by imitating other human beings. In such behaviour, the primal form of love, the priests of authenticity scent traces of the utopia which could shake the structure of domination.'
[2] J. S. Mill, 'On Liberty', in *Utilitarianism*, ed. Mary Warnock (1962), p. 187.

things, the meaning of words, etc. The teacher says "Stop interrupting and do as I tell you. So far your doubts don't make sense at all." ' – A stark warning to youthful admirers of Mill.)

Secondly, and from the standpoint of the educator, it means that in order to be able to recruit new participants to our total language-game, or form of life, we need to be ready to point to certain beliefs whose acquisition we are prepared to *call* 'learning' (which is, of course, a normative concept – like 'true', with which it is, in a Wittgensteinian sense, grammatically connected). Our role as educators is not to say 'Here are some ideas for your consideration: $p, q, r \ldots$', but to *assert* $p, q, r \ldots$ and to train our pupils to act in accordance with those propositions (cf. *OC* §144). The educational process essentially involves an exercise of rational subjectivity on the part of the educator – a readiness, once again, to 'put his mind where his mouth is' (cf. section 20 above). In the present case, this would be a readiness to identify oneself with a certain substantive conception of how the world is, and with the particular way of acting which corresponds to that conception.

If we consider our Wittgensteinian picture of linguistic training in its specific application to the transmission of the *moral* language-game, the resultant thought is that here, too, the educator must be in a position to equip the learner with an array of substantive beliefs. The beliefs in question would be of the type characterized as capable of providing non-hypothetical grounds for action (cf. section 13 above) in virtue of their bearing on the project of living a good life. From such an array of beliefs the learner will be able, as his sophistication increases, to abstract an array of moral *concepts* – that is, concepts to which he can appeal with a view to the non-hypothetical justification (or condemnation) of particular courses of action.[3] As moral educators, we have to ensure for our pupil, by the transmission of this repertoire of concepts, the 'possibility of the phenomenon' (*PI* I §90) of

---

[3] Such concepts are suited, in other words, to feature in a particular kind of 'desirability characterization'. Cf. Anscombe, *Intention*, §37.

there being a non-hypothetical point in doing anything (cf. section 49 below).

But since the pupil must acquire a system of moral *beliefs* before he can be said to possess a repertoire of moral concepts, this part of his education as much as any other provides a field of operation for the (benign) conformism which consists in imitating certain habits of judgement exemplified by his teachers. As Bradley puts it, 'To the question, How am I to know what is right? the answer must be, By the *aisthēsis* of the *phronimos* [the perception, or intuition, of the wise man]; and the *phronimos* is the man who has identified his will with the moral spirit of his community, and judges accordingly.'[4] If the language-game is to be sustained, the pupil must take the teacher's judgement as authoritative; but conversely, the teacher must present himself as a model of *sound* moral thinking – a competent exponent of the rules of a language-game which, for him, forms part of the content of *Sittlichkeit*.

The Wittgensteinian position we have been developing turns out, therefore, to allot an essential role to *historical continuity* in securing a meaningful life for individual persons. This again is in contrast with non-cognitive theories of ethics. Far from being able to bring moral order into our lives by the exercise of an autonomous will – a mysterious decision-making power with no discernible historical origins – we acquire the capacity for moral judgement, on the proposed realist view, by inserting ourselves into the historical process of using moral language.

───── 25 ─────

The specifically moral significance imputed here to continuity, authority, imitation, and kindred concepts is ultimately determined by certain more general considerations

---

[4] Bradley, *Ethical Studies*, p. 196. For the *aisthēsis* of the *phronimos*, cf. Aristotle, *Nicomachean Ethics*, 1106b 36-1107a 2; 1109b 20-3; 1143b 11-14; 1176a 15-19.

about the nature of theoretical change over time – considerations which flow from the idea of language-games as grounded in a form of life, i.e. a synchronically shared and diachronically continuous practice.

Wittgenstein argues in *On Certainty* that all we can lay claim to, in those areas where metaphysicians have traditionally sought a 'foundation' for human knowledge, are *propositions which one is unable to doubt:* the reason being that if we did doubt them, it would mean 'giving up all judgement' (*OC* §494). For example, we should then have to doubt the validity of every test which might be used to allay the original doubt (cf. *OC* §125). But 'global doubt' of this kind differs in a fundamental way from what we ordinarily mean by 'doubt', for in the normal course of things our inquiries – our *uncertainties*, in whatever field – take place against the background of a stable world-picture, or total theory, by reference to which we determine the truth or falsity of what is dubious; and it is only in relation to this background that they make sense as part of a project of trying to find out how things are. By contrast, a retreat from the beliefs which make up the background itself – i.e. which count, for us, as certainties – would not cohere with any such project: it would amount, rather, to an abandonment of the struggle to keep things under cognitive control (to 'stay in the saddle' (*OC* §616) in our capacity as transcendental subject of judgement).

Such an event is, of course, perfectly imaginable (for example, something 'really unheard-of' might happen (*OC* §513)). Indeed, there is at the best of times no sharp boundary, as regards the rational surveyability of the world, between our normal condition and one in which we should say we had gone mad (cf. Z §393). The 'mad' condition could not, however, be described in terms of *doubt,* for doubts 'form a system' (*OC* §126): a doubt implies recognition of the possibility of error, and (*OC* §74) 'when someone makes a mistake, this can be fitted into what he knows aright.' The condition of 'doubting' all our beliefs indiscriminately does not belong within theoretical activity at all, but represents an abdication from such activity.

There is a convergence here with Quine's view, discussed in section 23 above, that in making specific changes to our total theory of nature in the face of new experience, we are guided by considerations which are 'where rational, pragmatic'. Both Quine and Wittgenstein maintain that if we throw out too much of our intellectual furniture at once, we cease to have a habitable world-view at all; Quine's own explicit endorsement, in the light of this idea, of a policy of 'conservatism' with respect to scientific theory-change presumably reflects a modest view of human flexibility and inventiveness (cf. section 46 below).

The 'habitability' of a world-view, however, is not simply a function of its consequences for the individual subject as he interacts with his physical environment. It is also a function of the scope which that world-view offers him for intellectual and practical integration into the life of the community to which he belongs. The pragmatic disincentive to reject a *de facto* certainty – a proposition that lies near the centre of the total system which has been made plausible to us (cf. *OC* §140) – has a social dimension as well as a purely mechanical one: dissent from the 'agreement in judgements' which underlies communication contains an inherent danger, if carried far enough, of cutting us loose from the network of social relationships which constitutes our identity as rational beings. For the practical expression of my rejecting a proposition theoretically is my refusal to act in accordance with it (cf. *OC* §144): but if I refuse to act in certain sorts of ways which are essential to the character of the language-game played by my community (cf. *PI* I §568), I thereby expel myself from the game – and so from the 'shared form of life which (in my particular case) is constitutive of rationality itself.' This is what Bradley has in mind when he writes: 'The knowledge that as members of the system we are real, and not otherwise, encourages us more and more to identify ourselves with that system.'[1] The limiting case of this idea would be the view that *rational dissent* from the prevailing consensual world-view was a logical impossibility.

---

[1] Bradley, *Ethical Studies*, pp. 182-3.

It thus appears to follow from the non-foundational theory of knowledge associated with our proposed moral realist position that a certain measure of conservatism, or gradualism, in respect of theory-change is imposed on us by the material exigencies of 'finding our way about'. Our ability to do this depends not only on the internal coherence of our behaviour as individuals, but also on the sustainability of our relation to existing social institutions. It is the latter form of dependence which lays us open to what Nietzsche calls the 'argument from growing solitude': 'A cold look or a sneer,' he writes, 'on the face of those among whom and for whom one has been educated, is feared even by the strongest. What is it that they are really afraid of? Growing solitude! This . . . rebuts even the best arguments for a person or a cause.'[2]

Does this feature of non-foundational epistemology allow us to draw any conclusions about the appropriate attitude to adopt towards moral or political dissent in our own society? In section 22 above I suggested that our specific historical circumstances may present philosophers with a temptation to try to extract some lesson of this kind. It is now time to embark on a more detailed discussion of their possible train of thought.

––––– 26 –––––

It is sometimes suggested that to reject the empiricist view of language in favour of the sort of view we have been developing is to return to a doctrine of 'direct' or 'unmediated' realism, extending to all branches of epistemology. This suggestion is to be found, for example, in the paper by Davidson to which I referred in section 9:

> In giving up dependence on the concept of an uninterpreted reality, something outside all schemes and science, we do not relinquish the norm of objective truth – quite the contrary. Given the dogma of a dualism of

---

[2] Nietzsche, *The Gay Science*, §50.

scheme and reality, we get conceptual relativity, and truth relative to a scheme. Without the dogma, this kind of relativity goes by the board. Of course the truth of sentences remains relative to language, but that is as objective as can be. In giving up the dualism of scheme and world, we do not give up the world, but re-establish unmediated touch with the familiar objects whose antics make our sentences and opinions true or false.[1]

Michael Williams concurs with Davidson: 'Once we abandon the foundational view, our knowledge of the physical world is secure. There is a sense in which the no-foundations view amounts to a defence of direct realism. . . .'[2]

We saw in section 5 above that the organizing principle of empiricist moral philosophy is a dualism of 'fact' and 'value': on one side the (evaluatively dead) objective world, on the other the value we project on to it.[3] The scheme/content dualism criticized by Davidson can be seen as a more sophisticated version of the same idea, placing on one side an uninterpreted sensory manifold, on the other the system of categories that we impose on this manifold in order to talk about it. This general pattern of thinking embraces a variety of possible definitions of the sphere of 'value',[4] but its variant expressions are united by their common ancestry in the

---

[1] Davidson, 'On the Very Idea . . .', p. 20.

[2] Michael Williams, *Groundless Belief,* p. 179.

[3] For a recent statement of this view, cf. Mackie, *Ethics,* p. 42ff.

[4] Thus Wiggins ('Truth, Invention . . .') suggests that the fact/value distinction might be made perspicuous in terms of a contrast between predicates denoting primary qualities of the physical world – predicates which will not be eliminated from our language by the putative convergence of scientific theories on a single, explanatorily adequate account of that world – and all other predicates whatsoever. Such a distinction would not coincide with that on which twentieth-century non-cognitivism has been based, since it banishes from the domain of the factual all discourse about possible objects of human concern: the language of 'fact', on Wiggins' proposed account, 'does not even have the resources to pick out the extensions of "red", "chair", "person", "earthquake", "famine" . . .' (p. 363). However, that account also differs from the classical Kantian view that the structure of all thought about the phenomenal world is supplied by the categories of the (human) understanding.

111

Enlightenment concept of a self-defining subject set over against the natural world. That concept, as Charles Taylor has written, 'brought along with it an objectifying of things, that is, it debarred notions like "meaning", "expression", "purpose" as inappropriate descriptions of objective reality and confined them rather to the mental life of subjects'.[5] Its influence is to be seen in the characteristically empiricist thought that the meaning of our experience – whether these words are construed in their humane sense, or in more narrowly perceptual terms – is injected into it through the operation of our own minds.

The target of Davidson's criticism – the 'conceptual scheme' of which we can supposedly predicate commensurability, or incommensurability, with others of its kind – is represented as a system of linguistic categories such that it is only by 'organizing' their sensory input in terms of these categories that human subjects can gain any knowledge of the external world. (Compare the role of the Kantian concepts, without which intuitions are blind.) The 'scheme' in its entirety, then, is supposed to be 'projected' on to the world in the same sense in which, for the purposes of the non-cognitivists' 'fact/value distinction', the specific batch of categories picked out as *evaluative* were supposed to be projected (in keeping with the mind's 'propensity to spread itself upon external objects').

Now we have already noted Davidson's claim that if, as his transcendental argument from interpretative method indicates, we cannot make sense of the idea of a plurality of such conceptual schemes, then we cannot intelligibly speak of a single such scheme either. The foregoing discussion suggests another way of stating this claim, as follows: if we cannot make sense of the thought that the act of 'projection', which is held to be responsible for the entire conceptual articulation of our experience, might be carried out in distinct and mutually incommensurable ways by different human groups, then we can have no use, either, for the idea of a single, transcendentally real source of light whose interception by the various

[5] Taylor, *Hegel*, p. 14.

extant conceptual 'filters' would yield this putative assortment of world-pictures; and once we cease to postulate a space between light-source and filter, the concept of *projection* itself becomes redundant. That is how Davidson's line of reasoning leads us back to the idea of a simple, transparent relation of reference between language and the world: a relation perceived, now, as internal to language itself (since *what makes a sentence true* is the *obtaining of its truth-condition*, and the latter cannot be specified without recourse to language), but none the less adequate on that account to the needs of a realistic theory of knowledge.

And so Davidson seems to abolish the possibility of thinking that human beings somehow participate, through the language they use, in the construction of the world they talk about. He seems to negate the discovery which marks the beginning of the modern period in intellectual history – namely, that the 'world text' is (at least partly; at least under some aspect) *written by ourselves*. His exposition suggests that the abandonment of empiricist metaphysics will render invisible to us the activity of representation – the *fabricated* character of linguistic signs – and so confront us directly, or 'immediately' (cf. 'unmediated contact') with the realm of objects represented.[6] And these objects, be it noted, are none other than the 'familiar' ones: the relativity of truth to language means, as far as we are concerned, its relativity to the language we actually have.

---

[6] T. S. Eliot writes in 'The Cultivation of Christmas Trees', in *Collected Poems* (1974):

> There are several attitudes to Christmas, some of which
> we may disregard:

> The social, the torpid, the patently commercial,
> The rowdy (the pubs being open till midnight),
> And the childish – which is not that of the child,
> For whom the candle is a star, and the gilded angel
> Spreading its wings at the summit of the tree
> Is not only a decoration, but an angel.

The child in the poem is not concerned with the fact that the 'angel' is made, say, of plastic and comes from Hong Kong. He is not yet acquainted with the idea of representation as a human activity, generating symbols which

27

'Direct' or 'unmediated', as a predicate of the proposed (post-empiricist) type of realism, is unobjectionable if it simply means 'non-inferential'. By describing our understanding of some specified region of discourse as 'directly realistic' in *that* sense, we should only be registering our conviction that judgements relating to the subject-matter in question were not to be thought of as inferences from evidence which could be characterized independently of the system of concepts featuring in those judgements. For example, in the case of everyday discourse about our physical surroundings, the rejection of empiricist epistemology in favour of a 'direct realism' would involve denying the view of Ayer (cf. section 5) that straightforward perceptual judgements such as 'That is a pencil' embody an inference – albeit a tacit one – from the evidence furnished by sensory impressions. Similarly, we can imagine a moral philosopher embracing the proposed view as an alternative, say, to utilitarianism – which, as Platts has pointed out,[1] is also realistic in the sense that it represents moral judgement as answerable to truth. Such a theorist would be exchanging an *indirect* realism about moral language for a *direct* realism. He would be rejecting the idea of moral judgements as inferences from non-moral evidence, namely, evidence as to the effects of actual or possible courses of action upon human mental states; and he would be replacing it with the idea of such judgements as recording moral information, conceived now as presenting itself directly to our senses.

---

may or may not have a counterpart in the 'real world'. When he grows older he will learn that there can be representations of angels even though angels do not really exist (though that is not necessarily the end of the story, for Eliot's intentions in this poem are thoroughly Hegelian). For the moment, however, the child's perception of the angel is 'direct', in the sense that it is not 'mediated' by any explicit consciousness of the signifying function of the plastic object in front of him.

[1] Platts, *Ways of Meaning*, p. 243.

As stated in section 12 above, our conversion to a more liberal notion of the possible content of sensory input would not necessarily signal a return to the tactics of positing indefinite numbers of mental 'faculties', in terms of whose exercise our capacity for making certain sorts of judgement would then be explained. Suppose, for instance, that an exponent of our proposed realism were to refer, in moral contexts, to a distinctively moral 'vision' or 'perception' – the subjective counterpart, so to speak, of our impersonally expressed idea of moral evidence as directly accessible to awareness. In such a case we should understand the use of perceptual terminology, not as pointing towards a metaphysical explanation of our ability to think in a particular way (cf. Wittgenstein, *RFM* VI §31, 'Our disease is one of wanting to explain'), but merely as affirming a phenomenological fact about language. The relevant fact would be that one of the complex of techniques we acquire when we learn to talk is the technique of finding forms of words suited to the moral appraisal of situations with which we are confronted: an activity which proceeds 'directly' from the confrontation itself, instead of being 'mediated' by some prior appraisal of the facts in non-moral terms.

The Wittgensteinian moral realist will point out that his own justification for describing moral judgement in perceptual terms is to be found in the character of the moral language-game itself. He will join Michael Williams in '[declining] to set any *a priori* limits to the kinds of things on which, with suitable training, we might come to report directly';[2] and from a rationalist point of view, morality will be among the beneficiaries of this undogmatic attitude.

However, there is another sense in which it would be highly misleading to suggest that when we reject the empiricist dichotomy of scheme and content (or fact and value) in favour of this kind of realist view, we thereby 're-establish *unmediated* touch with the familiar objects' of discourse. Davidson's suggestion is open to a misinterpretation which would annul the very characteristic that renders the proposed

---

[2] Michael Williams, *Groundless Belief*, p. 180.

realism thinkable, in its application to morals, for ourselves as heirs of the Enlightenment. For our kind of realism is, precisely, 'mediated' by a form of reflective awareness which was absent from the pre-Enlightenment conception of a real, or natural, moral order. It is 'mediated' by the new dimension of self-consciousness which accrues to those who accept the expressivist vision of language embodied in Wittgenstein's philosophy. What we get from that philosophy is, as I shall try to explain, a further development[3] of the distinctively modern notion of the self-defining human subject: a transposition of the idea of autonomous subjectivity from the individual to the collective field.

To subscribe to Wittgenstein's view of language is to recognize language-use as an aspect of human behaviour. Despite the generally unsystematic appearance of Wittgenstein's later writings, we can find in this basic insight the key to his entire therapeutic strategy against the 'bewitchment of our intelligence by means of language (*PI* I §109). Wittgenstein shares the view expressed by Marx, that 'all mysteries which lead theory to mysticism find their rational solution in human practice and in the comprehension of this practice' (cf. section 7 above).

By the time he composed the *Blue Book*, Wittgenstein had already singled out the vice of linguistic fetishism[4] as the

---

[3] In terms of the general history of philosophy it was not, of course, left to Wittgenstein to perform this transposition. The work had been done, more than a century earlier, by Hegel and Marx. But as far as the adherents of non-cognitivism are concerned, it is as if that step had never been taken; and it is with reference to these theorists that I speak of Wittgenstein's thought as incorporating a 'further development' of the notion of self-defining subjectivity. The proposed moral realism develops that notion beyond the individualistic stage, which is as far as it has progressed within empiricist moral philosophy; and it is as a rival to empiricist moral philosophy that the proposed theory presents itself.

[4] Wittgenstein himself does not refer to 'linguistic fetishism', but a precedent for this way of describing our 'bewitchment by language' is to be found in the following passage from Nietzsche: 'Language belongs in its origins to the age of the most rudimentary form of psychology: we find ourselves in the midst of a rude fetishism when we call to mind the basic

characteristic source of philosophical confusion. 'The mistake we are liable to make,' he writes (*BB* p. 5), 'could be expressed thus: We are looking for the use of a sign, but we look for it as though it were an object *coexisting* with the sign.' And again (*BB* p. 28), 'a word hasn't got a meaning given to it, as it were, by a power independent of us, so that there could be a kind of scientific investigation into what the word really means. A word has the meaning someone has given to it.'

The error condemned in these passages consists in treating as a *natural phenomenon* (cf. 'object'; 'scientific investigation') what is really a product of our own actions, and hence, a manifestation of our own subjectivity. 'The use of a word' sounds like 'the leg of a table'; but this superficial analogy may deceive us by disguising the fact that 'the use of a word' is an abstract variant of 'how a word is used': and *using a word* is something that *we do*. Wittgenstein, then, rebukes the purveyors of traditional metaphysics for refusing the genuinely philosophical task of *self*-examination with respect to our ways of talking and thinking, and, consequently, for misrepresenting that task as one of exploring a certain problematic realm of *objective* entities – the realm of 'meanings'.

28

But this means that to gain a reflective awareness of the practical character of language – which is the fate of the theorist who exchanges non-cognitivism for our proposed form of moral realism – is to lose one's innocence with respect to participation in language-games. Any person who succeeds in emancipating himself from the linguistic fetishism condemned by Wittgenstein thereby 'falls', in a somewhat

presuppositions of the metaphysics of language . . . It is *this* which sees everywhere deed and doer; this which believes in will as cause in general . . .' (*Twilight of the Idols* (1889), trs. R. J. Hollingdale (1968), p. 38).

theological sense, into the knowledge that 'words are also deeds' (*PI* I §546). That is to say, he ceases to think of language primarily as a medium in which we *copy* reality, and comes to recognize the organic connection of each individual language with a specific *culture* – a complex of activities which, instead of being answerable (like a 'copy') to some norm or paradigm external to itself, may assume any (ecologically viable) form whatsoever.

Wittgenstein says that 'Commanding, questioning, recounting, chatting, are as much a part of our natural history as walking, eating, drinking, playing' (*PI* I §25). But it is clear that he sees linguistic phenomena as belonging to our cultural, or human, history as well as to that of our evolution as a natural species. The existing multiplicity of linguistic forms, he writes, 'is not something fixed, given once for all; but new types of language, new language-games, as we may say, come into existence, and others become obsolete and get forgotten' (*PI* I §23). It is our recognition of this fact, i.e. of the transience and replaceability of language-games, which confers upon our participation in the prevailing game a moral dimension that it did not previously possess. By acknowledging that we could do something other than what we actually do, we acknowledge the openness of our actual practice to a form of critical scrutiny which we could not previously have seen to be applicable to it.

A similar thought is expressed in Nietzsche's remark that 'all experiences are moral experiences, even in the realm of sense perception':[1] in other words, all reports on experience are morally significant, because our use of the particular words in which they are couched constitutes an act with a definite moral character; it exhibits our commitment to the scheme of values implicit in that vocabulary.

We are now in a position to see more clearly what was meant in section 7 above by the assertion that, on a Wittgensteinian view of language, the empiricist categories of 'fact' and 'value' coalesce in such a way that each must be

---

[1] Nietzsche, *The Gay Science*, §114.

thought of as pervading the entire declarative part of our discourse. We can now appreciate that if *objectivity* is everywhere (so that we can have the concept of 'moral reality' along with that of 'physical reality'), *subjectivity* is everywhere too. Each time we take part in the practice of talking about the objective world, under whatever aspect (moral, physical, etc.), we in effect identify ourselves with the institutions in which the relevant language-game is embodied: by 'putting our minds where our mouths are' – assuming, of course, that we are in fact doing this, i.e. that our participation in the language-game is ingenuous – we breathe into those institutions the 'spirit' without which they would be expressively dead (cf. section 20 above).

With these considerations in mind, we can say of linguistic practices – as Collingwood said of civilizations (cf. section 2 above) – that they depend for their survival on the continuing will of individuals to participate in them. And this is no less true of those language-games which lie towards the factual end of the fact/value continuum (cf. section 17 above) than of those which lie towards the evaluative end. Each one is, in principle, dispensable: just as 'any logic good enough for a primitive means of communication needs no apology from us' (*OC* §475), so any language-game – irrespective of its subject-matter – can be subtracted from our total repertoire 'without apology' if we can continue, as a community, to function without it. Subject to that one qualification, nothing constrains our choice of how to live or what linguistic systems to maintain in use; and to those who recognize this, their participation in any existing way of life will henceforward appear under the aspect of moral *complicity*.

The consciousness of that complicity cannot, of course, be expected to affect everyone in the same way – a point which has been well stated by Stanley Cavell. 'The reason why methods which make us look at what we say, and bring the forms of language (and hence our forms of life) to consciousness, can present themselves to one person as confining and to another as liberating is,' he suggests, 'understandable in this way: recognizing what we say, in the way that is relevant in

119

philosophizing, is like recognizing our present commitments and their implications; to one person a sense of freedom will demand an escape from them, to another it will require their more total acceptance.'[2]

29

The suggestion is, then, that in embracing Wittgenstein's philosophy of language we are adding a new determination (cf. section 8) to our conception of our own moral autonomy. Granted the Wittgensteinian picture, our actions turn out to possess moral significance not only in relation to the positive rules which govern our conduct as members of some particular community (the morality of 'rendering unto Caesar', so to speak), but also in relation to any canons of criticism which we may be able to bring to bear upon that set of rules (and hence upon our own submission to them).

The same construction could have been placed upon the claim made in section 14 that, with reference to the community as a whole, linguistic and other social norms are not prescriptive but descriptive: they are abstract representations of what is actually done by speakers or agents who are recognized as competent exponents of the relevant language-game. As far as individuals are concerned, the rules of the game are indeed compelling, but only 'in the same sense as other laws in human society', i.e. materially. But this implies that if, *as a community,* we did things differently, then the rules governing our thought and conduct *as individuals* would be different too. And so it looks, once again, as though we ourselves are answerable for the existence of the particular system of social constraints by which we find ourselves bound.

At this point a possible objection must be considered. The argument of the foregoing sections has suggested that the

[2] S. Cavell, 'The Availability of Wittgenstein's Later Philosophy' (1962), in Pitcher (ed.), *Wittgenstein: The Philosophical Investigations* (1966), pp. 166-7 n.

oppressively 'empty freedom' enjoyed by Iris Murdoch's 'Kantian man' (the paradigm of moral agency inherited by non-cognitivism; cf. section 4 above) will obstinately survive the abandonment of a non-cognitive theory in favour of our proposed Wittgensteinian moral realism, undergoing thereby nothing more disruptive than a transposition from the sphere of individual to that of collective behaviour. (This is, no doubt, the reason why expository writing about Wittgenstein tends to throw up curiously 'existentialist' turns of phrase, as, for example, when Dummett attributes to him the view that '*At each step* [in a piece of mathematical reasoning] *we are free to choose* to accept or reject the proof.'[1]) So much may be conceded; but how, it will be asked, does the freedom of a linguistic community to play any (ecologically possible) language-game – the absence of anything keeping *us*, collectively, 'on the rails'[2] – impinge upon the individual agent? In what sense does it yield the idea of individual moral *complicity* in a prevailing way of life?

Wittgenstein, as we have seen, is impressed by the necessity for us to 'accept many things' (*OC* §344; cf. section 25 above) – specifically, to maintain a posture of uncritical acceptance towards a certain core of intellectually authoritative institutions – if we are to be able to *think* at all, or (equivalently) to make sense of the world we inhabit. The anarchic spirit who undertakes too bold a programme of subversion endangers his own intellectual identity thereby, for he runs the risk of severing himself wholesale from all available models of sound judgement: that sort of freedom, to borrow a useful formulation from a different context, proves in the end to be just another word for nothing left to lose. It may therefore be objected that our Wittgensteinian premises make it appropriate, rather, to see the prevailing form of life as a kind of juggernaut, bearing us inexorably onward without regard for our wishes – the suppression of individual moral autonomy

---

[1] Michael Dummett, 'Wittgenstein's Philosophy of Mathematics', in *Truth and Other Enigmas*, p. 171 (emphasis added).
[2] The phrase is McDowell's, in 'Virtue and Reason', (cf. section 10 note 2 above); cf. also Wittgenstein, *PI* I §218, and context.

being, surely, no more than the price we agreed to pay in order to defend our own position against the irrationalist tendencies we detected in non-cognitivism. And that being so, the objection will continue, what sort of sense does it make to burden the individual with a responsibility for the conduct or ultimate fate of the whole?

A useful preliminary to the discussion of this problem might be to recall Wiggins' proposal (cf. section 20 above) that moral philosophy should now be trying to resolve the contradiction, inherent in non-cognitivism, between the 'inner, or participative' and the 'outer, supposedly objective' conception of ourselves as agents. That proposal, it will be remembered, was attended by a caveat: Wiggins holds out no hope of recovering by such means the 'intuitive certainty' which we may find enviable in the moral life of the past.

In the light of the suggestion made in section 28 – namely, that to accept a Wittgensteinian view of language is to become conscious of the historicity of one's own form of life, and consequently of the fact that it could be changed – the impossibility of recovering that kind of moral certainty is readily intelligible. Armed with our newly-acquired historicist insight, we can never again participate otherwise than *reflectively* in any language-game. From now on, we cannot speak at all without being aware of ourselves as *ipso facto* joining in a practice of speaking *in some particular way* – a practice enforced by our community's (ultimately material, cf. section 15 above) insistence on conformity to the going norms of judgement and argument.

How can we, with this knowledge, continue to participate in the game? For it might now be argued that we could never, on pain of surrendering all our dignity as autonomous moral subjects, consent to take our place in what we consciously recognized as a structure of relationships of material control and submission. In that case, the argument would continue, the likely outcome of our historicist insight would be a perpetual ironic standing-off from the social practices to which, before we gained that insight, we were able to bring a naïve conviction; or if we found the ironic pose too hard to sustain, we might be tempted just to reimmerse ourselves sentimentally in forms of behaviour which seemed to us to have offered a meaningful life to earlier generations – people who understood less than we do about the matters under consideration here.[3]

Now the considerations of section 20 suggest a possible response to this difficulty. They suggest the thought that we shall be able to integrate the so-called 'inner' and 'outer' viewpoints – to 'put our minds where our mouths are', while at the same time retaining our consciousness of the historicity of the language-game – just to the extent that we can 'find ourselves' in the public, or institutional, framework of the game. If we are to accomplish the desired integration, we need to be able to recognize the relevant institutions as an adequate expression of our 'true being', i.e. of the values and beliefs by which we define our identity. For the possibility of doing this can be equated with the possibility of regarding the prevailing form of life as *rational:* which is precisely what we must be able to do, if we are coherently to combine a practical commitment to that form of life with a reflective awareness of its replaceability by a different one.

―――― 30 ――――

At the moment when the individual gets the idea of the language-*game* – of language as a system of practices in which he participates – the expressive relation between himself and his community becomes problematic. The knowledge that 'words are also deeds' introduces the logical possibility of asking: do the available words represent deeds of a kind that I can perform without shame? (Are the constituted intellectual authorities the sort of partners whose guidance in the 'dance' (cf. *PI* I §172) of symbolic behaviour I can accept without

―――――――――――――――――――――――――――

[3] Wittgenstein sensed danger in this area. 'Everything ritualistic (everything that, as it were, smacks of the high priest) must be strictly avoided, because it immediately turns rotten', he wrote in 1930 (*CV* p. 8). 'Of course a kiss is a ritual too and it isn't rotten, but ritual is permissible only to the extent that it is as genuine as a kiss.'

indignity?) The philosophical exercise which brings our commitments to consciousness compels us, as Stanley Cavell points out (cf. section 28), to pass a rational judgement on those commitments, and so either to reaffirm or to renounce them.

Here we must add one more Hegelian concept to our repertoire – that of 'alienation', which can be characterized (from a psychological point of view) as the condition of those whose allegiance is no longer held by the values expressed in their cultural environment, and for whom, therefore, 'the world has the character of being something external, the negative of self-consciousness.' Such persons cannot entirely avoid making a contribution of sorts, in so far as they interact with others, to the social process which sustains *Sittlichkeit,* and so for them, too, as Hegel observes, the ethical order 'is the *work* of self-consciousness'; but 'it is also an alien reality already present and given, a reality which has a being of its own and in which [they] do not recognize [themselves].'[1] Consequently, they will cease to look to the public life of their community to provide them with a sense of their own identity, and will seek instead to realize themselves primarily as members of 'civil society' – the economic sphere in which order prevails, not because a universal law is willed by individuals, but because a universal dedication to selfish objectives gives rise to a system of activity displaying law-like regularities.

Following Cavell, we have admitted two possible responses – one positive and one negative – to the historicist discovery about language. The negative reaction, which occurs in the case where reflection reveals us as implicated in a system of practices which appear morally irrelevant (or even abhorrent), can now be identified as the bringing to consciousness of an 'alienated' condition. And that process in turn can be seen to comprise the following 'moments'. First, we come to see that the culture within which we have our being is only a specific instance of human society, characterized by many peculiari-

---

[1] Hegel, *Phenomenology,* p. 294. Cf. also Taylor, *Hegel and Modern Society,* p. 91.

ties belonging to its own time and place. We thus attain sufficient critical distance from these features to be able to say, where appropriate, that they detract from the rationality of the culture as a whole. When we begin to think in this way, 'Our immediate unity with [objective] Spirit . . . [our] trust, is lost': we come to regard the prevailing laws and customs as 'mere ideas having no absolute essentiality'.[2] Thus we place ourselves (as individuals judging by the criteria of a rationality which transcends the narrow vision of those who have not yet brought their *sittlich* commitments to consciousness) in opposition to the laws and customs to which our judgement addresses itself.

To the extent that the later Wittgenstein's conception of the task of philosophy is adequately captured in the maxim: 'Describe language-games', it will be true to say that our response – positive or negative – to what we can learn about ourselves by practising philosophy in a Wittgensteinian spirit will not, itself, be determined by philosophical considerations. It will be determined by 'what we want', in a sense illustrated by Wittgenstein's discussion (*RFM* VII §15) of the legitimacy of using rulers made of dough: 'Would that of itself have to be wrong? Couldn't reasons easily be imagined, on account of which a certain elasticity in rulers might be desirable? "But isn't it right to make rulers out of ever harder, more unalterable material?" Certainly it is right; if that is what one wants! "Then are you in favour of contradiction?" Not at all; any more than of soft rulers.' And this is as much as to say that it will depend upon what particular way of life we take to be recommended by the best reasons. For example, in the case of hard versus soft rulers, Wittgenstein evidently holds that the arguments for soft rulers are not compelling: he declares himself 'not in favour' of them. But it is, as he emphasizes, *imaginable* that (in different circumstances from our own) a case for such implements might be made out. Similarly, in the light of a historicist view of language, some will come to feel that they have been committed, albeit without their conscious knowledge, to a system of practices

---

[2] Hegel, *Phenomenology*, pp. 214–15.

which is not supported by good reasons, i.e. is irrational; others, discovering the same set of commitments to be implicit in their own behaviour (linguistic and otherwise), will be satisfied – as Wittgenstein is, with reference to hard rulers and to the general policy of avoiding contradiction in mathematics – with the rationality of the existing practice.

'It depends what one wants': but not necessarily in the irrationalistic sense which empiricist philosophers typically have in mind when they talk about 'wanting'. The relevant sense of 'wanting' here is one in which the objects of our desires are specified in terms of a system of evaluative *concepts,* in accordance with the model presented in sections 3-4 above. To assert the presence of a certain value-feature in a deliberative situation is, in that model, to give a non-hypothetical reason for acting in a certain way: no more needs to be said in order to show that the situation furnishes a rational agent with a motive for acting like that.[3]

But it was suggested in section 13 above, where we sought to make this account more perspicuous by bringing it into connection with the expressivist view of language, that moral values are *grounded in a form of life.* On that view, our competence with moral language (which is the objective manifestation of our moral rationality; cf. section 12 above) arises organically out of our personal experience of participation in the relevant social practices: it is the outcome of a domesticating process which gradually brings us within the ambit of the relevant institutions. How, then, could we ever find ourselves in a position to pass a negative verdict on the rationality of the commitments brought to light by philosophical self-scrutiny? How could there be such a thing as a *reasoned* rejection of those commitments? For it is precisely our personal history of participation in language-games

---

[3] A 'want', thus understood, conforms to Thomas Nagel's account of a 'motivated desire', i.e. a desire which is 'arrived at by decision and after deliberation'. Such desires are not conceived as mental *phenomena*, but are ascribed to a person in virtue of the fact that certain sorts of practical consideration turn out to weigh with that person. Cf. Nagel, *The Possibility of Altruism*, p. 29.

which, according to the present line of thought, equips us to reason about anything at all (cf. section 24 above).

In section 25, commenting on Bradley's doctrine that 'As members of the system we are real, and not otherwise', I remarked that the limiting case of this doctrine would be the view that rational dissent from the prevailing world-picture was a logical absurdity. But we have still to explore the possibilities which open up to us if we decline to push this kind of holism to the limit. Our discussion of the incompleteness of intellectual authority in respect of certain regions of discourse (section 17 above) gave grounds, after all, for resistance to the idea of a form of life – or of the rationality embedded in it – as a monolithic entity, possessing such a high degree of internal coherence that to disengage oneself from it at any point would be to forfeit one's membership altogether, and so to place oneself in the intellectually untenable position of the thorough-going 'anarchist' mentioned in the foregoing section. It would be perverse indeed to picture our own form of life as an arithmetical system in macrocosm, so that social interaction (and discursive thought) took on the aspect of techniques whose practitioners would require to be trained 'with endless practice, with merciless exactitude' (*RFM* I §4; cf. section 17 above). Adherence to an expressive conception of language does not mean that we have to represent ourselves as citizens of one of those 'devout, authoritarian, semi-primitive societies' (cf. section 23 above) which appear to have inspired the development of that conception: we can retain the idea of language as expression – of linguistic institutions as embodying the objective spirit of a community – without making fanciful claims about the degree of internal cohesion or harmony which can be attributed to our own form of life.

The importance of reserving philosophical space for a moderate, or pluralistic, interpretation of organicist views about language lies precisely in the power of such an interpretation to make sense, within the given theoretical context, of the phenomenon of rational dissent. For in a community where intellectual cohesion exists only in a low degree, there will be nothing to prevent individual members from rationalizing their distaste for a particular sub-set of the prevailing values (or institutions) in terms of an alternative or divergent scheme of values, through which they can sustain their identity as rational persons while renouncing the dominant mode of rationality. In this way, their criticism of the *sittlich* commitments of their fellow-citizens (which are also their own commitments, prior to reflection) will not necessarily prejudice their status as exponents of a way of life regulated by universal laws or principles. Any imperfectly coherent form of life necessarily encompasses the values which govern the thought of dissenters as well as those which govern the thought of the orthodox: it encompasses institutions which are dedicated to incompatible (or dubiously compatible) ends, and that is why there can arise within it competing habits of judging and reasoning – the habits grounded respectively in these competing institutions – whose exponents can engage in mutual rational criticism. The dissenting values, too, are grounded in the form of life whose partially alienated members draw upon them to articulate and justify their own alienated condition.

The following remarks by Collingwood are relevant: they occur in the exposition of his personal vision of metaphysics as the historical study of the absolute presuppositions of thought. 'The dynamics of history is not yet completely understood,' he writes,

> when it is grasped that each phase is converted into the next by a process of change. The relation between phase and process is more intimate than that. One phase changes into another because the first was in unstable equilibrium and had in itself the seeds of change, and indeed of that change. Its fabric was not at rest; it was always under strain . . . A civilization does not work out its own details by a kind of static logic in which every detail exemplifies in its own way one and the same formula. It works itself out by a dynamic logic in which different and at first sight incompatible formulae contrive a precarious co-existence; one dominant here, another there; the recessive formula never ceasing to

operate, but functioning as a kind of minority report which, though the superficial historian may ignore it, serves to a more acute eye as evidence of tendencies actually existing which may have been dominant in the past and may be dominant in the future.[4]

This passage helps us to understand why it is that a negative reaction to the commitments brought to light by philosophy would not necessarily involve rejecting the entire corpus of social experience to which, on the expressivist view, we owe our rationality. It implies that we need not think of such a reaction as tantamount to an act of intellectual or moral suicide, a 'turning of one's weapon against one's own heart' (Bradley; cf. section 22 above): that would be the case only if the working of our 'hearts' (or minds) instantiated, as Collingwood puts it, a single formula, so that by rejecting that formula we should incapacitate ourselves completely as participants in the language-game.

It was argued in section 28 that to gain reflective awareness of the practical character of language is come to see oneself as morally implicated in the form of life in which one participates. In the following section we considered an objection to that claim, namely that if one wishes to advance a conception of moral rationality centred upon the idea of the individual's submission, or allegiance, to intellectually authoritative institutions, one cannot then proceed to saddle the individual with a responsibility for the maintenance of those very institutions in sound rational order. But now it appears the objection was not well founded: we can retain the individual in his role as critic of the values and ends expressed in the public life of his community, and we can do so without condemning him once again to the 'empty freedom' of moral and political judgement which he possessed in the non-cognitivist picture. He will still be represented as recognizing certain intellectual authorities and as regulating his own judgement by reference to these: that is how he will manage to remain *rational*. At the same time, however, he will be able

---

[4] Collingwood, *An Essay on Metaphysics*, pp. 74-5.

(in virtue of the internal tensions or contradictions of his community's form of life) to subject certain features of the established *Sittlichkeit* to an appraisal in terms of evaluative concepts which have their institutional basis elsewhere within the culture: that is how he will manage to be a *critic*.[5]

The phenomenon of immanent critique in relation to forms of social life is discussed in more concrete terms by Richard Norman in his book, *Reasons for Actions*. Following Wittgenstein, Norman conceives of the giving of reasons for an action as an exercise in representing that action as an instantiation of some publicly acknowledged normative concept – a concept with a recognized place in the 'moral grammar' of the relevant community (as we might paraphrase Norman's view, in the language of section 16 above). This is, of course, the conception of practical rationality which we have seen to be associated with our own proposed moral realism; and Norman is especially concerned to show that that conception is applicable, also, to the rational advocacy of moral *change*.

As an example of the kind of moral change he has in mind (and this example, which comes at the end of the book, evidently embodies its central purpose), Norman discusses the possible substitution of socialist for liberal values. 'Although it is undeniable,' he writes,

> that different social groups do employ different evaluative concepts, the concepts are situated in, and draw their meaning from, a common language, and consequently the concepts associated with a particular social group are accessible to someone from outside that group . . . To recognize the existence of this common normative language is to see the concepts of the working-class ethic as a development and extension of pre-working-class normative concepts, and hence to see the change from one ethic to the other as a rational

---

[5] Cf. Adorno, *Minima Moralia*, p. 74: 'Nothing less is asked of the thinker today than that he should be at every moment both within things and outside them.'

change. Similarly . . . we can see the concepts of the socialist ethic as extensions of liberal normative concepts, and can therefore see this change too as a rational one. Finally, corresponding to this historical fact is the fact that a rational case can therefore be made for the socialist ethic which does not presuppose a prior acceptance of the ethic and which at the same time does not appeal to supposed 'independent transcendent norms' or 'impersonal neutral standards'. And this conclusion, if it is valid, seems to me to be of some importance.[6]

In the course of the process described in this passage, the consensual norms of judgement and argument operating

---

[6] R. Norman, *Reasons for Actions* (1969), p. 172. It is perhaps worth pointing out that in so far as Norman's theory of rationality is purely positive (i.e. in so far as it does not presuppose our subjective identification with any particular sub-set of the culturally available normative concepts), his conclusion with regard to the 'rationality' of the transition from liberalism to socialism is of less 'importance' than he imagines. Certainly it is of less comfort to socialists. For Norman's 'rationality' is opposed, not to *irrationality*, but to *non-rationality*. Thus when a practical proposal is described, in Norman's terms, as 'rational', no more can be meant than that the recommended course of action may be represented as falling under a normative concept which is in common use. There is no reason why this should not be true of a historical development in a direction unacceptable to Norman, say from a liberal to a *fascist* morality.

The only reassurance Norman offers us in respect of this risk is to be found in the argument by which he justifies his non-recognition of 'nigger' as a normative concept. An essential feature of any authentic such concept, he argues, is that it should hang together with others of its kind to 'make up a meaningful way of life'. 'But this,' he claims, 'is just what we *cannot* say about the evaluations implicit in the word "nigger". Of course, racialism can be, in one sense, a whole way of life. But the notion of colour has, in itself, no connection with any of the concepts which are relevant to the question of how one is to treat other people.' (p. 71).

This argument fails, since the appearance of the phrase 'in itself' in the last sentence signals a relapse into just the kind of appeal to 'independent transcendent norms' which Norman explicitly rejects. The constraints of (moral) grammaticality offer no protection against the occurrence of rude words. Racialist societies exist: therefore the conceptual connections denied by Norman exist also, in spite of his protests, and have as good a claim to the philosopher's recognition as any other linguistic phenomena.

within the relevant linguistic community undergo a development of the kind termed 'dialectical'; which is to say that although reasoned arguments may at any time take place between the partisans of the traditional and those of the innovative view – implying that at any given moment an appeal can be made to common criteria of sound reasoning – these criteria will themselves be different at the end of the process from what they were at the beginning. We can compare the classical definition of dialectical thought as *thought which calls its own presuppositions into question:*[7] the relevant Wittgensteinian image here is that of the river bed which shifts, or is eroded, over a period of time, though in relation to the water passing over it we think of it as static (*OC* §96-9).

—— 31 ——

We noted at the beginning of the foregoing section that enhanced self-consciousness about the workings of language renders problematic the expressive relation between ourselves (as theorists) and the language-games we play; or in other words, it prompts us to ask whether our own way of life offers the possibility of a reflective, or critical, reintegration of the 'inner' and 'outer' viewpoints. This is the question confronting anyone who exchanges non-cognitivism for our proposed form of realism; and it is the question which Davidson might be suspected of begging when he suggests that by abandoning scheme/content dualism in the theory of knowledge, we can place ourselves once again in direct contact with the *familiar* objects of discourse (cf. section 26). For unless it can be answered in the affirmative, we shall have to conclude that our present language-game needs to be amended; and if we are to go in for a different way of talking, the objects we shall find ourselves talking about will not be precisely the ones with which we are currently 'familiar'.

The question is a practical one: what do I want? (Bearing in

---

[7] Cf. Plato, *Republic*, 533c.

mind, of course, that the relevant notion of 'wanting' is the one explained in the preceding section: the theorist is not being asked to report on the character of any unmotivated 'passions' which may assail him, but to consider which are the *right* moral and political institutions to have.) And it gains urgency from an insight acquired in the course of the theorist's retreat from empiricism: namely, his discovery of the logical link between *objectivity* and *intellectual authority*, and of the embodiment of such authority in institutions which exert a coercive force upon individual participants in the language-game.

A recurrent theme within the tradition of thinking natural-istically about morals is that the idea of an *objective* moral view of the world arises only amongst persons of roughly equal material power. Thus Thucydides (V, 89) makes the Athenian speaker in the Melian dialogue say: 'We both know that, as far as human reasoning is concerned, the assessment of moral obligation occurs only where both sides are placed under the same constraints: the stronger do what they can, while the weak submit.' The same thought appears in Hobbes' deduction of the duty of political obedience from our equal misery in the imagined state of nature, and in Nietzsche's assertion that the trading mentality is the histori-cal source of 'all "good-naturedness", all "fairness", all "good will", all "objectivity" on earth': 'justice on this elementary level,' he continues, 'is the good will among parties of approximately equal power to come to terms with one another, to reach an "understanding" by means of a settle-ment – and to *compel* parties of lesser power to reach a settlement among themselves.'[1]

Let us suppose, with the naturalists, that it is only under conditions of material equality that the habit of reasoning in terms of an objective concept of right, or justice, can

---

[1] F. Nietzsche, *The Genealogy of Morals* (1887), trs. Walter Kaufmann (1969), p. 70. The joint appearance of the three authors mentioned in this paragraph is, of course, anything but coincidental. Hobbes translated Thucydides; and Nietzsche seems to have admired him more than any other Greek author: cf. *Twilight of the Idols*, p. 107.

spontaneously evolve and flourish. In that case, we could not reasonably expect to find anything like Quine's 'pull toward objectivity' (cf. section 15 above) functioning effectively, with respect to moral discourse, except where such conditions existed.

The end subserved by that 'pull', it will be remembered, is the production of new 'ideal observers' of moral reality – new exponents of the consensually-supported system of moral responses to experience; and the way it works towards this end is by weaning individual speakers away from what Quine calls the 'subjectively simplest rule of association' in applying concepts to objects, and so bringing it about that (in a massive proportion of cases) those speakers *agree with one another* as to how things stand in the world. The 'pull toward objectivity', then, tends of its very nature to eliminate individual peculiarities of judgement which would lead to dissent from the total consensual world-view.

Now in relation to the teaching of morality, this means that each prospective member of the community must be induced to look upon the moral world from a viewpoint in which, as with other objective areas of discourse, all individual viewpoints are supposedly fused. That is to say, the place where the 'ideal moral observer' is required to stand is one which he is supposed to be able to reach, whatever his starting-point, simply by emancipating himself from his own peculiar set of subjective (i.e., in the moral case, selfish) concerns.

The options are already clearly stated in Hume:

When a man denominates another his *enemy*, his *rival*, his *antagonist*, his *adversary*, hs is understood to speak the language of self-love, and to express sentiments peculiar to himself, and arising from his particular circumstances and situation. But when he bestows on any man the epithets of *vicious* or *odious* or *depraved*, he then speaks another language, and expresses sentiments, in which he expects all his audience are to concur with him. He must, therefore, depart from his private and particular situation, and must choose a point of view, common to him with others; he must move some universal principle of the human frame, and touch a string to which all mankind have an accord and sympathy.[2]

In this passage Hume recognizes two possibilities, and two only, with respect to 'standpoint' in judgements of moral character: on one hand a public standpoint which is both accessible to, and mandatory for, all persons in their moralizing capacity; on the other, the standpoint of self-love, from which the only considerations that will appear relevant are those bearing upon the purely private interests of the person judging. The picture set before us is one in which the agencies that work to win the individual to the public viewpoint (to gain a new member for the 'party of humankind against vice and disorder, its common enemy' – cf. section 1) serve only to harmonize a motley of private interests, between which, *qua* private, there is *nothing to choose*.

We might wonder whether this picture bears any relation to reality. That is to say, we might ask whether, in fact, 'our way of life' exhibits empirically the pure opposition posited *a priori* by Hume – an opposition between the 'universal' and the 'private'. The moral realism we are currently considering invites us to test against historical experience the formalistic account of objectivity which it seems to receive intact into its keeping from the empiricist tradition: an account alleging that the only interests or impulses from which individuals are required to detach themselves, in order to reach the standpoint of the 'ideal observer', are inherently selfish, anti-social impulses.

If this account is accepted as empirically accurate, we shall be unable to name any rational reason why any member of the community should fail to internalize the goal which is set before him by those to whom it falls to drill him in the community's moral 'grammar' (cf. section 14 above): namely, the goal of moral rationality, construed as 'the thoroughgoing unity of the universal and the single' (cf. section 20 note 11) with respect to the moral language-game. But if

---

[2] Hume, *Enquiry Concerning the Principles of Morals*, p. 272.

the Humian picture is rejected, such failures will make all the sense in the world, and by the same token, so will the spectacle of an interminable recourse to violence in the service of the 'pull toward objectivity' – interminable, in that there can be no solid hope of the trainee ever coming to 'understand' the rules and thereafter spontaneously carrying on in an acceptable way. For the imposition on a speech community of a false, or suppositious, 'universal standpoint' will always provoke resistance, and will depend for its continued success on the forcible suppression of behaviour expressing a refusal to occupy that standpoint.

Pessimism of this sort about our own methods of moral 'education' would cast doubt upon the possibility of a critical reintegration of the 'inner' and 'outer' viewpoints in relation to the moral language-game as currently constituted. This is one (familiar)[3] line of thought which might lead the possessor of our historicist insight about language to resist the attempts of certain advocates of moral realism – however much he might be in sympathy with their metaphysical position – to saddle him once more with the same old language-game, and consequently with the 'familiar objects' of moral discourse.[4]

---

[3] Marxists will be reminded of Marx and Engels' criticism of Bentham, to the effect that in his philosophy 'the bourgeoisie no longer appears as a special class, but as the class whose conditions of existence are those of the whole of society' (*The German Ideology*, p. 113).

[4] Davidson's position shares a defect with that of the 'compatibilists' in the philosophical debate about freedom of will. It is not the metaphysics of these latter theorists which is at fault (sc. their contention that the only notion of moral freedom available to us is the non-transcendent one, 'liberty of spontaneity'); what gives cause for complaint is their failure to surmount the positivity of the historical conditions under which retribution is meted out. The *theoretical* acceptability of compatibilism issues in *practical* acceptability only on the basis of a *historical* reunion of 'inside' with 'outside', i.e. of the retributive or judgemental attitude towards wrong-doers with the objectifying attitude which renders us sensitive to the cultural conditioning of wrong-doing. Compatibilism, in other words, becomes a 'liveable' doctrine only in a just society.

32

These reflections carry us far into the terrain of critical social theory, and may arouse curiosity as to how our idea of the immanent criticism of a form of life relates to the Wittgensteinian insistence that philosophy itself is neutral as between such forms – that it 'leaves everything as it is' (*PI* I §124). Students of Wittgenstein, after all, have long been familiar with the claim that alternative belief-systems – whether they succeed one another in time, or exist simultaneously in different places – do not lend themselves to evaluative comparison in terms of truth, rationality or moral worth. From this relativist picture it would seem to follow that the transition from one form of life to another, like the successive forms of life themselves, must be seen simply as an aspect of the 'given' – of 'what has to be accepted' (cf. *PI* II p. 226). Thus Peter Winch writes: 'Criteria of logic are not a direct gift of God, but arise out of, and are only intelligible in the context of, ways of living or modes of social life. It follows that one cannot apply criteria of logic to modes of social life as such.'[1]

The process by which the rules of socially meaningful behaviour change over time – the development and decay of specific configurations of intellectual authority – lends itself readily enough, it is true, to dispassionate description. It is a recognized part of the subject-matter of the historian, whose functions overlap in this area with those of the philosopher *qua* 'describer of language-games'. An example of this kind of subject-matter is supplied by Collingwood: 'If any group or community of human beings ever held a pan-magical belief about the world, it is certainly not "experience" that could shake it. Yet certainly it might be shaken. It might be shaken through the influence of a very powerful tribesman who found himself taking a different view; or by the prestige of some other community, accepted and revered in the first

---

[1] Peter Winch, *The Idea of a Social Science and its Relation to Philosophy* (1958), p. 100.

instance as very powerful magicians, and later found to reject and despise it.'[2]

Historical changes of this kind obviously differ with regard to 'physiognomy'; they range from the imperceptibly gradual to the catastrophic. We can represent these different patterns of evolution in terms of the varying stature and effectiveness of intellectually authoritative institutions in relation to the language-games they regulate.

The more familiar type of case is that in which some particular aspect of social practice is in a state of flux, so that there no longer exists (or does not yet exist) a firm consensus to determine what shall count as obedience to the relevant rules (cf. section 19 above). The individual participant in a practice of this kind (one whose rules display only a low degree of determinacy) discovers that in certain cases he must just *decide* to treat a certain judgement as sound, a certain inference as valid. Authoritative practical guidance will not always be available – a point on which Wittgenstein lays considerable stress (*OC* §326, 'But who says what it is reasonable to believe in *this* situation?').[3] And where it is unavailable, the unconstrained decision of the individual (as expressed in what he actually *does*) may contribute, by way of precedent, to the determination of a future pattern of practice – and hence of a future norm of judgement.

(It should be borne in mind that the weight of intellectual authority in respect of any given region of discourse is itself not always a strictly objective matter. Some speakers will consider themselves bound by the rules of the language-game to make one move rather than another; others will hazard a paradoxical or idiosyncratic interpretation, and (if they are not expelled from the game) will thereby change its character through the operation of the process sketched above. The individual must draw upon his own anthropological insight,

---

[2] Collingwood, *An Essay on Metaphysics*, p. 194.
[3] Such moments of decision are, of course, nothing but intensified experiences of a phenomenon which pervades the whole of natural language: *PI* I §68, ' "But then the use of the word is unregulated, the 'game' we play with it is unregulated". . .'

so to speak, in order to assess the chances that a particular form of behaviour will be found unacceptable in relation to a given rule, and in order to gauge the severity of the likely sanctions if the decision goes against him. (This may involve a delicate appraisal of power-relationships.) Finally, of course, his behaviour will reflect the extent to which he personally fears the penalty of 'growing solitude' (cf. section 25 above).)

Another mode of historical change in the rules of a language-game is also worthy of mention. I have in mind the sort of change which occurs when the material basis of the relevant rules has grown weak and liable to collapse. However strictly the practice of a game is regulated, the continued existence of that game (in a recognizable form; cf. *PI* II p. 226) hinges upon the feasibility of enforcing its rules, and of penalizing actions which are held to contravene them; and if an institution which has hitherto been acknowledged as a seat of intellectual authority ceases, for whatever reason, to hold people's allegiance, a single act of disobedience (whether individual or collective) may be all that is needed to put an end to the practice within which that institution exercises its dominance. Thus we may witness spectacular discontinuities of the kind described in this passage from Frazer's *Golden Bough:*

> Many days' journey to the north-east of Abomey, the old capital of Dahomey, lies the kingdom of Eyeo. 'The Eyeos are governed by a king, no less absolute than the king of Dahomey, yet subject to a regulation of state, at once humiliating and extraordinary. When the people have conceived an opinion of his ill-government, which is sometimes insidiously infused into them by the artifice of his discontented ministers, they send a deputation to him with a present of parrots' eggs, as a mark of its authenticity, to represent to him that the burden of government must have so far fatigued him that they consider it full time for him to repose from his cares and indulge himself with a little sleep. He thanks his subjects for their attention to his ease, retires to his own apartment as if to sleep, and there gives directions to his women to strangle him. This is immediately executed,

and his son quietly ascends the throne upon the usual terms of holding the reins of government no longer than whilst he merits the approbation of the people.' About the year 1774, a king of Eyeo, whom his ministers attempted to remove in the customary manner, positively refused to accept the proffered parrots' eggs at their hands, telling them that he had no mind to take a nap, but on the contrary was resolved to watch for the benefit of his subjects. The ministers, surprised and indignant at his recalcitrancy, raised a rebellion, but were defeated with great slaughter, and thus by his spirited conduct the king freed himself from the tyranny of his councillors and established a new precedent for the guidance of his successors.[4]

This episode illustrates Wittgenstein's remark (*PI* I §193) that bits of a machine can bend or melt or break off. Such an event can put the machine out of action, even though it is not allowed for in the operator's manual.

33

Winch is right, in the passage quoted above (p. 137), to connect the moral neutrality which Wittgenstein seeks to impose on philosophy with the Wittgensteinian view of moral (and other) values as grounded in a social practice. It is certainly implicit in Wittgenstein's general position that any evaluative judgement concerning the way of life of a particular community (or the particular habit of thought embedded in it) must be made from some definite *standpoint:* that is, from within a total world-view which is itself embedded in a historically specific form of life. For the mere act of committing oneself to a (would-be) objective judgement already displays one's allegiance to certain intellectual authorities – one's *sittlich* identification with some, at least, of the existing

---

[4] J. G. Frazer, *The Golden Bough*, abridged edn (1922) (Macmillan, 1971), p. 360. I owe this reference to Graham Ley.

institutions of discourse. At the same time, as we saw in section 9 above, Wittgenstein holds that the total world-view of a community of speakers is not itself based on grounds. 'What people accept as a justification – is shown by how they think and live' (*PI* I §325); but the repertoire of justifications available to a given community at a given time does not contain a (non-circular) justification for thinking and living as they currently do. Thus if I happen to *live through* the historical transition from one form of life to another, my evaluative assessment of the initial form of life will be different at the beginning of the process (when I was a participant in that form of life) from what it will be at the end (when I have transferred my allegiance to the new one): but what I shall *not* meaningfully be able to do will be to pass judgement on the actual process by which I have arrived at the system of beliefs within which I now operate. Nothing new can be discovered about my intellectual outlook by asking me the further question, 'Which judgement is correct – the one you made then, or the one you are making now?'

There is a parallel here with some remarks of Bernard Williams' about existential choice. Williams points out that whenever a person is faced with a decision which will affect the whole future course of his life, he is called upon to make that decision at a specific historical moment, in the light of the beliefs and values he then holds. He does not know, at the time of choice, what values and beliefs he will hold in the future, when the question may arise whether or not he chose rightly – indeed, it is possible that those future attitudes will themselves be conditioned by the choice he has yet to make. So 'there is no set of preferences both fixed and relevant, relative to which the various fillings of my life-space can be compared . . . The perspective of deliberative choice on one's life is constitutively *from here*. Correspondingly, the perspective of assessment with greater knowledge is necessarily *from there*, and . . . I cannot ultimately guarantee from what standpoint of assessment my major and most fundamental regrets will be.'[1]

---

[1] Bernard Williams, *Moral Luck*, p. 35.

If we think of a linguistic community under the aspect of an existential subject (cf. section 29 above), we can say that the community's perspective upon any proposed innovation in its way of life – and hence the perspective of its members, exercising their judgement in accordance with the going consensual norms – is constitutively 'from there', i.e. from its own historical situation. At any given moment, people can only ask themselves, 'Is the proposed change in our procedures acceptable to me?'; and their response will depend on 'what they want' (cf. section 30 above): that is, it will be framed in terms of the values to which, at that moment, they are committed. (If their system of rules falls short of perfect internal coherence, the question may of course elicit conflicting answers.) It is only in the light of the extended historical development of a mode of behaviour that those who initiated it come to be authoritatively described, *in retrospect*, as creative, ingenious, daring, etc. (laudatory words used of the supposed originators of currently valued modes of acting). This is evidently what J. L. Borges had in mind when he said: 'Every writer *creates* his own precursors. His work modifies our conception of the past, as it will modify the future.'[2]

Wittgenstein describes the following imaginary situation (*RFM* VII §11): 'Lists, rolls, of people are prepared, but not alphabetically as we do it; and in this way it happens that in some lists the same name appears more than once. – But now it can be supposed that this does not strike anyone; or that people see it, but accept it without worrying . . . But now times have changed and people (at first only a few) begin to demand exactness. Rightly, wrongly? – Were the earlier lists *not* really lists?'

We can, perhaps, identify ourselves imaginatively with the participants in this historically fluid practice of list-making, and with their (sometimes mutually incompatible) perceptions of the new method. The general situation is familiar enough: some will say that it is a fresh, exciting approach; others will call it tiresome, irrelevant, pedantic.

---

[2] Jorge Luis Borges, 'Kafka and his Precursors', in *Labyrinths*, ed. Yates and Irby (1981), p. 236.

In terms of rhetoric, however, the example has a different purpose. It exploits the fact that we ourselves are *not* under any strong temptation to take sides in the debate. Why should we care whether this tribe makes lists accurately, by our standards, or not? They got on all right before without doing it accurately, so what does it matter whether they change now? And our indifference with respect to this hypothetical case permits us to see the arbitrariness, *sub specie aeternitatis*, of our own intellectual location. The question, 'Rightly, wrongly?' is designed to be greeted with a shrug: *we* don't mind what they do, and we can see that *their* respective verdicts will simply be determined by the strength of their commitment to the existing practice. It is this last clause which displays the moral we are meant to draw in relation to ourselves.

The demand for a standpoint *outside history* from which to deliver judgements of value is linked with the demand for a standpoint *outside the body* from which to survey reality: for an embodied creature necessarily exists in time. Nietzsche saw the tendency towards a withdrawal of the former demand as 'Europe's longest and most courageous self-overcoming'.[3] In his eyes, our renunciation of the idea of culture-transcendent canons of judgement represented a victory for the authentically irreligious, or 'skin-covered',[4] view of the world (see section 47 below).

---

[3] Nietzsche, *The Gay Science*, §357: 'Looking at nature as if it were proof of the goodness and governance of a god; interpreting history in honour of some divine reason, as a continual testimony of a moral world order and ultimate moral purposes ... that is *all over* now, that has man's conscience *against* it, that is considered indecent and dishonest by every more refined conscience. . . . In this severity, if anywhere, we are good Europeans and heirs of Europe's longest and most courageous self-overcoming.'
[4] Ibid., §256: 'All people who have depth find happiness in being for once like flying fish, playing on the peaks of waves; what they consider best in things is that they have a surface: their skin-coveredness – *sit venia verbo*.'

34

The last two sections will have contained no surprises for anyone familiar with Wittgenstein's writings. But they raise a problem for adherents of a Wittgensteinian moral realism of the kind we have been developing. For the idea of a 'value-free' account of change in consensual norms invites an objection couched in terms of the opposition, which Wiggins (cf. section 20) introduces into his discussion of non-cognitivist moral philosophy, between an 'inner' and an 'outer' perspective on human existence. That opposition, Wiggins argues, is the site of a conflict within non-cognitivism which ultimately renders the theory incoherent. For it leaves us with a choice between two seemingly incompatible approaches to the (non-hypothetical) evaluation of human activities. One approach, characteristic of the 'outer' view-point, finds no *objective* difference between the projects of the (apocryphal) Southern pig-breeder, who spends his life 'breeding hogs to buy more land to breed more hogs . . .',[1] and those of the individual seeking to construct a *monumentum aere perennius;* from this viewpoint, there is nothing to choose, in respect of inherent value, between the various vital manifestations of human animals. The other approach, by contrast – that of the 'inner' viewpoint, i.e. the viewpoint of the participant in a human form of life – finds a world of difference between these two kinds of project. Wiggins objects to the gloomily biologistic spectacle seen from the 'outer' viewpoint (which the non-cognitive theorist elects, *qua* theorist, to occupy) that 'that is not how it feels to most people from inside.'[2] We should not be satisfied, he suggests, with a moral philosophy which represents the strictly rational individual as one who is too grand to see any point in doing anything. And this dissatisfaction issues, as we saw earlier, in the demand for a reunion of 'inside' and 'outside'.

---

[1] Wiggins, 'Truth, Invention . . .', p. 343.
[2] Ibid., p. 340.

The objection which we now have to face runs as follows: doesn't the Wittgensteinian denial of a transcendent standard of rationality with regard to moral and intellectual norms amount to much the same thing as the non-cognitivists' denial of 'objective' or 'real' variations, in point of intrinsic value, between different sorts of human activity? Wittgenstein offers us the picture of an unending succession of language-games, in relation to which it is senseless to ask questions about meaning or purpose or value. The business of philosophy, he affirms, is simply to offer a perspicuous description of the relevant facts about language-use: to set those facts before us in such a way that we shall no longer be tempted to look for a canon of rationality which would transcend all historical standpoints. This essentially reflexive exercise is not, in itself, supposed to involve us in the outward-looking function of reporting on the moral characteristics of the reality which it lays bare.

On the strength of the insight we have just been rehearsing, Wittgenstein's later philosophy is sometimes plausibly described as a 'subtle', linguistically-orientated, species of *positivism* – for like the blunt, natural-scientific species, it seems in the end to present us with 'nothing but the facts'.[3] There are forms of life, and there are the individual human beings who participate in them; and our shared form of life is said to be 'constitutive of rationality itself'. Wittgenstein's views imply, therefore, that if we wish to engage in any kind of rational thought or action we must immerse ourselves in a habit of mind which – in our philosophical capacity – we can recognize as historically conditioned. But now someone may protest that this is nothing but a global version of the non-cognitivist view that, in order to discover a meaning in life, we must immerse ourselves in the scheme of concerns supplied by our own (positive or negative) *feelings* about the world. Those feelings, too, are represented by non-cognitivism as historically conditioned; which is the very reason why non-cognitivism maintains that a person who remains open to their motivating influence must be looking at the world in a way which could not be justified in purely rational terms.

---

[3] Cf. Pears, *Wittgenstein*, pp. 170, 173.

Wiggins, we have noted, accuses the non-cognitivist account of moral agency of presenting, at the philosophical level, a picture which is at odds with our subjective experience as agents. It now looks as though the same criticism can be deployed against the Wittgensteinian, or expressivist, conception of rationality with which we propose to replace that account. The new opposition between philosophical and non-philosophical thinking seems to give rise to a similar tension between what we suppose we *know*, as theorists, about the status of the values implicit in our thinking, and what we *feel* as originators of the kind of thought in which those values have a place.

The tension declares itself in a curious way. Non-cognitivism is flawed, according to Wiggins, by its refusal to concede the presence of real value where the untheoretical human agent professes to find it. The proposed Wittgensteinian account of morality threatens to incorporate the converse flaw: when Wiggins speaks of rationality – and hence, *a fortiori*, of moral rationality – as *constituted* by our shared form of life, the 'untheoretical participant'[4] may be expected to complain of this (avowedly philosophical) idea that '*that* is not how it feels from inside' either; not at any rate to those of us who must confess to being participants in a form of life that is deaf to reason. Such thoughts are, moreover, evidently capable of coexisting with the notion of rationality as grounded in consensus – thus Wittgenstein, *CV* p. 44: 'If in life we are surrounded by death, so too in the health of our intellect we are surrounded by madness'; *CV* p. 6, 'I have no sympathy for the current of European civilization and do not understand its goals, if it has any.'

———— 35 ————

So we must now ask how exactly it does feel 'from inside', or in other words, what follows from a Wittgensteinian conception of language with respect to the kind of judgements the

---

[4] Wiggins, 'Truth, Invention . . .', p. 357.

individual can meaningfully make about the rationality of the social practices in which he finds himself implicated. In particular, we need to examine the consequences of holding that, as asserted by our proposed form of realism, rationality is 'constituted by a shared form of life'. If the philosopher is obliged to think of forms of life, and their historical mutations, as something simply 'given' (cf. section 33 above), won't the same be true of the untheoretical person? Or if we answer this question in the negative, shan't we lay ourselves open to the very charge previously lodged against the non-cognitivists – the charge of driving a wedge between the conception of ourselves with which we are to work when we are thinking philosophically, and the different conception we are to adopt for the purposes of practical life?

Non-cognitivism responded to this difficulty simply by condemning as 'fantastic' (cf. section 1) the fear that we might lapse, under the influence of a theoretical denial of the objectivity of value, into a state of mind in which we actually experienced the world as a place where nothing mattered. The theory lays particular stress upon the idea that evaluative judgement does not *describe* our attitudes, but *expresses* them, so that a capacity for value-perception would be the immediate outcome of our consenting to endorse the attitudes in question; and to withhold this consent would be perverse, for it would mean disowning the affective part of our nature.

We must acknowledge that the response offered by our proposed moral realism to the problem of 'inside' and 'outside' bears more than a superficial resemblance to the non-cognitivist solution which we have just been recalling. For it involves appealing to a distinction between *description* and *expression* which echoes the one on which non-cognitivism insists in specifically moral contexts. Our own use of this distinction will not, however, be so restricted, and the argument of the following sections (to 38) is intended to lend force to an idea introduced earlier in this book, viz. that an expressivism which extends to the whole of our discourse can clear itself, merely in virtue of its global character, of the irrationalist taint which it carried when it was asserted only in respect of a limited subject-matter.

To see how the crucial distinction is employed within Wittgenstein's philosophy, we can begin by reminding ourselves of a point which was made in section 9 above. It was noted in that section that although (in Wittgenstein's view) it is an agreement, or congruence, in our ways of acting that makes objective discourse materially possible, this agreement does not itself 'enter into' the relevant language-game: when we ask a question about some aspect of reality, we are not asking for a report on the state of public opinion with regard to that question, we are asking to be told the *truth* about it. (Cf. Z §431, 'Does human agreement *decide* what is red? Is it decided by appeal to the majority? Were we taught to determine colour in *that* way?') The idea of rationality as resting upon consensus, then, does not imply that the *fact* of consensus need carry any weight with us in any particular piece of thinking about the objective world: a point which is demonstrated by the absence of any logical (or 'grammatical') objection to statements of the form: 'I'm right and everyone else is wrong.'

The logical possibility of saying this kind of thing 'belongs with' the critical, or normative, concepts (truth, reality, rationality, goodness, right, etc.). And it is a possibility on which we must continue to insist if we are to remain within the spirit of the Wittgensteinian manifesto discussed in section 11 above: 'Not empiricism and yet realism in philosophy, that is the hardest thing.' Empiricism is rejected as soon as we get the idea that there is no external authority to validate the norms of judgement and argument enforced within a linguistic community; thereafter, realism can be retained only on condition that we cease to hanker after such an authority and are content, instead, to keep on using critical concepts in the conscious knowledge that 'a word hasn't got a meaning given to it . . . by a power independent of us . . . [it] has the meaning someone has given to it' (cf. section 27 above). And the task of determining criteria for the application of such concepts is one to which every language-user can aspire to make a contribution (cf. section 38 below).

We noted earlier that the view of language presupposed by our Wittgensteinian moral realism is a 'naturalistic' view, in the sense that it represents linguistic behaviour as 'part of our natural history'. But it does not on that account involve us, any more than did non-cognitivism, in the 'naturalistic fallacy' which G. E. Moore condemned with reference to 'good'. Moore's criticism, as is well known, was directed against *reductive* naturalism in ethics – a mistaken line of thought against which the proper defence, according to Moore, is to remember that 'propositions about the good are all of them synthetic and never analytic';[1] and this is a view with which Wittgenstein's vision of language is in no way in conflict, since it does not incorporate an *analysis* of normative propositions in terms of propositions about consensus. (Cf. *BB* p. 18, 'it can never be our [sc. philosophers'] business to reduce anything to anything.')

Wittgenstein's idea of the relation of consensus to critical concepts may be compared with his idea of the relation of pain-behaviour to pain-discourse. The possibility of the language-game with the word 'pain' is conditioned by certain uniformities in the way human beings react to the impact of external conditions on their bodies, or to events and processes inside their bodies. Wittgenstein suggests that it is by exploiting these uniformities that we draw new speakers into the game: *PI* I §244, 'Words are connected with the primitive, the natural, expressions of the sensation and used in their place. A child has hurt himself and he cries; and then adults talk to him and teach him exclamations and, later, sentences. They teach the child new pain-behaviour.' But he explicitly denies that the word 'pain' *means* crying: 'The verbal expression of pain replaces crying and does not describe it.' (For the idea of speech as a natural extension of the language of gesture, cf. section 12 above.)

Similarly, the presence in a language of normative or critical terms reflects the material fact that (if not always, then at least overwhelmingly often) the people who speak that language *agree* in accepting certain modes of thought and conduct as correct, and rejecting others as incorrect. That is to say, it reflects the existence of intellectual and moral norms within

---

[1] G. E. Moore, *Principia Ethica* (1903), p. 7.

the community in question. But this does not imply that when we call a proposition 'true' we *mean* that it commands general agreement, or that when we call something 'good' we *mean* that it is generally approved of. To suppose that a reduction of this kind was implicit in Wittgenstein's treatment of critical concepts would be to make a mistake exactly analogous to the one made by his imagined interlocutor at *PI* I §244, who tries to interpret his treatment of the concept of pain as a form of behaviourism.

John McDowell[2] has drawn attention to a passage in which Wittgenstein brushes aside the demand for an independently intelligible account of what we are saying about a person when we say that he is in pain – an account, that is, which could be offered to someone who did not yet know what 'pain' meant, and from which he could find this out: *PI* I §393, ' "When I imagine that someone who is laughing is really in pain, I don't imagine any pain-behaviour, for I see just the opposite. So *what* do I imagine?" – I have already said what.' The same point could be made in relation to critical concepts, for example in ethics: 'When I say that a generally accepted form of behaviour is vile and contemptible, I am not saying that people who go in for it are penalized, for I see just the opposite. So what am I saying? – Do you want me to become repetitive as well as moralistic?'[3]

In each of these cases we can point to a certain feature of what Wittgenstein might call the 'natural history' of human beings, such that if that feature were absent the relevant language-game would not exist. But once the game is in existence, the concepts that figure in it acquire a measure of autonomy *vis-à-vis* the material circumstances in virtue of which we were able to learn their use. Thus there would be no pain-discourse without pain-behaviour – but having learned to talk about pain, we can make sense of the idea that a person

---

[2] McDowell in Hookway and Pettit, p. 141.
[3] Cf. also Wittgenstein, *RFM* VII §40: 'I don't make use of the agreement of human beings to affirm identity. What criterion do you use, then? None at all. To use the word without a justification does not mean to use it wrongfully.'

may be in pain even though he doesn't flinch. Similarly, there would be no normative discourse unless certain ways of proceeding had consensual backing and were physically enforced – but once we have learned to talk about true and false, right and wrong, rational and irrational, we can make sense of the idea that the values upheld by the consensus are sometimes at fault.

36

These considerations are relevant to a much-debated question belonging to the philosophy of social science, namely: how are we to understand the phenomenon of confrontation between belief-systems, or between an established belief-system and the dissenting opinions which may be held by individuals operating within it? Should we see the rival views as competing in respect of *truth*, or merely in respect of *material dominance*?

In sections 32-3 we considered what a Wittgensteinian theorist of language might be expected to say, in global terms, about this kind of situation. At that stage, the position seemed to be that if there is no authority to which both parties are prepared to submit their dispute for arbitration, then there is no standpoint from which the rights and wrongs of the case can be settled in a manner that both will recognize as *objective*. And it seemed to follow that when this happens, the conflict must be resolved *without* recourse to authority – which means, in effect, that it must be resolved by a trial of strength. Thus *RFM* IV §56 (quoted in section 19): 'A contradiction might be conceived as a hint from the gods that I am to act and *not* consider.' Our proposed moral realism does not look so different, in this light, from the non-cognitive theory with its insistence upon the voluntaristic defence of a morality which lacks the warrant of reason (cf. section 1). On one view the canons of rationality are presented as immanent in human practice, on the other as transcending that practice; but even the 'immanent' conception, which reimposes the constraints of reason upon moral

151

judgement, leaves open the possibility that rationally irre-soluble disputes will arise when (publicly acknowledged) moral reasons 'give out' (cf. *PI* I §211, and context).

In the foregoing section, however, the emphasis was reversed and the contrast between the two positions was once again in evidence. We saw there that nothing in Wittgenstein's view of language places us, as *participants* in a rationally irresoluble conflict of opinion, under any logical obligation to withdraw our claim of *truth* for our own beliefs. The point can be stated as follows: suppose I believe that p, and another person believes that q, and p and q are mutually contra-dictory. Now if I am sufficiently certain that p, it will be impossible (theoretically, at least) for me to accept as valid the judgement of any allegedly impartial authority which may pronounce that the truth lies 'somewhere between p and q', or indeed anywhere except where *I* think it lies: for to do that would be to betray my own, as I see it, *better* judgement. And, of course, the same applies to the other person with respect to q. But since I hold that his belief is wrong, his refusal to acknowledge any authority which might pronounce in favour of *my* beliefs will not alter the picture at all as far as I am concerned: I shall say that this is simply part of his error, and, once again, he will say the same thing about me. When we reflect upon this state of affairs – when, that is, we undertake to describe it for philosophical purposes – we can see that the attitude of each party displays a commitment to a certain total theory of the world. But this does not detract from the right of either to say what he does say. It makes perfectly good sense to assert of another person that he has *failed to grasp the force of a valid argument* against his own mistaken view.

Thus Wittgenstein's philosophy turns out to encompass two ideas which have traditionally presented themselves as diametrically opposed. We might label these respectively as the 'relativist' and the 'absolutist' conceptions of rationally irresoluble theoretical conflict. 'Relativism' is a name com-monly given to the view that such conflict must be under-stood in terms of a struggle between partisans of the rival theories for control over the relevant social practices. The contrasting, 'absolutist', view would be that no philosophical considerations can legitimately undermine our natural inclination to say (in our capacity as partisans of a particular theory) that that theory is *true,* and any theory which contradicts it, *false.*

Wittgenstein declines to choose between these positions. In keeping with his wider treatment of the mind/body relation, he rejects the question whether a confrontation between language-games, or forms of life, should be seen as theoretical or practical. His view is that any extensive theoretical confrontation must also be a practical confrontation, if it matters at all: for, as we saw in section 7, he equates 'learning to believe certain things' with 'learning to act in accordance with these beliefs' (cf. *OC* §144).

This is not the same position as the relativism which maintains, with reference to some specified type of situation in which a discrepancy in outlook comes to light, that 'there is no such thing as a theoretical conflict here; the only conflict that enters into the matter is a practical one.' Wittgenstein's view is offered as an insight into the *nature* of theoretical conflict – just as his consensual notion of rationality is meant to provide an insight into the nature and workings of critical concepts, not to dissuade us from critical thinking. We might, in fact, adapt the manifesto discussed in section 11 above to give the maxim: 'Not scientism and yet rationalism in anthropology, that is the hardest thing.'

Consider the following passages from *On Certainty:*

(a) 609. Is it wrong for [people] to consult an oracle and be guided by it? – If we call this "wrong" aren't we using our language-game as a base from which to combat theirs?
610. And are we right or wrong to combat it? Of course there are all sorts of slogans which will be used to support our proceedings.
611. Where two principles really do meet which cannot be reconciled with one another, then each man declares the other a fool and a heretic.
612. I said I would 'combat' the other man, – but

153

wouldn't I give him *reasons*? Certainly; but how far do they go? At the end of reasons comes *persuasion*. (Think what happens when missionaries convert natives.)

(b) 286. We all believe that it isn't possible to get to the moon; but there might be people who believe that it is possible and that it sometimes happens. We say: these people do not know a lot that we know. And, let them be never so sure of their belief – they are wrong and we know it.

If we compare our system of knowledge with theirs then theirs is evidently the poorer one by far.

There is no difference between these two cases in terms of the kind of historical situation we are invited to imagine. The missionaries will have said of the natives, just as 'we' say of the moon people: 'They are wrong and we know it.' ('We', after all, *are* the missionaries.)

The one factor which has changed in the second example is that the reader is now being asked to construe the situation from the 'inner' point of view. It is no longer a question simply of the physiognomy of the dispute, but of the reader's willingness to identify himself intellectually with the missionaries (or, as it may be, with those who want to spread the good news about western physics).

—— 37 ——

The transition from a philosophical to a participatory stance with respect to the language-game – from describing it as a historical phenomenon, to joining in it – is explicitly indicated at *OC* §281, where Wittgenstein says he is certain that his friend hasn't got sawdust inside his head: 'To have doubts about it would seem to me madness – of course, this is also in agreement with other people; but *I* agree with them.'

Wittgenstein stresses the point that in order to *use* sentences of a language (as distinct from just mentioning them – for instance, by designating them as object-language expressions in the theorems of a recursive theory of meaning), I must draw upon my own conception of how the world is – i.e. upon the particular 'totality of judgements' which has been made plausible to me (cf. *OC* §140). Thus, the formal identity between the two situations discussed at the end of the last section implies that sooner or later one will have to answer the question: which 'slogans' (cf. *OC* §610), in your opinion, constitute *valid reasons*?

To confront this question is to descend from the philosophical, or reflexive, level of thinking into some non-philosophical arena of debate – to engage in the business of talking about the world, and of acting in the ways that standardly accompany such talk. When we were doing philosophy, we were not thus engaged; the machine of language (cf. *PI* I §132) was merely, so to speak, servicing itself. Sooner or later, however, it must go back to its routine work, which is to describe extra-linguistic reality.[1] If, for example, the point at issue is whether human beings can go to the moon, the views we advance will not be reflections on the functioning of language, but propositions of physics, physiology, etc.

'I really want to say,' writes Wittgenstein (*OC* §509), 'that a language-game is only possible if one trusts something (I did not say "can trust something").' With this remark in mind, we can say that the first-person proposition in the above passage from *OC* §281 ('This is in agreement with other people; but *I* agree with them') has the force of a declaration of trust, in the relevant sense, with regard to a specified feature of the prevailing language-game.

Now this 'trust' which, on a Wittgensteinian view, ultimately characterizes our relation to any first-order theory of

---

[1] Cf. Marx and Engels, *The German Ideology*, p. 103: 'Philosophy and the study of the actual world have the same relation to one another as masturbation and sexual love'; ibid., p. 118, 'For philosophers, one of the most difficult tasks is to descend from the world of thought to the actual world. *Language* is the immediate actuality of thought. Just as philosophers have given thought an independent existence, so they had to make language an independent realm . . . The problem of descending from the world of thoughts to the actual world is turned into the problem of descending from language to life.'

objective reality within which we consent to operate cannot fail to recall the 'trust' which non-cognitive theorists of ethics (cf. section 35 above) exhort us to place in our own moral convictions. Yet there is a crucial difference between the two philosophies in respect of the role allotted by each to the 'trusting' attitude. The difference is that our proposed Wittgensteinian position, unlike non-cognitivism, recognizes nothing with which that attitude could be intelligibly contrasted – no region of objective discourse which does *not* require from those who participate in it an acknowledgement of their merely finite status. And the reason this difference is crucial – the reason it suffices, phenomenologically, to clear the way for a descent from philosophical to 'outward-looking' thought in ethics – is that it addresses itself directly to the root cause of that mental 'stammer' (cf. *PI* I §433) which afflicts many people when they try to view the world, as required by non-cognitivism, from the standpoint of affectivity.[2] For by denouncing the whole array of hier-archical dualisms in terms of which empiricism is compelled to represent the fact/value distinction (e.g. adult/child, section 2; male/female, section 22), our proposed moral realist position releases the evaluative region of discourse from the stigma of inferiority objectively attaching to it in the empiri-cist model. (I say 'objectively' because it is important not to be misled by chivalrous flannel about the 'different but equal' status of value-judgement; cf. section 1.)[3]

---

[2] '. . . vocibus et gestu cum balbe significarent/imbecillorum esse aequum misererier omnis' (Lucretius, *De Rerum Natura*, V 1022-3).

[3] Jacques Derrida has a word for the mental set which churns out these dualisms: he calls it *'le phallogocentrisme'* (see e.g. his contribution to *Politiques de la philosophie*, ed. Dominique Grisoni (1976)).
Nietzsche, though scarcely to be remembered as a critic of phallic values in general, declines to avail himself of this particular way of expounding them. Thus, for instance, he says that if human-relative perception partakes of the character of a dream, then there is no such thing as being awake. 'I have discovered for myself that the human and animal past, indeed the whole primal age and past of all sentient being continues in me to invent, to love, to hate and to infer. I suddenly woke up in the midst of this dream, but only to the consciousness that I am dreaming and must go on dreaming lest I perish' (*The Gay Science*, §54).

Wittgenstein's appeal to the concept of 'trust' is anticipated by Hegel, as we discovered in section 30 when the idea of 'alienation' was introduced. Hegel states that 'the single, individual consciousness as it exists immediately in the real ethical order, or in the nation, is a solid unshaken trust in which Spirit has not, for the individual, resolved itself into its *abstract* moments ... The individuality of self-consciousness is, it is true, a moment in universal Spirit itself, but only as a vanishing quantity which, appearing on its own, is at once resolved within universal Spirit, and enters consciousness merely as trust.'[4]

The 'I' of the Wittgensteinian declaration ('*I* agree with them') is, I think, a 'vanishing quantity' in the sense intended by Hegel in this passage: it is necessary for the philosopher to *declare* his agreement with others (e.g. in the matter of heads not being packed with sawdust) only for the purpose of putting it on record that he has passed through a certain phase in what Hegel would have termed the self-unfolding of Spirit – that phase, namely, which consists in acquiring conscious-ness of one's own individuality in its potential opposition to the universal ethical order, or *Sittlichkeit*.

In terms of Wittgenstein's philosophy, the acquisition of this consciousness may be identified with our discovery of the moral dimension of language-use: for that (as I argued in sections 29-30) was a discovery of the individual's moral complicity, each time he participates in a language-game, with the institutions in which the prevailing form of life is embodied. Thus when Wittgenstein says 'Other people believe so and so – and *I* agree with them', his intention is to make it clear that although the speaker has grasped the historical character of the language-game, and has confronted the moral question which this raises with regard to his own participation, yet he declines the option (which his thought about language has made logically available to him) of dissociating himself from the game as currently constituted. Bearing in mind that 'we can never do better than occupy the

[4] Hegel, *Phenomenology*, p. 214.

standpoint of some theory or other',[5] he elects to occupy the standpoint of the received theory rather than to try to replace it by a different one. But once he has registered his disinclination to dissent, nothing remains to be done but to *assert* the proposition on which he and the rest of the world are in agreement; and that assertion will not contain any reference to himself. The 'I' of Wittgenstein's 'declaration of trust' makes its appearance only to be 'resolved' in the orderly process of the language-game, just as the 'individualityof self-consciousness', according to Hegel, is resolved in universal Spirit.

But this condition, it will be remembered, is posited either as the logical starting-point of a thought-process, or as its imagined end-point – i.e. as the goal which rational action has to realize. I suggested in section 29 that an adherent of Wittgenstein's view of language should equate that goal with the establishment of a language-game in which we could participate ingenuously, while retaining our awareness of it as a specific historical formation. A community in which such a language-game was played would be one which had succeeded in integrating the 'outer' conception of human subjectivity (that of the philosopher, standing 'outside' the language-game and reflecting upon it) with the 'inner' conception (that of the 'trusting' participant). That is to say, it would be a community whose members understood their own form of life and yet were not embarrassed by it.

---

[5] Cf. Quine, *Word and Object*, p. 23 (on the status of objects referred to in scientific theories): 'To call a posit a posit is not to patronize it . . . Everything to which we concede existence is a posit from the standpoint of a description of the theory-building process, and simultaneously real from the standpoint of the theory that is being built. Nor let us look down on the standpoint of the theory as make-believe; for we can never do better than occupy the standpoint of some theory or other, the best we can muster at the time.'

We have seen that expressivism is not obliged to make it a necessary condition of rationality that one should enjoy a *sittlich* relationship with the particular set of linguistic institutions which happen to be dominant within one's own community. It will not be surprising, therefore, from the point of view of that theory, if ordinary language proves to contain devices enabling 'alienated' speakers to express their disengagement from the institutions concerned.

One such device – the ironic, or 'inverted commas', use of words whose normal function is to commend or condemn – is discussed by Hare in *The Language of Morals*, and again in *Freedom and Reason*. A speaker who uses a normally evaluative word in this way is not making a value-judgement himself, according to Hare, but 'alluding to the value-judgements of other people':[1] its meaning, in his mouth, is 'purely descriptive' (which means that his audience is to understand it as denoting the same empirical property, or cluster of properties, as in standard use, but not as expressing the standard practical orientation with regard to things possessing that property). Thus if I become disenchanted with the moral quality celebrated in my language under the name of 'courage', I may make an announcement of the following form: 'What I shall actually do . . . is to use the word "courageous", but to make it clear by my tone of voice or by putting quotation marks round it, that I am using it in a purely descriptive sense, implying thereby no commendation whatever.'[2] Hare also says (cf. section 4 above): 'It is true that there is no single evaluatively neutral word which in the present case can be used to describe [courageous] actions without committing the describer to any evaluation: but we *could* have such a word.'

The difficulty with this view, as McDowell has suggested,[3]

---

[1] Hare, *The Language of Morals*, p. 124.
[2] Hare, *Freedom and Reason*, p. 189.
[3] McDowell, 'Are Moral Requirements Hypothetical Imperatives?', p. 20;

is that it is far from self-evident that we 'could have' an array of evaluatively neutral words with precisely the same extensions as our current moral concepts. We have no business to assume that the individual language-learner could grasp the unifying principle which brings together various phenomena under the concept of 'courage', unless at the same time certain systematic feelings of respect, admiration, etc. were being imparted to him. It may rather be that the technique of classifying actions in terms of our various *de facto* evaluative categories is one which can be taught and learnt only as the linguistic vehicle of a specifically moral or aesthetic sense. (Compare the way in which the acquisition of competence with moral language was represented in section 8 above, where we saw that the 'semantic depth' of moral words could be understood naturalistically, sc. in terms of the learner's ability to participate in social practices of progressively greater complexity.)

We can accept McDowell's criticism of the 'two-part' analysis of value-terms, since the moral realist position we have been developing incorporates his rejection of the empiricist view of practical rationality – the view according to which beliefs and desires combine in a mechanistic way to generate action. But the validity of that criticism should not lead us to overlook the phenomenon which Hare singles out for attention in the passages cited above.

We can grant that, as Wittgenstein puts it (*OC* §160), 'doubt comes after belief', and hence that the possibility of using moral words in Hare's 'inverted-commas' sense is dependent on some prior experience of their naïve use.[4] On this view, it is only our personal history of participation in language-games which provides us with anything to be

---

cf. also his 'Non-Cognitivism and Rule-Following', in Holtzman and Leich (eds.), *Wittgenstein: to Follow a Rule* (1981), pp. 144-5.

[4] I do not mean to imply that the ironic use of any *single word* requires a background of this kind in respect of the particular word in question; a historical or anthropological study of its use may be all that is needed. But we could not undertake an anthropological study of the values of others unless we had a system of values of our own, in terms of which to interpret the alien system (cf. section 9 above).

alienated *from*. The alienated speaker will be able to use his ironic predicate, 'courageous', with the appropriate extension only because his parents and teachers once inculcated in him a non-ironic appreciation of courage (and related qualities); and the words of Milton's Satan, 'Evil be thou my good',[5] owe their power precisely to the semantic depth which the speaker's former status confers on them. ('Was not that Lucifer an angel once?'[6]) In short, there is an experiential background not only to those uses of moral words which Hare calls 'prescriptive', but also to his so-called 'purely descriptive' uses.

The force of these expressivist considerations about language-acquisition does not, however, alter the fact that doubt and disaffection can sever the individual from the community to which his education was intended to bind him (cf. *OC* §298). Such a person will be unable to participate without irony in any language-games which may be affected by his dissenting attitudes: with respect to those games, he will be unable to make the transition from the 'objective' to the 'participant' standpoint, as exemplified at *OC* §281 (cf. section 37 above).

Individual speakers can give partial expression to this kind of dissent simply by rooting the unacceptable concepts out of their own idiolects (cf. Oscar Wilde's assertion, in an anecdote cited by Hare, that 'blasphemous' was not 'a word of his').[7] Hare's remarks about 'courage' are easy enough to paraphrase in expressivist terms: 'What I shall do . . . is to use the word "courageous", but to make it clear . . . that I am using it in an alienated spirit, in no way implying that I can "find myself" in the prevailing form of life in so far as that form of life expresses itself in the language-game with the

---

5 Cf. Hare, *The Language of Morals*, p. 175.
6 Marlowe, *Doctor Faustus*.
7 Hare, *Freedom and Reason*, p. 189n. It is accepted, even by those who insist on the notion of impersonal rules of evidence in moral argument, that such rules apply only on condition that a particular moral vocabulary is accepted. Cf. Foot, *Virtues and Vices*, p. 104: 'Calling an action "rude" is using a concept a man might want to reject.'

word "courage".' Nor need the decision to accept or reject any given moral concept be an arbitrary one, for the person concerned can offer a rational justification of his refusal to use one such concept (e.g. 'blasphemy') in terms of another for which he does have a use (e.g. 'hypocrisy'). We saw in section 30 that adherence to a non-standard scheme of values does not restrict one, in one's capacity as a moral agent, to the exercise of an existentialist 'empty freedom' of the kind whose influence on ethical theory is deplored by Iris Murdoch and others.

A special difficulty arises, however, in connection with certain abstract concepts which encapsulate the norms that regulate our thinking in a more general way. Examples would include 'true', 'rational', 'reasonable', 'realistic', 'good', 'beautiful', 'intelligent'. These concepts cannot just be excluded from the vocabulary of the dissident individual; if he were sincerely to say, for instance, ' "Rational" is not a word of mine', he would forfeit his claim to be listened to. Yet in so far as he fails to discover his own 'true being' in the shared way of life which determines how these concepts are to be applied, he will be unable to participate in that way of life in a non-ironic spirit; and so these words too – where they occur in his speech – will tend to be hedged about with inverted commas, or other devices expressing critical distance from the consensus. (Thus *OC* §254, 'Any "reasonable" person behaves like *this*.') The attitude of the alienated individual towards concepts such as 'rational', whose function within the language-game is a global one, will therefore oscillate between irony and non-irony, and in this way he will situate himself critically in relation to the various regions of discourse spanned by the concept.

Now we noticed a moment ago that this person's rejection of certain concrete value-terms, such as 'blasphemy', was not an arbitrary movement of revulsion, but a logical consequence of the values to which he actually subscribes. The same thing, I suggest, will be true of his ironic attitude towards the dominant language-game with the abstract normative concepts of truth, rationality, etc. In distancing himself from certain aspects of the prevailing usage of these words, he seeks to record the fact that he has his own views about their proper use; in this case the target of his irony is the way the words are actually applied, *not* the very idea of a form of life in which they would have a place (for that, as stated earlier, would be self-contradictory in so far as he himself is concerned to speak the truth, act rationally, etc.) His irony expresses the thought that within the dominant language-game those concepts, are, so to speak, in a fallen condition; and it gets its point by implied opposition to the idea of a 'redeemed' language-game in which they could be used without irony.

Sometimes the alienated person will engage in this imagined language-game in a prefigurative way. If his own dissenting attitudes are those of a sizeable minority of participants in the established way of life, the 'prefigurative' nature of his contribution may be relatively inconspicuous, but we can see it increasingly clearly as that minority diminishes in size: thus Wittgenstein's declaration that 'in the health of our intellect we are surrounded by madness' demands to be read as an appeal to those isolated representatives of mental health, in whose existence (as its own potential audience) Wittgenstein's remark expresses faith.

We saw in section 35 that even if I believe myself to be the only person in possession of the truth about any given subject, I shall still be entitled (on a Wittgensteinian view) to regard my own opinion as true *sans phrase:* that is to say, the fact that I appear to be in a minority of one does not make it necessary (or even legitimate) for me to resort to subjectiviz-ing qualifications ('true for me', etc.). What I shall believe is that *I am right and they are wrong;* and this belief, as we have seen, can coexist with the philosophical idea that intellectual norms are grounded in a common practice, just as our insistence on the distinction between *real pain and a perfectly convincing imitation* can coexist with a Wittgensteinian understanding of our knowledge of other minds.

The belief that 'I am right and everyone else is wrong' prefigures, through its implicit realism, a condition in which others will have come to share my own current practice with regard to the application of normative concepts – to share, in other words, my own values and beliefs. A world in which that condition obtained would be one where 'reality' in the positive sense (i.e. that which is fixed by the content of the propositions comprised in the consensual world-view) had come to coalesce with 'reality' in the critical sense (i.e. that which is fixed by the content of the totality of propositions that *I* hold true). By contrast, the 'purely descriptive' use of value-terms discussed by Hare is a symptom of the state of mind experienced by someone for whom these two senses of 'reality' have come apart in respect of a particular region of discourse.

The grammatical admissibility of the statement 'I am right and everyone else is wrong' is bound up with the historical possibility of the sequence of events imagined by Wittgenstein in connection with the tribe that develops a new way of making lists (cf. section 33 above). My subjective situation, when I make such a statement, parallels that of the (hypothetical) *first person* to advocate the new method. For Wittgenstein envisages a process of change in which the revision of the existing practice is demanded, at first, by 'only a few'. Those few speakers will initially have to engage, without reference to any already constituted authority, in a language-game which they themselves have invented – a game regulated by norms which, as yet, lack the kind of institutional backing enjoyed by the norms that regulate the dominant practice. But if they succeed in drawing in the bulk of the community, the time will eventually come when they will be described – with all the authority of the altered consensus which it is their purpose to create – as the far-sighted pioneers of an altogether superior approach to the list-making question. This is the material possibility in which critical thinking is grounded.

'Dialectical reason,' writes Theodor Adorno, 'is, when set against the dominant mode of reason, unreason: only in encompassing and cancelling this mode does it become itself reasonable.' But he adds in another place: 'No sunrise, even in mountains, is pompous, triumphal, imperial; each one is faint and timorous, like a hope that all may yet be well, and it is this unobtrusiveness of the mightiest light that is moving and overpowering.'[8]

—— 39 ——

The early part of this book was concerned with the implications of abandoning non-cognitivist moral philosophy in favour of a moral realism based on expressivist notions of language and society. Later, it was argued that because the passage from the former to the latter type of theory proceeds by way of a disclosure of the historical dimension of language, and hence of the moral significance of our participation in specific language-games, this passage could not constitute a simple movement of return to the condition of 'unmediated contact' with the current objects of our discourse. The suggestion that it could do so was likened, in section 26 above, to a claim that our proposed (post-empiricist) philosophy of language would place us in the position of the child in T. S. Eliot's poem about Christmas trees: a position in which it would be as if we had not yet begun to acquire consciousness of the human activity that goes into the construction of linguistic systems. This state of mind, however, as Eliot insists, must be distinguished from that of the 'childish' adult, i.e. of one who declines to yield himself to the mediating process which would *re*-establish contact between mind (or language) and its objects at a level appropriate to his own seniority.

The distinction just drawn has a bearing on the attempt to derive a conservative moral or political philosophy from the kind of moral realism we have been developing. That realism, as we have seen, incorporates the Wittgensteinian idea that in doing philosophy we are trying to confront our own sub-

---

[8] Adorno, *Minima Moralia*, pp. 72, 111. Cf. Wittgenstein, *OC* §141, 'Light dawns gradually over the whole'; also Nietzsche, *The Gay Science*, §260, '*One* is always wrong, but with two, truth begins.'

jectivity as it is manifested in the medium of language (and of social practice generally): the purpose of philosophical activity, according to Wittgenstein and various other express- ivist thinkers, is to oppose the drive of our intellect towards a fetishistic misunderstanding of its own operations (cf. section 27 above). However, where we find expressivist premisses issuing in conservative conclusions, we shall also, I think, find evidence of a resistance to this counter-drive towards 'enlightenment' which animates expressivist theories of language in so far as such theories can be held to fall within the rationalist tradition.

In order to appreciate this connection it will be helpful to examine the mode of operation of the 'anti-enlightenment' tendencies postulated above. Bradley's essay on 'My Station and its Duties', which we examined in section 20, provides a suitable case-study.

The main thesis of the essay, it will be remembered, is that it is only within a community that the individual can 'realize himself', or endow his life with meaning. Bradley offers this thought as an antidote to the way in which the self-realization theme is apt to be treated within the empiricist tradition, where 'society' plays a somewhat negative role and may even be seen, first and foremost, as a potential oppressor – a coercive agency constantly threatening to encroach upon the individual's personal space. The *locus classicus* for such a view is, of course, Mill's essay 'On Liberty' (though this too was influenced by a developmental concept of 'individuality' derived from the German Romantic movement).[1]

The empiricist picture is exposed to criticism both for its assimilation of personal identity to an item of property, and conversely for its failure to attach any concrete meaning to the idea of *universality* which has to be set over against that of private interest for the purposes of moral reasoning (cf. section 31 above; section 43 below). Thus Bradley maintains that 'if anybody wants to realize himself as a perfect man without trying to be a perfect member of his country and all his smaller communities, he makes what all sane persons

---

[1] Cf. Steven Lukes, *Individualism* (1973), p. 69.

would agree to be a great mistake.'[2] Similarly, T. H. Green argues that 'the love of mankind . . . needs to be particularized in order to have any power over life and action. Just as there can be no true friendship except towards this or that individual, so there can be no true public spirit which is not localized in some way.'[3]

Many of Bradley's remarks about the relation between individual and community present themselves simultaneously as philosophical and as sociological, or historical ones. In terms of its method, therefore, the essay may be seen as a contribution to the Wittgensteinian project of trying to gain an understanding of the phenomenon of linguistic meaning (specifically, of morality conceived as a symbolic system; cf. section 16 above) by 'assembling reminders' (cf. *PI* I §127) about the way language works. And the sociological observations which define the physiognomy of the moral language-game as perceived by Bradley relate, above all, to the *feasibility of dissent* from consensual morality.

Bradley does not wish to encourage optimism in this area. Individual 'ideals', he points out, have a shadowy existence and are ill-fitted to survive competition against the might of actual institutions. The moral organism is 'stronger than the theories and practice of its members against it':[4] so much so that it can allow itself the luxury of a tolerant attitude towards

---

[2] Bradley, *Ethical Studies*, p. 201.
[3] T. H. Green, *Lectures on the Principles of Political Obligation* (1895), p. 175. (It should be pointed out that these remarks of Green's are sandwiched between statements to the effect that 'it is utterly false to speak as if the desire for one's own nation to show more military strength than others were the only or the right form of patriotism', and that 'there is no reason why . . . localized or nationalized philanthropy should take the form of a jealousy of other nations or a desire to fight them, personally or by proxy.')
[4] Bradley, *Ethical Studies*. All the passages cited in this and the following paragraph occur on pp. 199-201. For the idea of toleration as a function of the strength of a society, cf. Nietzsche, *The Genealogy of Morals*, p. 72: 'As the power and self-confidence of a community increase, the penal law always becomes more moderate; every weakening or imperiling of the former brings with it a restoration of the harsher forms of the latter. The "creditor" always becomes more humane to the extent that he has grown

'new theories and youthful opinions that everything would be better upside down'; even, it seems, towards 'star-gazing virgins with souls above their spheres, whose wish to be something in the world takes the form of wanting to do something with it.' Experienced persons 'are intolerant only of those who are old enough, and should be wise enough, to know better than that they know better than the world.'

It is, he concedes, legitimate – in fact, it is a duty – 'standing on the basis of the existing, and in harmony with its general spirit, to try and make not only oneself but also the world better, or rather, and in preference, one's own world better.' But a merely invented, or imagined, condition of moral perfection – an idea which generates opinions that do violence to consensual morality – may be recognized *eo ipso* as a vehicle of delusion. 'The moral world, with its social institutions, etc., is a fact; it is real; our "ideals" are not real.'[5]

Moreover, Bradley suggests that in the higher interests of the community as a whole – notably in time of war – everyone will in fact condone the suspension of the individual freedoms cherished by liberal theory: at such times we regularly see 'what are called "rights" laughed at, "freedom", the liberty to do what one pleases, trampled on, the claims of the individual trodden underfoot, and theories burst like cobwebs.'[6]

It is in passages like these that Bradley's account of moral discourse approximates most closely to the position I characterized in section 25 as the limiting case of the holistic conception of rationality: the view, namely, that rational

richer; finally, how much injury he can endure without suffering from it becomes the actual *measure* of his wealth. It is not unthinkable that a society might attain such a *consciousness of power* that it could allow itself the noblest luxury possible to it – letting those who harm it go *unpunished*. "What are my parasites to me?" it might say. "May they live and prosper: I am strong enough for that!"'

[5] Bradley was following Hegel closely in this. Cf. *Philosophy of Right*, p. 11: 'If [a philosopher's] theory really goes beyond the world as it is and builds an ideal one as it ought to be, that world exists indeed, but only in his opinions, an unsubstantial element where anything you please may, in fancy, be built.'

[6] Bradley, *Ethical Studies*, p. 184.

dissent from the established world-view is a logical impossibility. A community of which this was true would be one that construed any unorthodoxy in theory or practice as an act of social suicide – a sufficient reason to debar the person concerned from that shared way of life in which every individual must participate if he is to sustain his identity as a rational subject. In making out moral dissent to be a peculiarity of those who are not sufficiently identified with the existing social institutions to count as 'real' for the purposes of moral discussion, Bradley is inviting the reader to think of himself as a member of a community of just this kind.

'My Station and its Duties' purports, then, to give a kind of empirical refutation of the liberal notion of moral autonomy – the idea of a personal morality embraced by the individual regardless of, or even in defiance of, convention. This purported refutation rests upon an appeal to facts about social life which will be acknowledged (according to Bradley) by any thoughtful person not in the grip of individualist dogma. The suggestion is that the 'worshippers of the individual' have simply failed to appreciate certain objective features of the moral language-game and of the institutions in which it is embodied.

—— 40 ——

However, if we look more closely at the 'sociology' which records these supposedly objective phenomena, we shall find that it is a typical product of the fetishistic, or reifying, tendency criticized by Wittgenstein. In fact, we shall find that it is open to an objection which is implicit in any expressivist account of language or of social institutions.

Bradley, as noted earlier, insists upon the strength of the 'moral organism' against dissent. Yet he himself, in supplying us with the concept of 'objective spirit', invites us to point out that the poor prospects of changing anything – of winning acceptance for any proposed adjustment to an established form of life – are not independent of the behaviour of those who affirm these 'facts' with such relish. The moral community, as presently constituted, may indeed be 'stronger than the theories and practice of its (dissenting) members against it'; but that strength, as philosophical reflection shows, is derived entirely from the commitment of its *other* members, the ones who remain loyal; from the continual obligation they acknowledge to sustain and renew the institutions in which their moral world is embodied. The stability of existing institutions, then, is owed to the *sittlich* attitude of individuals towards them, and to the readiness of individuals to undertake a militant defence of those institutions against attempted subversion.

There is, of course, nothing inherently irrational in a determination to resist change. Such a determination is irrational only if the proposed innovation is more rational than what currently exists. In order to establish whether that is so in any given case, it is necessary to examine both types of arrangement and make up one's mind – on the basis of reasons – which of the two is preferable. We are supposing, with Wittgenstein, that this is not a philosophical exercise (cf. section 37).

Departures from moral tradition may be labelled alternatively as 'evil' or as 'progressive'. The choice of label will depend, as we have seen, on the degree to which one identifies oneself morally with the traditional practice as against any proposed alternative. To a person whose identification with the existing order is total, moral obligation will appear solely in the guise of a demand upon him to sustain that order: it will seem, in other words, to be entirely of a *sittlich* character. Such a person will recognize nothing in the nature of the Kantian *Moralität,* or obligation to realize what does not yet exist (cf. section 16 above). His system of values will thus constitute a 'morality of *mores*', to borrow the term Nietzsche was fond of using: under a moral system of this kind, says Nietzsche, *change* is perceived as 'the very essence of immorality and pregnant with disaster'.[1]

By contrast, it is not surprising to find that where the

---

[1] Nietzsche, *The Genealogy of Morals,* p. 114.

relevant identification is lacking, expressivist theories of language and culture yield very different results from those reached in 'My Station'. Nietzsche, for instance, anticipates the Wittgensteinian idea that to construct a reality is to play a game[2] – the game of using linguistic signs which have an objective reference. It is true that for him, as for Wittgenstein (cf. sections 11, 35; and section 37 n.2), this 'game' is set apart from others by the fact of our inability in principle to put it away and give our minds to something more serious. But that fact does not suffice to purge the 'game' idiom of all ethical significance: Nietzsche certainly interprets his own express-ivist views as pointing a moral for intellectual life, namely, that the reality which is the objective correlate of our discourse should not be elevated into a ' "world of truth" that can be mastered completely and forever with the aid of our square little reason.'[3] For an essential characteristic of games is that their rules can at any time be modified, at the will of any or all the players, with a view to making the game more enjoyable to play. Such changes may, moreover, be initiated by experimental behaviour on the part of an individual player, who – like Paul Feyerabend's 'epistemological anarchist' a century later – 'can assert anything he wants and often will assert absurd things in the hope that this will lead to new forms of life.'[4]

The abyss which divides Nietzsche and Bradley reflects a divergence not so much in the metaphysical positions of the two thinkers, but rather in their individual responses to moral

---

[2] For 'play', cf. *The Gay Science,* §382; other kindred images are 'dreaming' (ibid. §54; cf. section 37 above), 'poetic creation' (§301), 'dancing' (§347) and 'acting' (§356).

[3] Ibid., §373.

[4] P. K. Feyerabend, *Science in a Free Society* (1978), p. 210 n. 2. Cf. also Nietzsche, *The Gay Science,* §51: 'I favour any *scepsis* to which I may reply: "Let us try it!" '; also Mill, *On Liberty:* 'Originality is a valuable element in human affairs . . . It is good that there should be differences, even though not for the better, even though, as it may appear to them [the public], some should be for the worse' (pp. 193, 204); also Wittgenstein, *CV* p. 80: 'For a philosopher there is more grass growing down in the valleys of silliness than up on the barren heights of cleverness.'

anomalies. It is the contrast between a man whose relationship with his social milieu is one of tender domesticity ('. . . what I have to do I have not to force on a recalcitrant world; I have to fill my place – the place that waits for me to fill it'),[5] and one who could describe himself as 'homeless in a distinctive and honourable sense' ('We children of the future, how could we feel at home in this today? We feel disfavour for all ideals that might lead one to feel at home in this fragile, broken time of transition; as for its "realities", we do not believe that they will *last*.')[6] These different attitudes tend to produce an emphasis, respectively, on the *static* and on the *dynamic* aspects of the social formation in which our talk about 'moral reality' is grounded. The expressivist conception of language, however, does not in itself determine either emphasis as more legitimate than the other.

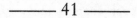

—— 41 ——

According to Wittgenstein's conception of language, which we took as the basis of our proposed moral realism, mutual understanding presupposes the common acceptance of some 'totality of propositions' – the theoretical counterpart of a common way of acting (cf. section 9 above). What we call 'rationality', too, turns out on this account to be a quality ascribed to individual persons just in so far as they are held to be capable of taking part in rule-governed forms of behaviour – notably, the practice known as *reasoned argument,* with its characteristic rules of inference. Essential to the Wittgensteinian picture is the idea that people whose behaviour is psychologically alien to us will to that extent fail to qualify as candidates for participation, along with ourselves, in a shared language-game: i.e. that in order to communicate with other people we need to be able to 'find our feet' with them (*PI* II p. 223).

---

[5] Bradley, *Ethical Studies,* p. 180.
[6] Nietzsche, *The Gay Science,* §377.

Now these alleged truths of reflection supply no information whatsoever as to the possibility of 'finding our feet' with specific individuals or groups. They do not tell us at what point a cultural divergence becomes so wide as to make any attempt at understanding pointless; neither do they tell us what to do in any actual situation where we may find ourselves unable to achieve understanding. In such a situation, we cannot turn to the above-mentioned parts of Wittgenstein's philosophy either for authority to lynch anybody, or for authority to insist upon toleration. And the same seems to be true of other brands of historicism about moral and intellectual norms: such doctrines are equally well-qualified to accompany a tolerant, experimentalist cast of mind, or a defensive and authoritarian attachment to tradition.

We might make use of a pair of familiar terms, 'conservative' and 'liberal', to denote two contrasting positions which are available to the expressive theorist of language. (There is, of course, a further position which, following Feyerabend, we might designate as 'anarchist', but I shall not consider this option explicitly: my remarks about 'liberalism' may be understood to refer to it by extrapolation.) The adherents of these different positions should, I believe, be seen as advocates of different *policies* towards deviant or *unsittlich* behaviour. The liberal commends a policy of toleration – of keeping an open mind as to whether the anomalous way of acting can be brought into connection with established social practices; the conservative, by contrast, calls for a strict policing of *Sittlichkeit* and demands positive disciplinary measures against the author of any anomaly. The relevant discipline consists in a withdrawal of the recognition previously extended to that person as a serious participant in the language-game.[1]

The distinction between recognition and non-recognition

---

[1] Perhaps the force of the word 'serious' here can best be conveyed by way of an elaboration of the 'game' metaphor. Thus, a group of children playing may turn out on inspection to contain a hard core (the older children, say) whose moves are acknowledged as making a difference to the course of the

of a given individual as a serious participant in the language-game may be understood as a variant upon the Kantian opposition between treating persons as ends and as means. That opposition has, in fact, been presented to modern readers (by P. F. Strawson in his British Academy lecture, 'Freedom and Resentment') in terms of a contrast between the so-called 'participant' and 'objective' attitudes towards persons. To adopt the 'objective' attitude, in Strawson's scheme, is to see another person not as an equal (a fellow-citizen in the Kantian 'kingdom of ends'), but as something to be 'managed or handled or cured or trained' – a phenomenon in the natural world, our interest in the latter being assumed to be motivated by a hankering after manipulative power.[2] The 'participant' attitude, on the other hand, accords to the other person a status which makes him an appropriate object of emotions such as 'resentment, gratitude, forgiveness, anger, or the sort of love which two adults can sometimes be said to feel, reciprocally, for each other.'[3]

The position I have designated as 'liberal' is that of the person who forbears to respond to moral dissent (or deviancy, as we may call it if it has no rationale that we can understand) with an objectifying strategy whose effect is to restrict the dissident's possibilities of taking part in social activity – and thus (in the long term) to undermine his status as a rational person. (Cf. Bradley: 'As members of the system we are real, and not otherwise.') Such a person will advocate a looser code of practice: refusing to take mere non-conformity as a ground for expelling anyone from the rational community,

---

game, while the younger ones run about on the fringes, imitating the others and calling out to them, but largely ignored by the core group. The members of this core group are the 'serious' players, in the sense I have in mind; the others, not.

[2] Cf. Hobbes, *Leviathan*, p. 161: 'I put for a generall inclination of all mankind, a perpetual and restlesse desire of power after power, that ceaseth only in Death.'

[3] P. F. Strawson, 'Freedom and Resentment', in *Freedom and Resentment and Other Essays* (1974), p. 9. Strawson's position in this essay, of course, owes as much to Hume as to Kant, for his 'reactive attitudes' are directly descended from Hume's 'moral sentiments'.

he will demand a more rigorous criterion (in Mill's case, for example, 'harming others'; sc. physically, or at least in some fairly tangible way). The conservative, meanwhile, is prone to think that deviation from the main channel of the language-game is a sufficient ground for the objectification of the deviant – the progressive annulment of any previously existing 'participant attitude' towards him.[4] That is to say, he is prone to assimilate the physiognomy of language-games as such to that of specific language-games, such as arithmetic (cf. section 17 above), in which any deviation from the consensus constitutes an *error* and is to be treated accordingly.

We might express the difference between the conservative and the liberal by saying that each has his own distinctive view about the sort of behaviour which is to be expected from a *rational person:* rational either *sans phrase,* or in relation to some specified region of discourse. Having said this, however, we must recall that 'rational' is a *word,* and a word – on the present conception of language – 'has the meaning someone has given to it': words stand in need of our criteria, and in the case of 'rationality' these criteria are grounded in our material acceptance or rejection of certain modes of thought and conduct.

Wittgenstein writes (*PI* II p. 178): 'My attitude towards him is an attitude towards a soul. I am not of the *opinion* that he has a soul.' We might wish, on occasion, to echo this thought as follows: 'My attitude towards him is an attitude towards a person whose values and beliefs are worthy of consideration.' With regard to certain individuals whose behaviour conflicts in some sense with the spirit of the existing form of life, the liberal will be prepared to say this, and the conservative will not; and their different attitudes will find expression in different behaviour.

In the light of these remarks we can recognize Bradley's argument in 'My Station and its Duties' as a presentation, not

---

[4] Cf. Patrick Devlin, *The Enforcement of Morals* (1965), p. 90: 'Naturally he [the law-maker] will assume that the morals of his society are good and true; if he does not, he should not be playing an active part in government.'

simply of the expressivist doctrine of 'objective spirit', but of that doctrine as refracted through the medium of the 'conservative' attitude identified above – the medium, that is, of the theorist's own somewhat inflexible commitment to the moral and political order within which he lives. And this insight helps us to find a response to Bradley's suggestion that anyone who resists the idea of an all-embracing moral and political consensus is simply failing to register certain *objective* sociological facts (cf. section 39 above). For it allows us to see those same facts under their *subjective* aspect, sc. as facts about the way in which human beings exercise social control over one another. It allows us to see that without that element of disingenuity which deflects attention from the role of human agency in sustaining *Sittlichkeit*,[5] Bradley would be unable to appeal to expressivist considerations about morality in support of his own repressive attitude towards moral anomalies. The practical inference that Bradley wishes to draw from his expressivist premises can be drawn from them only at the cost of a fetishistic distortion.

An analogous distortion of Wittgenstein's views about language might be inspired by his remark at *PI* I §242: 'If language is to be a means of communication, there must be agreement not only in definitions, but also . . . in judgements.'

---

[5] This is a form of disingenuity which Bradley's readers today should have no difficulty in appreciating. Compare, for instance, recent studies documenting the process of reification at work in orthodox political journalism, which encourages us to see as impersonal facts of political life what are really the effects of identifiable human actions. In this way it comes about that 'rationality and hard "realism" appear to be the prerogative of the dominant view', as 'the pragmatism of the "actual" world is set against the "political" demands of the left . . .' The latter, meanwhile, 'stays out on a limb where it has always been – purveyed to the public as an unwholesome bunch of dreamers or subversives. The TV companies are content to acknowledge that they do, indeed, give more serious and extensive coverage to the policies of the centre and right: after all, they would argue in self-defence, are not the views of these people the dominant views? Apparently they imagine this state of affairs developed quite independently of their own actions as broadcasters.' (G. Philo, J. Duffy and J. Buchanan, 'An Illusion of Balance', in *New Statesman* (18 April 1980).)

Philosophy would be doing nothing more unusual than re-enacting its past history, were this remark to be invoked as a cover for some *decision* not to concede the status of rational subjectivity to persons who place themselves outside a tacitly acknowledged moral consensus – tacitly acknowledged, that is, by those who remain within it.

Adherents of Wittgenstein's view of language, we have said, seek to elucidate the idea of rationality in terms of participation in a common way of life; and no objection to this picture has been raised in the course of our discussion. But what has emerged from that discussion is that such theorists must also be prepared, in the light of their own philosophical views, to endorse reflectively the procedures which currently determine how the word 'rational' is to be used. For here, as elsewhere, Wittgenstein's expressivism makes our relation to those procedures morally problematic (cf. sections 28-31 above).

I must stress that when I spoke of a 'fetishistic distortion', whose effect was to conceal the role of human activity in maintaining order within the language-game, the target of my protest was the concealment and not the activity concealed. We long ago, in rehearsing Wittgenstein's rule-following considerations, confronted the fact that committed partici-pants in a social practice – those who, in Hegelian terms, are 'within the ethical substance' – will take steps to excommuni-cate from that practice any person who persists in flouting the *sittlich* obligations which go with his participant status. Their readiness to do this is a logical corollary of their own participation, as naturalistic moral philosophers have under-stood since the time of the Sophists:[6] it 'belongs with' the idea of morality as such. What is at issue is, rather, the consent of those encompassed by *Sittlichkeit* to examine the content of their *sittlich* commitments and to recognize explicitly what sort of collective life such commitments presuppose: a recog-

---

[6] Cf. Plato, *Protagoras* 322d: in the mythical narrative assigned to Protagoras, Zeus is represented as saying, 'Take it as a law from me that anyone who is unable to share in conscience and justice is to be killed as a plague upon the city.'

nition which would have to extend, *inter alia*, to the way in which we mark out the domain of possible behaviour for a serious player of our own language-game.

If we were to conduct an inquiry into this process of demarcation, our subject-matter would be highly concrete in character. The question would be: what sort of conduct or outlook on the part of another person am I accustomed to treat as grounds for switching from a *participant* to an *objective* attitude towards that person? (At what point, or in what circumstances, does my attitude towards him cease to be an 'attitude towards a soul'?) To ask such questions, is, of course, to engage in that reflective activity which was identified in section 28 as distinctively philosophical, according to Wittgenstein's conception of the purpose of philosophy. And success in this activity would mean, not that we were able somehow to transcend all practical commitments, but only that we disengaged ourselves in the course of it from any commitments which appeared incompatible with a practical orientation embodying a reflectively acceptable set of criteria for the application of the concept 'rational'.

Acknowledging this, we shall hesitate to make loud statements to the effect that on an expressivist view of language, the moral dissident – the person who distances himself from 'ethical substance' – thereby 'sets his weapon against his own heart' (Bradley; cf. section 22 above). We shall hesitate, because we shall now understand that the destruction of the dissident is brought about by the actions of individual persons who could, in principle, choose to do something other than what they currently do; and this understanding will lead us to anticipate the comment that the apparent *penchant* of dissenters for self-mutilation may be no more than a reflection of the violence emanating from within the moral organism.

We shall get a better idea of the meaning of our own responses to moral anomalies if we follow up a suggestion contained in Strawson's description of the 'objective attitude'. That attitude, says Strawson, defines its object as something to be 'managed'. What does this tell us about the state of mind of the person who adopts it?

In the foregoing section I maintained that the way we react when we become aware of a discrepancy between our own moral beliefs and those of other people should be seen as the expression of a distinctive policy on our part. Wittgenstein's challenge at *RFM* VII §11, whose purpose is to dispel our sense of *not having a choice* at a certain sort of conjuncture in mathematics, is surely no less applicable to the moral aspect of life: 'But you can't allow a contradiction to stand! – *Why not? . . .* "We take a number of steps, all legitimate – i.e. allowed by the rules – and suddenly a contradiction results. So the list of rules, as it is, is of no use, for the contradiction wrecks the whole game!" *Why do you have it wreck the game?*'[1]

It happens not infrequently that because of the incompleteness of intellectual authority within the moral language-game (cf. section 17 above), 'contradiction' arises in the course of that game even though none of the players can be said to have broken the rules (the latter not being sufficiently determinate to allow us to say this). In other words, people may disagree about the instantiation of moral concepts (about what is permissible, or obligatory, or in bad taste, etc.) without it being possible to refer the dispute to any kind of arbitration which will command general assent. In these circumstances none of the disputants can be *authoritatively* identified as having violated the rules for the application of the concept; or, to put the same point in material terms, the use of the relevant word is not subject to the control of any single agency which could enforce a single, coherent practice in connection with it.

---

[1] Emphasis added.

Now it is in this kind of situation that the policy of an individual or group towards moral contradiction is revealed. Once the stock of arguments on each side is exhausted, and rational debate is therefore at an end, we can *choose* either to 'let the contradiction stand', or to continue to treat it as a theoretical challenge – an anomaly which detracts in an unacceptable way from the intelligibility of the world, and for which, accordingly, an explanation must be found.

A view about what needs explaining is an evaluative view. This is especially obvious in the overtly moral or political sphere. For example: a student of sociology might think it was worth looking into the reason why it was considered acceptable, within some ethnic minority group, for women to be rather vague and offhand about the paternity of their various children. The same person, if he were fairly unsophisticated, might never take it into his head to ask why the indigenous population did not in general find this acceptable. If he did not think of asking the latter question, this would provide evidence of his own assent to certain practical norms concerning reproduction and the family. Another example: a student of psychology might think it was important to find out what constitutional or developmental factors cause people to become homosexual. This (in the absence of a parallel interest in the process by which heterosexuality is established) would show that he, the student, did not look upon homosexuality as something which he himself might perfectly well go in for. Another: in economic theory, it is possible to treat military expenditure either as an aberration or as a *prima facie* rational use of resources. Thus a Marxist may seek to account for such expenditure, for example, in terms of the absorption of surplus; while a conservative may not recognize anything here that calls for a non-trivial explanation (we need bombs, he may say, so we make them). These two approaches display different evaluations of a given state of affairs in respect of rational intelligibility: one registers a source of mental discomfort where the other does not.

Nietzsche makes the following helpful remarks about the subjective significance of theory-building:

I asked myself: What is it that the common people take for knowledge? What do they want when they want 'knowledge'? Nothing more than this: something strange is to be reduced to something *familiar*. And we philosophers – have we really meant *more* than this when we have spoken of knowledge? What is familiar means what we are used to so that we no longer marvel at it, our everyday, some rule in which we are stuck, anything at all in which we feel at home. Look, isn't our need for knowledge precisely this need for the familiar, the will to uncover under everything strange, unusual and questionable something that no longer disturbs us? Is it not the *instinct of fear* that bids us to know?[2]

This passage recalls Wittgenstein's conception of the activity of thinking – of making judgements – as part of a continuing exercise in *finding one's way about* (cf. Z §393). According to that conception, our attempt to understand the world (whether under its natural or under its human aspect) is an attempt to equip ourselves with a system of beliefs, and a corresponding system of behaviour, such that we shall not come seriously unstuck either in our interaction with the physical environment or in our relations with other people. To succeed in this attempt would be to arrive at a world-view which was 'habitable' (cf. section 25 above) both in a cognitive and in a practical sense – our cognitive control of things being, of course, grounded (on a Wittgensteinian view) in our ability to control them practically.

I suggest that the strength of our compulsion to *explain* any discrepancies which may come to light between our own moral beliefs and those of others corresponds to the degree of insecurity, or fear, that we feel when confronted by such

---

[2] Nietzsche, *The Gay Science*, §355. Cf. John McDowell, 'Physicalism and Primitive Denotation: Field on Tarski', in Platts (ed.), *Reference, Truth and Reality*, pp. 125-6: McDowell describes natural-scientific explanation as 'a kind [of explanation] in which *events are displayed as unsurprising* because of the way the world works'; while 'intentional explanation *makes an action unsurprising* . . . as something which the agent can be understood to have seen some point in going in for' (emphasis added).

discrepancies. The different policies we can adopt in response to moral contradiction reflect the varying extent to which our cognitive control is threatened by the existence of the alternative view. Thus if the threat is severe, we may prefer not to 'let the contradiction stand', when reasoned argument fails us, but to switch to an objectifying treatment of the anomalous opinion which will enable us to consider it in terms of its causal origins.[3] If the threat is slight or negligible, on the other hand, we may not see fit to give the matter any more thought. For instance, a rationally irresoluble disagreement as to whether it is fun to ride on the big dipper is a contradiction of a kind which we habitually allow to stand.

Sometimes our sense of insecurity in the face of moral differences is well-founded. To deny this would be to commit ourselves to a policy of acquiescence in any and every form of human barbarity.[4] At other times it merely betrays a closed mind and a bad conscience – as with the (fictional) immigration officer who says: 'We call them integrated when they are indistinguishable from ourselves.'[5] An ability to tell the first kind of case from the second is the goal of that department of moral and political theory which considers 'how to realize in human nature the perfect unity of homogeneity and specification';[6] how to establish within society a system of 'differentiation, meaningful to the people concerned, which at the same time does not set the partial communities against each other, but rather knits them together in a larger whole.'[7]

Libertarian thinkers are sensitive to the workings of a

---

[3] Platts (*Ways of Meaning*, p. 248) makes a bold (or maniacal?) claim for the primacy of this type of response: 'The "simple fact" of differences of moral judgement does not yet imply the falsity of moral realism. In moral judgements, as in others, people can, and do, make mistakes. What realism requires is that their errors be *explicable* – in realistic terms.'
[4] Cf. R. G. Collingwood's reference to the ' "liberals", such as John Stuart Mill, who argued that people ought to be allowed to think whatever they liked because it didn't really matter what they thought' (*An Autobiography* (1939), p. 152).
[5] Cf. *The Swissmakers (Die Schweizermacher)*, a recent film directed by Rolf Lyssy.
[6] Bradley, *Ethical Studies*, p. 188.
[7] Taylor, *Hegel and Modern Society*, p. 117.

mechanism which has been named the 'segregation of dissent'.[8] This 'segregation' is the badge of a community in which the dominant criteria of rationality – and especially of moral or political rationality – are such as to call into question the participant status of any person who expresses unorthodox or non-consensual opinions.[9] In this kind of community, deviation from the moral consensus will be treated as a sufficient ground for expulsion from the language-game. The deviant individual, simply on the basis of his deviation, will be held to have forfeited his right to be treated 'as a soul'. This is, of course, the situation represented by 'conservative' exponents of our expressivist moral realism as obtaining universally, in virtue of the essentially social nature of rule-governed practices in general; but I have argued that, so far from being a corollary of any such general (ahistorical) facts about language-use, it is the outcome of a distinctive response to moral dissent, which may or may not be displayed by a particular community at a particular time.

Those who believe in the 'segregation of dissent', as a historical phenomenon to be observed within existing societies, believe also that that phenomenon is a morbid one. They think that the disposition to apply 'intolerant' criteria of moral and political rationality – criteria whose effect is to banish dissenting individuals from the 'rational' community – is, in general, symptomatic of an attitude of mind which perceives dissent as a threat to the community's intellectual and practical security, and as requiring, therefore, to be

---

[8] Originally the title of an essay by E. P. Thompson (1961), reprinted in *Writing by Candlelight* (1980).

[9] For a simple illustration of this tendency, cf. the following paragraph from *Radio Times* (10-16 May 1980), p. 39: 'Defence has always been a world where decisions are taken in the darkest corridors of power. Public debate has been of little consequence. Any protest movement has invariably been tarnished with a "fringe" or "leftish" label. Yet today, in East Anglia, small groups of ordinary people are demanding the right to discuss openly just what military planning might mean for our future . . .'

The structural opposition between 'ordinary' and 'leftish' here makes at least as significant a contribution to the total meaning of the paragraph as the explicit statement that 'ordinary' people as well as lefties are now concerned about the problem under discussion.

'managed'. Such an attitude is not necessarily irrational from the standpoint of the conservative, for the primary loyalty of the latter is to the 'solid fact of a world so far moralized' – and if he ever comes to have doubts about the 'strength of the moral organism against dissent', he will be acting rationally, *qua* conservative, in seeking to *stifle* dissent. In absolute terms, however, his position exhibits not only the irrationality (such as it may be) of the social order to which he is committed, but also that of repressing a variety of moral and political tendencies which are not in fact hostile to the cohesion of the community as a whole. This repression may be seen as indicative of a wrong approach to the problem of reconciling the social values of 'homogeneity and specification'.

The defence of an established way of life – regardless of the wisdom or unwisdom of such a policy in given historical circumstances – depends for its success, as expressive theorists have often noted, on the attitude of the community at large. It is assisted by the prevalence of an objectifying reaction to any item of human expression which differs from what people are used to: any attempt to extend an existing symbolic system, or to propose some unfamiliar kind of behaviour as a new way of acting in accordance with the rules. Conversely, it is obstructed by any inclination to adopt a 'participant' attitude towards experimental or dissident thinking, i.e. to treat the dissenting views as possibly valuable or true; to compare them on merit with one's own. Materially speaking, these contrasting responses are expressed in terms of the extent to which the community's channels of communication, and its intellectually authoritative institutions, are made accessible to dissidents.

Those whose beliefs and values run counter to a consensus are obliged at every moment to resist the process of objectification. They cannot consent to become the target of a 'management' policy conceived and executed by the representatives of 'common sense'; for the aim of that policy will be precisely to forestall the process outlined in section 38, whereby a recessive mode of rationality 'encompasses and cancels' the dominant one. Such people have to seek to remain

184

'inside' the rational community; to retain their status as serious participants in the language-game; to be talked *to* rather than *about*. They have to insist on their right to be seen as members of the 'party of humankind' rather than as exemplars of 'vice and disorder, its common enemy' (cf. section 1 above). An awareness of this necessity is reflected in the concept of 'marginalization', meaning the condition of a (radical) political movement which is not assigned participant status in relation to the 'serious' or 'real' political life of the community. It is reflected, too, in the struggle to maintain public recognition of certain social tensions as being of a political character, and not to allow them to be classified as problems of 'law and order'.

——— 43 ———

A time-honoured method employed by linguistic communities in controlling their dissident elements is that of 'divide and rule'. As far as theoretical ethics is concerned, this manifests itself in a refusal to recognize any middle course between, on one hand, submission to the dominant intellectual authorities; on the other, mere selfish individualism – an attitude of indifference to moral considerations.

I referred in section 31 to the opposition set up by Hume between motives traceable to self-love, and those flowing from 'some *universal* principle of the human frame'. Subsequent writers have continued to assume that failure to see the moral world 'objectively' – that is, as it is seen by the 'ideal' moral observer – indicates a moral sense distorted by straightforwardly egoistic bias. Thus Bradley writes of a moral universal which 'wills itself in us against the actual or possible opposition of the *false private self*';[1] Kolnai alludes to the 'anarchic *self-assertive* impulses of individuals and minority groups';[2] Iris Murdoch thinks that 'in the moral life the enemy is the fat relentless ego', and that 'moral philos-

---

[1] Bradley, *Ethical Studies*, p. 180 (emphasis added).
[2] Kolnai, *Ethics, Value and Reality*, p. 162 (emphasis added).

ophy is properly . . . the discussion of this ego and of the techniques (if any) for its defeat'.[3] It seems, in fact, to be characteristic of objectivist moral philosophy to attribute any rejection of the demands of consensual morality to the dissidents' assertion of their own private claims at the expense of the common good.

There is an obvious ideological incentive to portray dissent as a peculiarity of isolated individuals. This story goes some way towards concealing the fact of internal strain within a form of life: tension between competing 'formulae', as Collingwood puts it (cf. section 30 above), which threaten to issue in the development of moral or political subsystems within the body of the larger 'moral organism'. Moral theories that incorporate the 'private/universal' opposition in its *a priori* form, as documented above, express a refusal to recognize the existence of such sub-systems; they represent the latter, at best, as shadowy entities, 'between being and not-being', devoid of any organic relation to a viable form of life.

Two distinct species of mystification can be seen at work here. In the first place, there is the reifying tendency discussed above (sections 39-42), which serves to obscure the theorist's (and the reader's) complicity in a form of life that happens to be antagonistic to moral experiment. The 'unreality' of a recessive moral formula, we said, is not a fact of nature, but a reflection of certain habits of thought and behaviour which happen to prevail in the community at large. It is the moral commitment of the theorist, and of others like him, which ensures the truth of his claim that dissenting attitudes are unlikely ever to find expression in materially effective institutions; unlikely, therefore, to generate new sources of intellectual authority that would command widespread respect. And so it is this same commitment which lends plausibility to the suggestion that any person who disregards his *sittlich* obligations – who rejects, in other words, the moral demands grounded in the established form of life – thereby reveals himself as indifferent to moral considerations altogether. It

---

[3] Murdoch, *The Sovereignty of Good*, p. 52.

makes that suggestion plausible, because it helps to maintain in the real world a state of affairs in which the one and only objective morality is, indeed, 'the' consensual one – all others having been chased from the scene; and to the extent that such a state of affairs obtains, it will be difficult or impossible to point to an *objective justification* for defying consensual morality in any respect.

Phenomena as diverse as the Dada and surrealist styles in art, the Baader-Meinhof style in politics, and assorted 'repulsive' styles in popular culture may all be understood as ironic responses to what is perceived as a too cohesive moral, political or aesthetic rationality. The exponents of these styles may be thought of as taking up the challenge which society, in their view, presents in due course to each of its members – a challenge relating to the consensual scheme of values, which is felt to be on offer only as a package: either you buy it, or you accept the status of a moral and intellectual outlaw, an 'unreal' person for social purposes. In these circumstances, to opt deliberately for outlaw status is merely to answer the question in the terms in which it was posed, even though the content of the answer may not be what was expected.[4]

The second mystificatory feature of the 'private/universal' polarity in ethical theory is that it involves a *historical* fabrication – a panoply of unsupported assertions about the actual configuration of intellectual authority within the community to which the theory is supposed to apply. As I suggested in section 30, we should not be too quick to concede the monopolistic claims which are sometimes made on behalf of 'our' consensual value-system. It is in any case far from clear how one would set about assessing the truth of such claims. The 'conservative', for example, tells us that recessive institutions are powerless to provide the material basis for a different, yet habitable, moral world-view, or to

---

[4] The concept of the 'outsider' has also, of course, had a large part to play within philosophy itself, especially in the existentialist tradition. To look no further afield, however, cf. Nietzsche on 'homelessness' (section 40 above); also Wittgenstein, Z §455, 'The philosopher is not a citizen of any community of ideas. That is what makes him into a philosopher.'

bring us by a non-standard route to the point of being able to participate rationally in moral and political discourse. But how would he know that? How would he, or indeed anyone else, *know* anything at all in this area? (Cf. Wittgenstein, *CV* p. 45: 'Go on, believe! It does no harm.'[5])

The fact is that at this point moral philosophy is engaged, not in the disinterested investigation of a certain historically specific sign-system, but rather in a propaganda war. For the philosopher happens to be particularly well placed to convey to alienated members of his community, individually and severally, the idea that the blame for their condition lies with themselves; that their disaffection from consensual morality is, at bottom, merely a symptom of 'fat relentless egoism'. In propounding a holistic account of rationality, it can easily be suggested that 'we', the orthodox, form an organic unity in virtue of our possession of a common way of life; while 'they', the dissidents, are nothing but an aggregate of rootless individuals, lacking any shared practice which might offer competition to 'ours'. This message will tend to discredit any moves that the dissidents might variously have been contemplating which would have tended, objectively, to bring them together in the service of that historical process whereby 'dialectical reason' progressively encompasses and cancels the dominant rationality. By telling the disaffected person that he is in a minority of one, the moral philosopher can help to ensure that he remains so.

There is, incidentally, nothing mysterious about the content of the 'historical fabrication' we have just been discussing. To say that a certain ethical theory is misleading because it denies, or glosses over, the existence of 'recessive' elements within a wider social practice – elements which are at variance with the general character of that practice – is just to say that the theory misleads us by denying the internal tensions of society itself. The degree of cohesion or fragmentation of a linguistic community in respect of its criteria of rationality

---

[5] Ibid., p. 60: 'Who knows the laws according to which society develops? I am quite sure they are a closed book even to the cleverest of men. If you fight, you fight. If you hope, you hope.'

may be read off directly from such phenomena as, for instance, the frequency with which discussion is abandoned in favour of confrontation. Mathematicians, Wittgenstein remarks, 'don't come to blows' over whether a rule has been obeyed or not (*PI* I §240): this is the kind of fact in which the absence of contradiction in mathematics – of rivalry between different intellectual authorities – is displayed. But there are other matters over which people do come to blows, either figuratively or literally; and that kind of occurrence in turn displays the extent to which, as a community, we fall short of having a unified rationality for the purposes of morals, politics, or whatever it may be. The latter type of fact is immanent in the former: the individuation of forms of life, and of the respective modes of rationality grounded in them,[6] is one more field in which 'everything lies open to view' (*PI* I §126).

———— 44 ————

In the context of an expressivist view of language, a connection comes to light between the 'divide and rule' tendency we have just been considering, and the suggestion (which Iris

---

[6] Wittgenstein's philosophy has attracted a good deal of ill-judged criticism on this score. Thus Roger Trigg writes (in *Reason and Commitment* (1973), p. 72): 'Neither Wittgenstein nor any of those influenced by him have given any clear indication of how a form of life is to be identified . . . It [sc. the idea of a form of life] can only be confusing if applied to the area of contemporary religion and morality in order to explain the fundamental disagreements which undoubtedly exist. We have only to ask whether religion, Christianity or a particular Christian denomination such as Catholicism should be regarded as a form of life. There is no clear way of answering such a question . . .'
There is also no *need* to answer it, for the attack is misdirected. The concept of a 'form of life' is no more suited to feature in *explanations* of the phenomenon of moral disagreement than e.g. that of 'sameness of sense' is suited to feature in *explanations* of the fact of inter-substitutability in opaque contexts (cf. McDowell, 'On the Sense and Reference of a Proper Name', p. 157). The urge to give epistemic priority to the first term in each pair is, once again, a symptom of the 'disease of wanting to explain' (cf. section 27 above).

Murdoch cites approvingly from Simone Weil) that as moral agents we have to seek to 'control and curb imagination'.[1] I will try in this section and the next to demonstrate that connection.

The need to 'curb imagination' is presented as part of the more general programme of putting the rumbustious 'Kantian man' (cf. section 4 above) under sedation: moral excellence, it is asserted, consists not so much in the exercise of an unconditioned personal will as in the ability to assess situations justly and without self-deception. Murdoch maintains that we need to think of our obligations as contextually determined: 'A philosophy which leaves duty without a context and exalts the idea of freedom and power as a separate top level value ignores this task [sc. the task of coming to see the world as it is] and obscures the relation between virtue and reality.'[2] Yet it seems that we exercise no control over the context of our duty, but must humbly accept it in all its violence; for virtue, in the Murdoch world, is typically displayed in gloomy surroundings. Hardship, oppression, even wartime atrocities provide the backdrop for her chosen examples of morally admirable behaviour: witness her approval of the 'virtuous peasant' and of 'inarticulate, unselfish mothers of large families', not to mention the revelation that her personal vision of saintliness is a vision of unselfish behaviour in a concentration camp.[3]

The same thought is to be found in Bradley. 'Practical morality,' he writes, 'means singlemindedness, the having one idea; it means what in other spheres would be the greatest narrowness. Point out to a man of simple morals that the case has other sides than the one he instinctively fixes on, and he suspects you wish to corrupt him. And so you probably would if you went on. Apart from bad example, the readiest way to debauch the morality of anyone is, on the side of

---

[1] Murdoch, *The Sovereignty of Good*, p. 40: 'As moral agents we have to try to see justly, to overcome prejudice, to avoid temptation, to control and curb imagination, to direct reflection.'
[2] Ibid., p. 91.
[3] Ibid., pp. 74, 53, 73.

principle, to confuse them by forcing them to see in all moral and immoral acts other sides and points of view, which alter the character of each . . .'[4]

This kind of talk may cause the reader to wonder how the concentration camp originally came to be built – and to suspect that what made such an aberration possible was, above all, the fact that the citizens at large were tied up with Strength through Joy, Winter Help, and other blamelessly inarticulate activities. A little more 'imagination' might have helped them to get the measure of events; but then, as Bradley observes, 'The non-theoretical person, if he be not immoral, is at peace with reality.'[5]

Here we find ourselves in an impasse, and it is natural to seek a way out by concluding that after all one had better not insist too much on humility in ethical matters, or allow oneself to be cheaply consoled for the existence of concentration camps by the fact, however moving and impressive, of unselfish behaviour on the part of some of their inmates. Our real need, we might argue, is for a world in which that kind of virtue would not be required. However, if the word 'imagination' means anything at all, it hardly seems open to dispute that the task of constructing such a world would make large demands on our imaginative powers – the very powers which certain moral realists apparently want to bring under control. Why, then, are these writers so anxious that the ordinary person should take a 'narrow' view of things?

The temptation to answer this question in a cynical vein grows stronger when one places Bradley's rationale for 'narrowness' side by side with Richard Norman's account of rational value-change, which we considered in section 30. Norman describes a process whereby new modes of behaviour, together with the values they embody, are made generally intelligible by plotting their position relative to the habits and value-concepts already current in a linguistic community: using the familiar concepts, in other words, to advocate unfamiliar courses of action. In giving this kind of

---

[4] Bradley, *Ethical Studies*, p. 197n.
[5] Ibid., p. 183.

presentation to a new 'ethic', Norman suggests, we are *'ipso facto* providing possible reasons for adhering to it – not reasons which consist in deriving it from something else which is external to the ethic, but reasons which consist simply in showing what the ethic is.'[6]

This is, of course, merely a special case of the process by which individuals (notably children learning their native language) are introduced to new moral concepts: for example, 'the meaning of "dishonest" can be explained only by indicating its position within a whole nexus of ethical concepts . . .'[7] The mechanism discussed by Norman diverges from the basic educational procedure only in so far as it implies that moral understanding – competence with moral language – is not a static condition, but a perpetually evolving one (cf. the considerations of section 8 above on semantic depth). Yet the latent power of this mechanism must not be underrated, for Norman tells us that it promises to accomplish a dialectical transition – within the framework of a common normative language – from liberal to socialist morality.

We seem to have located a possible tension within the type of realist doctrine constructed in this book. The problem is that by encouraging the imaginative exploration of social experience, geared to discovering novel moral aspects of situations and thus achieving a more adequate grasp of moral reality, the philosopher is sowing the seeds of a critical tendency which he cannot undertake to control: the tendency towards a state of affairs in which the 'moral fabric' of the community is perpetually being demolished and rebuilt. For,

---

[6] Norman, *Reasons for Actions,* p. 170.

[7] Ibid., p. 70. The same method of moral education, incidentally, is commended by Platts, who says that 'the procedure for understanding another's moral view is that of leaving oneself open to his efforts to draw our attention to the (distinctive) features [sc. of situations] he claims to detect'; also that 'discussion with others, like self-reflection, may prompt the attention that is needed, both to focus upon particular moral aspects of a given case that would otherwise have been overlooked and to see instantiations of novel moral concepts of which we previously had no grasp.' (*Ways of Meaning,* pp. 251, 252)

as Bradley observes, when people begin to consider customary forms of behaviour from unfamiliar points of view, their assessment of such behaviour at a more abstract level of evaluation is liable to alter also. The implications of a change of perspective may therefore be far-reaching: it may become necessary, in order to restore coherence to one's total moral outlook, to qualify or even withdraw one's previous unreflective endorsement of some existing moral institution. In this way the initial, bland-looking imaginative exercise of 'trying to see different sides of the case' may open a path to the more contentious project of applying one's imagination to the construction of alternative institutions – and that project, in turn, may come to be seen as involving a radical re-ordering of the material basis of the relevant language-games.

From the point of view of those who would like to insure against this risk, it makes sense to argue that imagination should be cultivated just to the degree required for competence in a simple form of moral discourse which is, as far as possible, free from the contagion of 'recessive formulae'. Thus with regard to 'collisions of duties' – situations in which one seems to detect objective reasons for pursuing each of a number of mutually incompatible courses of action – Bradley suggests that 'these are avoided mostly by each man keeping to his own immediate duties, and not trying to see from the point of view of other stations than his own.'[8] This is essentially in keeping with the views of Iris Murdoch, as illustrated by the passages cited above; and in both writers it seems safe to attribute the advocacy of an 'unimaginative' morality to a politically-motivated sense of unease at the direction the moral language-game might take, if allowed full scope to unfold itself dialectically.

I spoke just now of a process of demolition and reconstruction of the 'moral fabric' of the community. In this connection, it is interesting to notice that contemporary radical movements do in fact make extensive use of a deliberately inculcated resistance to the forces which constitute Quine's 'pull toward objectivity' in the moral and political spheres: a

---

[8] Bradley, *Ethical Studies*, p. 198 n. 5.

conscious refusal, that is, to take up one's moral position on the spot designated by society as the standpoint of the 'ideal observer'. Quine himself mentions the way in which *artists* may seek to recall to consciousness the 'cues' which cause their expressive responses to sensory input to conform to those of other people.[9] This wilful undoing of the socializing process involves an emancipation from *objectivity* – a (partial) reversal of that earlier emancipation from *subjectivity* which endowed us with our social identity (cf. section 15 above). As such, it has a place in politics as well as in art; though politics can hardly rest with the mere deconstruction of the identity we have acquired, but must show us how to construct a new one, based on a different conception of publicly observable moral reality. (Nietzsche again: 'We can destroy only as creators.')[10]

45

We noted in section 26 the advisability of a cautious response to the idea that non-cognitivist ethical theories might be supplanted by a doctrine of 'direct' or 'unmediated' realism. These epithets, although there is indeed a harmless way of reading them, may also (and less innocently) serve to divert attention from the special character of a moral realism arrived at, like our own proposed version of that theory, by exchanging the empiricist conception of language (cf. section 5 above) for an expressivist conception of the kind developed here. The latter view of language, we found, makes visible the moral dimension of our participation in the prevailing culture (sections 27ff.), and consequently forces us to recognize that any future reintegration of the 'inner' and 'outer' perspectives on human activity must be an *achieved* reintegration, i.e. must result from the consciously willed establishment of an expressive relationship between ourselves and our public institutions.

---

[9] Quine, *Word and Object*, pp. 7-8.
[10] Nietzsche, *The Gay Science*, §58.

Now it will also be remembered that our proposed moral realism derives from Wittgenstein the idea that not just moral discourse, but every area of discourse, rests upon a common system of social *activity*. Just as non-cognitive theories of ethics contain an activist, or voluntarist, theme (cf. section 1), so the realist doctrine which is to replace non-cognitivism must preserve that theme, while insisting that it holds good not only for morality but for every subject-matter impartially (cf. section 10 above).

The importance of this activist theme lies in the fact that any moral realism which fails to incorporate it necessarily condemns us to an unending commerce with the *'familiar* objects' of thought – a constraint which can no longer be accepted, once we recognize that in order to achieve the desired reunion of 'inside' and 'outside' it may be necessary to undertake a critical reconstruction of the institutions in which the moral spirit of our community is currently embodied. For any such reconstruction is liable to involve an exchange of the 'familiar objects' of discourse for other, novel objects.

Suppose we do undertake to substitute a different way of life for our familiar one. In this situation, the different way of life envisaged by us may be one which has never actually existed. It may simply be something which we represent to ourselves in thought – a product of our (moral or political) 'imagination'. Yet as long as the extant criteria of moral and political rationality are not so rigid that any innovation in the relevant discursive practices is automatically condemned to be perceived as an *error,* the language in which we express the thought of that different way of life can be the one made available to us by the way of life in which we have been brought up to participate (cf. section 30 above). In other words, our experiential grasp of the moral institutions of our community is enough to equip us with a moral imagination which transcends the range of concrete experience that can be had within a community dominated by institutions such as those. Our acquisition of the concepts we shall use as participants in *Sittlichkeit*, or customary ethics, also provides us with all the intellectual resources we need for the purposes of *Moralität* – that part of ethics which concerns our obligation to bring about, not what already exists, but what ought to exist.

Any appearance of paradox here can be dispelled by a line of argument parallel to the one followed in section 19, where we considered a possible verificationist objection to the idea which is characteristic of realism in the general theory of meaning: viz. that we can have the conception of a circumstance which may remain permanently inaccessible to our awareness. The verificationist, we said, argues that linguistic training cannot in principle consist of anything more than the transmission from one person to another of a complex system of skills, the overall effect of these skills being an ability to produce suitable linguistic responses to circumstances presented to the speaker's consciousness. And he queries the suggestion that this training can impart to the language-learner any conception of a state of affairs which may obtain even though it never is thus presented – or, consequently, any conception of the meaning of statements purporting to record such states of affairs.[1]

In the theoretical and the practical sphere alike, the realist is exposed to the same kind of verificationist challenge: a challenge to make the phenomenon of *speculative thinking* intelligible. And in each of these spheres his response can take the same form. As competent users of language in general, he can point out, we are able to speculate about putative states of affairs which obtain (if at all) beyond our awareness; moreover, our ability to do this is wholly consistent with a naturalistic account of the language-learning process, since we possess it simply in virtue of our competence with a certain vocabulary and with certain principles of sentence-formation. For example, there is no more to possessing the conception of a (possibly recognition-transcendent) historical circumstance than the possession of competence in the use of the past tense. The same is true, he can then go on to argue, of our capacity for speculative thought of a practical character. We can respect the quasi-verificationist requirement that an acceptable theory of meaning for moral language must

---

[1] Cf. McDowell in Hookway and Pettit (eds.), p. 128.

represent mastery of such language as dependent upon initiation into the way of life of one's community, through practical experience and participation; but we can simultaneously insist that nothing more than this is needed in order to render intelligible our ability to see the morally compelling qualities of a way of life never yet realized in practice – or conversely, the morally unacceptable features of a way of life that currently exists. In each of these cases, what we shall think of ourselves as having come to perceive is an objective reason for seeking to bring about a change in the material, or institutional, basis of our moral world. Yet the possibility of that perception must indeed derive from our earlier induction into the moral world *as currently constituted*. The language (or, more broadly, the system of meaningful behaviour), mastery of which constitutes us as participants in consensual morality, must itself provide the apparatus we need for the purposes of critical thinking about moral questions; and conversely, our competence in the routine moves of the moral language-game (assuming that that game is not so regimented as to be devoid of creative possibilities) must suffice, in principle at least, to ensure that we are able to entertain 'recessive' moral ideas.

This is the picture which T. H. Green seems to have had in mind when he wrote:

> The general principle that the citizen must never act otherwise than as a citizen, does not carry with it an obligation under all conditions to conform to the law of his state, since those laws may be inconsistent with the true end of the state as the sustainer and harmonizer of social relations. The assertion, however, by the citizen of any right which the state does not recognize must be founded on a reference to an acknowledged social good . . . The condition of [such a right's] being so claimable is that its exercise should be contributory to some social good which the public conscience is capable of appreciating, not necessarily one which in the existing prevalence of private interests can obtain due acknowl-

edgement, but still one of which men in their actions and language show themselves to be aware.[2]

We have been considering 'imagination' in its role as the vehicle of speculative thinking, and we have equated speculative thinking in the practical sphere with the Kantian *Moralität* as understood by Hegel (with ideal as opposed to customary ethics). But if our capacity for a type of thought which transcends our experience is to be conceived, in general, as a linguistic capacity – a product of our ability to manipulate a finite repertoire of concepts and syntactic rules in creative ways – then 'imagination', in the sense which concerns us here, must also be thought of as manifesting itself in our use of language. It must be *language* that allows us to perform the function which Collingwood, in the passage cited in section 19 above, assigns to *imagination:* that of '[constructing] possible worlds, some of which, later on, thought will find real or action will make real.' And such a view is, indeed, expressed by Wittgenstein at *PI* I §441: 'The fact that some event stops my wishing does not mean that it fulfils it. Perhaps I should not have been satisfied if my wish had been satisfied . . . Suppose it were asked "Do I know what I long for before I get it?" If I have learned to talk, then I do know.'

'Knowing how to talk' – either absolutely, or with reference to some specified subject-matter – is something that admits of degree; the effect of our discussion of semantic depth (section 8), and of the way moral facts can transcend individual awareness (section 18), was to support just this conclusion in respect of morality. Also, we can work on our discursive skills and build them up. For example, the process of seeking out new moral perceptions by cultivating a receptive attitude towards the perceptions reported by others (section 44 above) is essentially a matter of enhancing one's ability to *talk* intelligently about questions of value; and this again is in keeping with our proposed reinterpretation in linguistic terms of the idea of a 'moral sense' (section 12).

But, granted the relation of immanence which we have

---

[2] Green, *Lectures on the Principles of Political Obligation*, pp. 148, 149.

posited between imaginative and linguistic activity, it follows that the intensity of the former within any given linguistic community will vary directly with the license enjoyed by its members to talk to one another in certain ways; and conversely, that the 'curbing of imagination' (cf. section 44) will consist in a curtailment of that license. And this insight can help us, I think, to a more systematic understanding of the kind of moral realism expounded by Bradley and Murdoch. It can help us to see how their concern with strict obligation, singleness of purpose, even 'narrowness', converges with the implicit 'divide and rule' policy in respect of moral rationality which I attributed to them in section 43.

It is not to be expected that an ethical theory which finds moral goodness, above all, in 'simple' people (cf. Murdoch's 'inarticulate, unselfish mothers of large families') will favour the unrestricted development of the moral 'imagination' of those people – the unrestricted advance, that is, of the process by which they come to see things from unfamiliar moral points of view. That process can only result in their becoming less simple, with consequences no one can predict. For example, it might turn out to be a bad day for 'moral reality' as we know it if the women whom Murdoch singles out for praise were to learn to conceptualize their possible resentment of the conditions of their life in some other terms than those of 'fat, relentless egoism'. ('If I hadn't been so inarticulate I wouldn't have had ten children,' they might say to themselves in a moment of heightened dialectical acuity.) To this extent, then, the ideological motive behind Bradley's and Murdoch's type of moral realism, with its emphasis on strict obligation and on an 'unimaginative' notion of virtue, is transparent. But when we make the postulated connection between *imagination* and *expressive skills,* we can go further and suggest that philosophical depreciation of the former function should be referred back to a more general tendency displayed by the kind of realist position we have labelled as 'conservative' (section 41 above). This was the tendency to construct theoretical models within which resistance to the 'objective' demands of morality is atomized, and thus effectively prevented from appearing under the aspect of dissent.

We can think of the policy of 'curbing imagination' as converging with the 'divide and rule' policy in the following sense. On general expressivist grounds we have identified the faculty of moral 'imagination', by which speakers represent to themselves how things might be different and better, as a distinct species of linguistic competence. But this implies that it is a faculty which cannot be exercised in isolation, but only within an organic grouping of persons who are participants in a common mode of activity. Now the 'conservative' moral realist seeks, *ex hypothesi,* to forestall any discursive process which might tend to 'debauch' those humble, simple people who provide him with his models of virtue – i.e. any elaboration of a deviant moral or political perspective upon their own experience, in the light of which they might claim to be able to discern an objective justification for ceasing to behave in the ways applauded by himself. Correspondingly, as regards the 'body of the moral world,' our 'conservative' is obliged to resist any attempt on the part of such people to regroup themselves within alternative moral institutions of their own devising, and, under the protection of those institutions, to construct a language-game incorporating different and (from his point of view) unacceptable criteria of rationality and truth (cf. section 38 above). And one thing he can say which is in keeping with this overall strategy is that the worthiest people are those who are too 'narrow' to conceive of any such project.

Thus the 'unimaginative' theme in certain variants of moral realism expresses, at the theoretical level, a feeling of displeasure induced by the vision of the world's virtuous peasantry 'learning to talk', for its own purposes, about moral and political questions. This is what motivates the suggestion that if ever the peasants do attempt a dialectical development of their existing conceptual resources, with a view to finding out 'what they want' (cf. section 30 above) in advance of actually getting it, they will be doing something which is at odds with the true requirements of morality – requirements such as humility, 'singlemindedness', and an unswerving respect for the duties that go with one's 'station'.

46

At an earlier stage of this discussion (notably, in sections
14-20) we were concerned to develop a certain philosophical
conception of what *objectivity* amounts to in moral and
political discourse. That conception was one which I tried to
show to be implicit in the later writings of Wittgenstein.
I believe that it is the only account of objectivity which can
support a plausible, and non-mystificatory, moral realism.

In the light of such an account, we can see moral and
political *conflict* as arising out of tension between the
partisans of a given mode of intellectual authority (and of the
institutions which form its material basis), and those who
seek to replace that mode of authority by another. We can
think of it as a confrontation between rival habits of thought,
each regulated by its own norms, and resting upon the
material forces it can call in to enforce those norms.

Our proposed account of objectivity implies that any (non-
disruptive) engagement in an existing language-game displays
complicity with the social practice which constitutes playing
that game. Where the practice in question is one that we
regard as sound (one that is acceptable to us on reflection), we
shall find no fault with that complicity: critical thinking will
not then have the effect of placing us outside the established
'ethical substance', or *Sittlichkeit*, but will leave us at liberty
to make the 'descent' mentioned in section 37 above – a
descent from (philosophical) description of the language-
game to (practical) participation in it. It will allow us to say,
in the spirit of *OC* §281: 'People in general think like this; and
I agree with them.' On the other hand, if reflection leads us to
condemn existing institutions, we shall of course regard any
kind of complicity with them as *prima facie* irrational or
wrong.

Even if no one within a particular community actually
possesses this philosophical conception of moral and political
conflict, outside spectators (e.g. historians) can still, where
appropriate, describe the experience of that community in the
terms which it suggests – in terms of a struggle, that is,

between those forces tending towards a 'breakdown of ethical substance', and those resisting such a tendency. These processes can, and often do, take place without any articulate plan of action on either side. For example, Wittgenstein's story of the tribe that develops a new way of making lists (cf. section 32 above) leaves it open whether, or to what extent, the behaviour which initiated this change was prompted by a reformist *theory* of list-making.[1] However, if our philosophical considerations about objectivity are consciously accepted within a given community, it follows that any members of that community who subsequently set out to realize – or carry on trying to realize – an alternative form of social life will necessarily be conscious participants in the 'breakdown of ethical substance'. Their attempt to subvert established modes of intellectual authority (the 'solid fact of a world so far moralized') will take the form of an effort to *initiate* the kind of situation which also occurs spontaneously when intellectual authority gives out: a situation in which 'the rule is explained by the value, not the value by the rule' (Z §301; cf. sections 19, 32 above). Such persons will express in their actions a disdain for the constituted authority-relations – as if the latter already enjoyed only a feeble, attenuated existence – and an implicit claim that it is their actions which now specify, in concrete terms, how the relevant social practice is to be carried forward. They will use Wittgenstein's 'Who says what it is reasonable to believe in *this* situation?' (OC §326) as a rhetorical question rather than an innocent one (an expression of defiance rather than of disorientation).

Now the idea of a calculated assault upon *Sittlichkeit* may prompt the objection that, according to the argument of section 25 above, Wittgenstein's view of language makes our very identity as rational beings contingent upon our being bound together, as a community, by a shared system of beliefs and a shared way of life. This (the objection will run) implies that the project of dismantling our customary scheme of values, whether in the practical or in the theoretical sphere,

---

[1] Frazer's story about the King of Eyeo is equally opaque in this respect. Did *he* see himself as striking a historic blow against the tyranny of custom?

will have an inherent tendency to cut off the branch on which it sits: to leave those who undertake it in a position of disengagement from *every* social formation that wields intellectual authority. To be in this position is to have lost the power to question or criticize anything at all, for in order that any part of my total world-view may be called into doubt, it is necessary that the rest – or much of the rest – should 'stand fast': 'If I want the door to turn, the hinges must stay put' (*OC* §343).

The objection, we concluded, is valid in respect of an *all-embracing* scepticism: it does indeed follow from our proposed holistic notion of rationality that one cannot doubt *everything*, on pain of what we might call 'cognitive collapse'. But it is misleading, once again, in so far as it suggests that there are only two possible stances one can adopt in relation to intellectual authority (in morals or elsewhere), namely an attitude either of total defiance or of total surrender. The effect of polarizing our options in this way is, of course, to make the price of deviancy appear so high that an unreserved incorporation into *Sittlichkeit* will appear inviting by comparison. However, as we noted in section 43, this Manichean picture of the relation between 'inside' and 'outside' is best understood not as a candid philosophical record of subjective experience, but rather as an opportunistic abuse of the metaphysical idea that 'our life consists in our being content to accept many things' (cf. *OC* §344). It is in fact a matter of experiment how much we have to 'accept' – how far our 'agreement in judgements' with other members of our community can be dismantled by critical thinking before we begin to be in danger of losing the sense of our own identity, or of ceasing to be able to occupy the position of a subject of judgement.

This is equally true of individuals and of societies. At the individual level, it is evidently a matter of intersubjective variation how many 'unshakeable convictions' one needs in one's life: 'needs', that is, in the sense of not otherwise being able to find things rationally surveyable. (This seems to be the sort of thing Wittgenstein is referring to at *OC* §616: 'Would it be *unthinkable* that I should stay in the saddle however much the facts bucked?') And at the collective level, too, we accept that different communities will vary with regard to the degree of fluidity that can be accommodated within their respective world-theories (and associated practices). We do not expect to find stability and instability present in the same proportions everywhere, or a single opinion everywhere as to how much of the total theory must 'stand fast' at any given moment if judgement or meaningful inquiry is to be possible. It is up to the community concerned to decide when *anomie* has gone too far – when people's behaviour has begun to 'stammer' unacceptably. It will depend on 'what they want' in the way of intellectual and moral regimentation.

The ability, or will, to 'stay in the saddle' without the support of a ponderous array of 'certainties' (beliefs which 'lie apart from the route travelled by enquiry' (*OC* §88) might be thought of as a moral dimension of personality. We saw in section 40 something of the way this theme is developed by Nietzsche; but it also occurs in non-philosophical literature, e.g. in Strindberg's Preface to *Miss Julie* (1888), where he expresses impatience with the 'man of character' as portrayed in bourgeois fiction and drama, and admiration for the type he describes as the 'skilful navigator of life's river'.[2] This is the ethical analogue of the transition from a foundational to a non-foundational theory of knowledge.[3] Empiricist moral

---

[2] 'The word "character" has, over the years, frequently changed its meaning. Originally it meant the dominant feature in a person's psyche, and was synonymous with temperament. Then it became the middle-class euphemism for an automaton; so that an individual who had stopped developing, or who had moulded himself to a fixed role in life – in other words, stopped growing – came to be called a "character" – whereas the man who goes on developing, the skilful navigator of life's river, who does not sail with a fixed sheet but rides before the wind to luff again, was stigmatized as "characterless" (in, of course, a derogatory sense) because he was too difficult to catch, classify and keep tabs on.' (Strindberg, *The Father, Miss Julie and The Ghost Sonata*, trs. Michael Meyer (1976), p. 94)

[3] It might be argued that the effect of that transition is merely to allow an older insight to rise to the surface. Cf. N. Machiavelli, *The Prince*, trs. W. K. Marriott (1908), ch. 25: 'I believe also that he will be successful who directs his actions according to the spirit of the times, and that he

philosophy, by contrast, shows a continued emphasis on moral *principles* and on *consistency*.

The quality of being able to renounce 'certainties' gracefully is, I think, a valuable one for ourselves. We could regard it as a distinctively modern form of *asceticism*. A person who displayed this ascetic quality in his relations with *Sittlichkeit* might be said to possess the same attitude to *culture* which the modern artist, according to Paul Klee, possesses to *nature*:

> [The artist] does not attach such intense importance to natural form as do so many realist critics, because, for him, these final forms are not the real stuff of the process of natural creation. For he places more value on the powers that do the forming than on the final forms themselves.
>
> He is, perhaps unintentionally, a philosopher, and if he does not, with the optimists, hold this world to be the best of all possible worlds, nor to be so bad that it is unfit to serve as a model, yet he says:
>
> 'In its present shape it is not the only possible world.'
>
> Thus he surveys with penetrating eye the finished forms which nature places before him.
>
> The deeper he looks, the more readily he can extend his view from the present to the past, the more deeply he is impressed by the one essential image of creation itself . . . rather than by the image of nature, the finished product.

---

whose actions do not accord with the times will not be successful . . . I conclude therefore that, fortune being changeful and mankind steadfast in their ways, so long as the two are in agreement men are successful, but unsuccessful when they fall out. For my part I consider that it is better to be adventurous than cautious . . .' (Why? '. . . because fortune is a woman, and if you wish to keep her under it is necessary to beat and ill-use her', etc.)

Machiavelli, as we know, was ahead of his time. It has been left to the writers of a much later period to 'dismantle the edifice of our pride' (cf. Wittgenstein, *CV* p. 26) in the matter of moral subjectivity. See also section 49 n. 4 below.

Then he permits himself the thought that the process of creation can today hardly be complete and he sees the act of world creation stretching from the past to the future.[4]

—— 47 ——

A different and more traditional asceticism is, however, the target of Wittgenstein's criticism in his later philosophy. The sickness which that philosophy sets out to treat (the 'bewitchment of our intelligence by means of language' (*PI* I §109) has its origins, he implies, in the incomplete acceptance of our embodied condition, and in our failure to acknowledge the significance of that condition for the reflective understanding of such topics as *meaning* and *rationality*.

Wittgenstein mounts a two-pronged attack on philosophical antipathy towards the body. On one side, there is his insistence on the sensuous character of linguistic communication – its 'superficial' character, if we can free that word from the negative connotations it usually carries. I am referring here to the idea attributed to Wittgenstein in section 12 above, namely, that of language as an extension and formalization of our natural repertoire of expressive behaviour. According to this picture, meaning is a surface phenomenon in the sense that once I have offered the world a particular composition in the spatio-temporal medium of language (for instance, by making certain sounds, or marking a sheet of paper in certain ways), I have done everything in which the disclosure of the relevant mental contents could in principle consist: 'The great difficulty . . . is not to represent the matter as though there were something one *couldn't* do' (*PI* I §374). Conversely, from the point of view of the audience, Wittgenstein's views underwrite the thesis of Evans and McDowell that 'it is essential to language as we know it that our understanding of meanings should normally be a *perception* of meanings, and

---

[4] Paul Klee, *On Modern Art* (1924), trs. Paul Findlay (1948) (1979 edn), p. 45.

hence precisely *not* a matter of inference'[1] (*sc.* to some logically private mental state or process of which the linguistic utterance provides *evidence*).

Resistance to this idea – the idea of language as part of the expressive repertoire of the human species – would also account for the difficulty of the programme announced as 'not empiricism and yet realism in philosophy' (cf. section 11 above). There, too, our problem was to stop thinking that if the use of language is *only a game* (or a social practice, or a motley of noises: any naturalistic designation will do to set this line of reasoning in train), then we can never hope to see the world as it *really is*, but only as it *appears to us* through the filter of words. If we think in this way it can indeed seem that there is 'something one can't do' – viz. get to know the 'thing in itself'. But Wittgenstein, as I tried to explain in section 35, seeks to break the link between naturalism and scepticism; to challenge the presupposition that 'truth' must be the name of something we could not attain without transcending our animal status.

Wittgenstein's critique of the metaphysical opposition between body and mind, or body and soul – a critique summed up in his statement that the former is the 'best picture' of the latter (*PI* II p. 178) – illustrates the anti-ascetic tendency of expressive theories of language in general. Such theories, as we saw in section 7, identify language itself as an artistic medium: that is to say, they emphasize the analogy between language and other media which we habitually classify as art forms.

The notion of language as art, and hence of talking about the world as an occupation displaying in some degree the characteristics of poetic composition, may be contrasted with the (positivist) ideal of a *non-interpretative* representation of reality. The latter incorporates a fundamentally different vision of what we are trying to do when we use language descriptively: it sets before us the goal of a theory of nature which could be stated in terms of 'concepts which are not

---

[1] Gareth Evans and John McDowell (eds.), *Truth and Meaning* (1976), p. xxii.

peculiarly ours [i.e. not anthropocentric], and not peculiarly relative to our experience.'[2] It was this model of intellectual activity which prompted Nietzsche to write in *The Genealogy of Morals*: 'That general renunciation of all interpretation (of forcing, adjusting, abbreviating, omitting, padding, inventing, falsifying, and whatever else is of the *essence* of interpreting) – all this expresses, broadly speaking, as much ascetic virtue as any denial of sensuality (it is at bottom only a particular mode of this denial).'[3] The rejection of any such model by the later Wittgenstein makes itself felt in the all-pervasive notion of the language-*game*. This idea marks Wittgenstein as an inheritor of that strain of Romanticism which maintains, with Schiller, that 'Man only plays when he is in the fullest sense of the word a human being, and he is only fully a human being when he plays.'[4]

However, Wittgenstein's insistence that we should think of language-use as a vital function (cf. *OC* §475, 'I want to regard man here as an animal', etc.), has not only a hedonistic but a practical aspect. This is the other side of what I have called his 'two-pronged attack' on the ascetic syndrome in philosophy, i.e. on that system of philosophical error whose governing principle is mind-body dualism. It emerges from the way in which Wittgenstein gives us to understand that although a language-game is, *qua* game, something that is *played*, it is also (typically) integrated with the performance of *work* – for example, the physical manipulation of slabs, pillars and beams (cf. *PI* I §2ff.).[5] Wittgenstein holds that our

---

[2] Cf. Bernard Williams, *Descartes: The Project of Pure Enquiry* (1978), p. 244.

[3] Nietzsche, *The Genealogy of Morals*, p. 151.

[4] F. Schiller, *On the Aesthetic Education of Man*, ed. Wilkinson and Willoughby (1967), Letter XV §9. Compare Wittgenstein's own opinion that 'a serious and good philosophical work could be written that would consist entirely of *jokes* (without being facetious)' – reported by Norman Malcolm, in *Ludwig Wittgenstein: a Memoir* (1958), p. 29; also my remarks on the 'game' idiom in section 40 above.

[5] Wittgenstein's idea of language as a tool-kit (cf. *PI* I §11) might be thought to display something of the instrumentalism which we attributed (in section 5 above) to the empiricist tradition, but of course he diverges

failure to appreciate this feature of the context of language-use is responsible for the kind of confusion which philosophy, as he conceives it, must try to dispel: 'The confusions which occupy us,' he writes (*PI* I §132), 'arise when language is like an engine idling, not when it is doing work.' That is to say, such confusions do *not* arise when we are using language to *make moves* in a language-game: to carry forward a performance in which words and actions are interwoven (cf. *PI* I §7).

This aspect of Wittgenstein's thought recalls the view of Marx and Engels in *The German Ideology* that we misunderstand the functioning of language because of the social division between mental and material labour. From the moment such a division appears, they argue, 'consciousness *can* really flatter itself that it is something other than consciousness of existing practice, that it *really* represents something without representing something real; from now on consciousness is in a position to emancipate itself from the world and to proceed to the formation of "pure" theology, philosophy, ethics, etc.'[6] However, we can deflate these pretensions, and penetrate the 'mysteries which lead theory to mysticism',[7] by coming to realize that since we possess consciousness only in virtue of possessing language, 'consciousness is . . . from the very beginning a social product'[8] – and hence a product of those operations on which society depends for its continued physical existence.

---

from empiricism precisely in his refusal to set up an absolute, or metaphysical, distinction between 'work' and 'play' with regard to the functions of language.

[6] Marx and Engels, *The German Ideology*, p. 52.
[7] Cf. Marx, '8th Thesis on Feuerbach'; and section 7 above.
[8] Marx and Engels, *The German Ideology*, p. 51.

'Words,' writes Charles Taylor in expounding Herder, 'do not just refer, they are also precipitates of an activity in which the human form of consciousness comes to be.'[1] We have seen that for Wittgenstein, too, language is a 'precipitate' of the shared activity of a certain species of embodied creatures, and it remains only to comment on the connection between this idea and another which we touched on some time ago: that of the natural limits to our capacity for making sense of the behaviour of other intelligent beings.

Now I suggested in the foregoing section that the later thought of Wittgenstein could be characterized, in general terms, as an *anti-ascetic* philosophy – that is, one designed to remove misunderstandings (of the kind which give rise to traditional metaphysical constructions) by compelling our recognition of the bodily aspect of language. Accordingly, the 'form of life' within which we learn language, and hence acquire rational subjectivity, must ultimately be a form of *biological* life; and the beliefs and concerns of which we need to be able to find some counterpart in any community whose behaviour we hope to interpret will necessarily be the beliefs, etc. of creatures with a certain physical constitution and a certain ecological location. But from this it follows that our acceptance of the idea that the 'limits of the world', in so far as we can talk about it, are determined by the limits of 'that language which alone we understand' (cf. *T* 5.62) amounts to an acknowledgement that all we shall ever be able to say about the world will be said from a point of view which is essentially that of creatures thus constituted and located. And this in turn amounts to an acquiescence in what we might describe as a 'transcendental parochialism': a renunciation of the (ascetically-motivated) impulse to escape from the conceptual scheme to which, as creatures with a certain kind of body and environment, we are transcendentally related.

'Parochialism' is a name we commonly give to the attitude

---

[1] Taylor, *Hegel*, p. 19.

of mind found in people who are satisfied with their own ways of going on, and have no curiosity about alternatives. This attitude expresses itself, in particular, in a disdain for critical challenge; and such disdain might be said to be just what is implicit in the dogmatic statements to which we are bound to resort in the Wittgensteinian situation where 'justification comes to an end' – statements such as *Z* §309, '*This* is how we think. *This* is how we act. *This* is how we talk about it.'

But the 'dogmatism of ordinary language', to recall the label I attached to this phenomenon in section 9, appears in the context of Wittgenstein's philosophy not as a vice (in the way that ordinary, empirical dogmatism counts as a vice), but rather as something benign. To try to surmount it is, in effect, to revolt against one's membership of a community for whom, despite their unique achievement in constructing the institutions of rational discourse, 'the end of giving grounds is' (nevertheless) 'an ungrounded way of acting' (*OC* §110).

It is this fact of our insertion into the natural world which ensures, for Wittgenstein, that the Socratic project of essentialist definition – of formulating rules such that anyone who had mastered them could reproduce the array of naturally acquired behaviour which constitutes the correct use of a word – cannot be realized without residue. Because the use of language is interwoven with our wider physical life, no explanation of a word in terms of other words – and no justification of any aspect of social practice in terms of *reasons*, the offering and accepting of which is itself a social practice – could be successful if it were not for the fact that that life encompasses the person to whom the explanation is given, as well as the one who gives it. Every such step towards representing our words and actions as part of a rational structure rests, ultimately, on an appeal to sub-linguistic consensus: 'Adopt whatever model or scheme [of interpretation] you may,' writes Wittgenstein (*BB* p. 34), 'it will have a bottom level, and there will be no such thing as an interpretation of that.'

Compare the following anecdote from Collingwood's *Principles of Art*: 'There is a story that Buddha once, at the climax of a philosophical discussion, broke into gesture-language as an Oxford philosopher may break into Greek [this was written in 1937!]: he took a flower in his hand, and looked at it; one of his disciples smiled, and the master said to him, "You have understood me".'[2] The present Wittgensteinian point could be expressed by saying that whenever we respond to another person's demand for something we do or say to be made intelligible to him, the exchange always ends – if it ends successfully – with an event analogous to the smile of *tacit* understanding in the Buddha story; though whether such an 'event' has in fact taken place, we shall ultimately judge by what the person in question *goes on to do* (cf. *PI* I §180, and context).

Holding these considerations in reserve, however, something must now be said to redress the balance of emphasis as regards the 'dogmatic' theme in Wittgenstein's philosophy. What needs to be stressed is this: the fact that Wittgenstein identifies a form of dogmatism, or parochialism, which is 'benign' (in the sense indicated above) does not mean that his conception of language cannot also accommodate the more familiar idea of a *harmful* dogmatism. That conception, which claims to make our ordinary linguistic practice immune to philosophical criticism, must also place beyond criticism the habit of thought within which 'dogmatism' features as the name of something bad – an undesirable quality whose incidence we record in the course of our (non-philosophical) thinking about human mental life. This quality might be labelled 'empirical dogmatism' (or 'empirical parochialism'), in contrast with the 'transcendental parochialism' to which, as I have suggested, Wittgenstein's reflections on language are meant to reconcile us.

It was stated in section 41 that the expressivist notion of rationality as grounded in a common form of life does nothing to commend any specific *policy* towards groups or individuals whose practices diverge from our own. That notion cannot, therefore, offer any justification for an attitude of hositility or contempt towards 'what lies beyond our

<hr>

[2] Collingwood, *The Principles of Art*, p. 243.

horizon', as Nietzsche puts it[3] (in a phrase which interestingly recalls the 'sunrise' imagery of Wittgenstein and Adorno, introduced in section 38 in the context of 'dialectical reason'). In so far as our expressivist considerations issue in the idea of a benign form of dogmatism, they relate not to the *historical* but to the *natural* 'limits of our language'. They are not concerned with the kind of intellectual limitation which can be imputed to an attitude or a policy – something we could change – but with the way in which our powers of 'making sense' are constrained, regardless of our own good or bad faith as interpreters, by our physical constitution and conditions of life. Accordingly, they do not supply any defence of the (empirical) dogmatism which may lead us, as mainstream exponents of a given language-game, to withhold participant status from any person in respect of that game. For this withholding will be an *act*, and as such will have a moral dimension; which means that philosophy, on the present view of that activity, cannot pronounce on it.

'Transcendental parochialism', as I have characterized it, is not an attitude or a policy – except in the purely negative sense that it consists in declining the attempt to transcend the human perspective.[4] It is this attempt which Wittgenstein's philosophy is intended to discredit. For example, when we read at *BB* p. 28 that 'ordinary language is all right', the contrast is with a perfect language as conceived by certain formal logicians, free from vagueness of sense, etc.; in denying that we need such a language, Wittgenstein should not be taken to suggest that ordinary language (and the life in which it is grounded) is 'all right' as it happens, historically, to be, and that it would be a mistake to try to change anything. Wittgenstein in his capacity as a philosopher of

---

[3] Nietzsche, *The Gay Science*, §373: 'Above all, one should not wish to divest existence of its *rich ambiguity:* that is a dictate of good taste, gentlemen, the taste of reverence for everything that lies beyond your horizon.' It is this 'dictate' which informs Wittgenstein's words at *OC* §645: 'I can't be making a mistake, – but some day, rightly [N.B.] or wrongly, I may think I realize that I was not competent to judge.'
[4] But this assessment of the outcome of Wittgenstein's philosophical therapy as 'purely negative' will be superseded in section 50 below.

language would not have presumed to offer an answer to this question.

I wish to suggest that it is the failure to distinguish empirical from transcendental parochialism which accounts for the proneness of holistic conceptions of rationality to the kind of distortion discussed in section 22 above. The distortion I have in mind involves an appeal to the holistic ideas to sanction a specific practical policy – that of the moral conservative, whose notion of morality is largely or entirely *sittlich* in content and who consequently regards any deviation from established patterns of conduct as 'the very essence of immorality and pregnant with disaster' (cf. section 40 above). This improper application of a doctrine which is neither ethical nor political, but metaphysical (in the wholesome sense of being about the relation of language to the world), results from our omitting to *anchor* the dogmatism which follows upon the 'end of justification'. It results from our allowing that dogmatism to float freely, so to speak, and to attach itself at random to any arbitrary historical configuration of social practices; whereas, by bringing it into connection with the embodied nature of speakers, we can insulate it from tendentious claims of philosophical authority for the specific corpus of moral institutions which happens to have been arrived at.[5]

The physicalist tendency of Wittgenstein's philosophy demands to be appreciated, for the powerful reason that if we slide over it carelessly we may thereby come to see Wittgenstein as a purveyor of the kind of activist doctrine which is essentially anti-rational, chauvinistic and violent in character. What we must understand, in order to avoid such an error, is

---

[5] I commend this thought to the attention of anyone who is inclined to believe in a link between repressive forms of sexuality and authoritarian politics – an idea, incidentally, which has long been familiar to conservatives, though the language in which they express it is sometimes a little quaint: thus Devlin, *The Enforcement of Morals*, p. 111: 'A nation of debauchees would not in 1940 have responded satisfactorily to Winston Churchill's call to blood and toil and sweat and tears.'

With reference to Wittgenstein, these remarks as always are by way of philosophical, not psychological commentary.

that 'justification comes to an end' for Wittgenstein not because we get bored with it, but because rational discourse unfolds within a setting not chosen by ourselves. The steady perception of this fact could perhaps be equated with the condition described by Wittgenstein in the *Notebooks* (8 July 1916) as one of being 'in agreement with the world', or 'in agreement with that alien will on which I appear dependent' – the condition which is the goal of ethics, in so far as 'ethics is transcendental' (*T* 6.421).

Failure to anchor the idea of legitimate, or benign, dogmatism to that of embodiment encourages a reading of Wittgenstein which would echo these words of the narrator in Anita Loos' book, *Gentlemen Prefer Blondes*: 'I always think a lot of talk is depressing and worries your brains with things you never even think of when you are busy';[6] or, again, this passage in a speech by Margaret Thatcher to the Foreign Policy Association, New York: 'Self-questioning is essential to the health of any society, but we have perhaps carried it too far . . . . The time has come when the West – and above all Europe and the US – must begin to substitute action for introspection. . .'[7] That is to say, it can make Wittgenstein seem to lend his authority to a glorification of action at the expense of thought. But that is not what Wittgenstein has in mind when he says that 'it is our acting which lies at the bottom of the language-game' (*OC* §204). What he rejects is, rather, the kind of pseudo-thought typified by bad (transcendent) metaphysics, where language is 'like an engine idling'; and he rejects that kind of exercise in favour of *genuine* thought, which, as he conceives it, may belong to one of two kinds: it may refer to external reality (in which case the machine of language is performing its primary function), or else it may refer to *itself* – as in philosophy, the language-game which takes other language-games as its subject-matter, and which I compared in section 37 to the action a machine would perform (if such a thing were possible) in servicing

---

[6] Anita Loos, *Gentlemen Prefer Blondes* (1925; Picador, 1974, p. 36).
[7] *The Guardian* (19 December 1979). She went on to explain that 'action' means 'modernizing our defences'.

itself. What distinguishes these two legitimate uses of language, as recognized by Wittgenstein, from its illegitimate use is that in the former, but not in the latter, the machine is *doing something*: either its routine tasks, or a maintenance operation whose aim is to improve the machine's performance of those tasks.

It is not a consequence of Wittgenstein's views that in any particular case we are wrong to try to provide ourselves with an explicit account of our behaviour as a community – whether that behaviour relates to the use of a particular word (as in dictionary definition), or to the general conduct of our lives (as in the case of moral rules or principles). The mistake consists only in idealizing the results of this work – that is, in supposing that they encapsulate a kind of knowledge which could be possessed quite independently of our insertion into a material world. Thus the Socratic impulse to render articulate our grasp of abstract concepts, and to discourage reliance on a residue of sub-linguistic (i.e. purely practical) understanding, should not necessarily be seen as a symptom of the ascetic error discussed above. It may, rather, reflect legitimate resistance to the idea of a wholly *sittlich*, and therefore wholly static, relation between ourselves and the language-games we play. For the (reasoned) pursuit of change demands that we *intervene,* from time to time, in the practice which constitutes the approved use of certain sensitive terms: in particular, the 'essentially contested concepts' of moral and political discourse. Such change is one of the 'particular practical purposes' (cf. *PI* I §132) which may motivate an attempt to draw artificially sharp boundaries (cf. *BB* p. 19) around the concepts in question, and so to privilege a specific sub-set of the established uses of a word as against the rest; for our success in abolishing the unwelcome uses would imply success, also, in modifying the life of the community at large in accordance with our desires.[8]

It is perhaps worth observing that on the proposed

---

[8] Thus we see that there is something true in Stevenson's theory of 'persuasive definitions' (cf. his paper of that name in *Mind* (1938), reprinted in *Facts and Values*, p. 32).

expressivist account of language, the goal of our attempts to transcend *empirical* parochialism will actually be identified as a condition in which the boundaries of our conceptual scheme will have been pushed back, through critical reflection, to a *transcendental* limit. This point may be understood in the following way.

Our Wittgensteinian considerations clearly imply that the idea of a partial, or capricious, viewpoint makes sense only in relation to that of a universal, or public, viewpoint which belongs to some specific totality of persons. Thus, in the case of moral judgement, they imply that we cannot meaningfully speak of 'moral blindness' except in relation to the 'normal' moral vision of some historically existing community. If we consider a given local world-picture without reference to some wider one which transcends it, there will be no more scope for calling that picture 'parochial' than there is, according to Wittgenstein, for imagining the social practice of a community of mental defectives 'under the aspect of disorder' (Z §372; cf. section 8 above): a succession of 'viewpoints', each arrived at by transcending the local peculiarities of the one before, should be seen as constituting a 'scale of forms' in which each level of understanding, until we go beyond it, represents the culmination of the series.

But now, it is important to notice that this thought can be counterposed: as long as we can form the concrete conception of a less arbitrary description of the world – as long as we can find other rational persons or communities, by reference to whose world-view new symptoms of (empirical) parochialism in our own world-view can be identified – there will still be ground to cover in order to emancipate ourselves from such parochialism. Only when we have exhausted the supply of dialectical material may we follow the Quinean course of 'acquiescing in our mother tongue and taking its words at face value' (cf. section 23 above). For practical purposes, this means – in the words of a Marxist writer whose thought characteristically incorporates the Enlightenment ideal of a cosmopolitan rationality – that 'Man knows objectively in so far as knowledge is real for the whole human race *historically* unified in a single unified cultural system. . . . There exists

217

therefore a struggle for objectivity (to free oneself from partial and fallacious ideologies) and this struggle is the same as the struggle for the cultural unification of the human race.'[9]

Acceptance of an expressivist view of language commits us, then, to interpret the idea of an 'absolute conception of reality'[10] not in transcendent, but in immanent terms – not as a conception of reality from which all traces of human perspective would be excluded, but as one in which the individual or local perspectives of all human beings would be able to find harmonious expression. To arrive at an 'absolute conception of reality' in this immanent sense would be to attain to an intellectual condition in which the only form of parochialism of which we could be convicted would be the benign, transcendental kind. And the practical counterpart of

---

[9] From Gramsci, *Prison Notebooks*, quoted in Alex Callinicos, *Althusser's Marxism* (1976), p. 24. See, however, section 35 above for the distinction between reductive and non-reductive conceptions of the linkage between truth, or objectivity, and consensus. I have tried to show that Wittgenstein's account of this linkage is of a non-reductive character.

[10] For the transcendent interpretation, cf. Bernard Williams, *Descartes*, pp. 240ff. Here the 'absolute conception of reality', which Williams plausibly regards as 'something presupposed by the possibility of knowledge', is introduced to us by way of a highly contentious process of extrapolation. The familiar and indispensable opposition of *being* and *seeming*, Williams points out, implies a contrast between 'the world as it really is' and 'the world as it seems to any observer in virtue of that observer's peculiarities'. This contrast yields the thought that there can be 'a conception of reality corrected for the special situation or other peculiarity of various observers'. But now, by the ever more rigorous application of this notion of 'correction', we arrive at the idea of a conception of the world 'as it is independently of the peculiarities of any observers': a conception, says Williams, 'which, if we are not idealists, we need' (and an idealist, he warns, is 'something that there is reason not to be').

According to this interpretation, then, the special characteristic of predicates which can feature in the 'absolute description of reality' is supposed to be their freedom from human-relativity (cf. section 47). On the deeper values implicit in this ideal, compare Williams: 'The Platonic presupposition that it is as pure rational intelligences that men have their real worth and purpose, and that although we find ourselves with bodies, we must recognize that fact as a limitation . . . is highly characteristic of Descartes's metaphysics . . .'

that condition would be a form of life which was in agreement, as the Hegelian idiom would have it, with 'universal reason'.[11]

— 49 —

I have referred several times to Wittgenstein's assertion (*OC* §204) that 'it is our *acting* which lies at the bottom of the language-game.' Now this relation of 'lying at the bottom' may be compared with that of the eye to the visual field – an image used by Wittgenstein at *T* 5.633 to clarify the relation of the solipsistic self to the world with which it is coordinated. Although I know that I have eyes and that they are my organs of vision, I do not actually see my own eyes because they do not lie within my field of vision, but determine its limits. Similarly, although as reflective beings we can form the idea of our own language (and consciousness) as grounded in a sub-linguistic consensus – an 'agreement in form of life' – we cannot make the content of that consensus explicit because it is not part of the possible subject-matter of our discourse, but determines what does and what does not fall within that subject-matter.[1]

This metaphysical analogy with the *Tractatus* points us towards another, which bears more directly upon our interests as moral philosophers. In order to grasp the ethical analogy which I have in mind, it will be helpful to recall once again the thought introduced in section 2 above, sc. that if we are to find life meaningful, we need to be able to point to objective reasons for the will to engage itself in one kind of activity rather than another; or, in other words, that we need to be able to participate ingenuously in a language-game whose goal is to record the real evaluative properties of situations, and thus to identify practical reasons which are both *objective* and *non-hypothetical*.

---

[11] Cf. Taylor, *Hegel and Modern Society*, pp. 92, 124.

---

[1] Cf. *T* 7, 'What we cannot speak about we must pass over in silence.'

The argument of section 2 suggests a new way of formulating what our proposed moral realism has to tell us about the philosophical problem of the meaning of life. Our new formulation will appeal to a distinction drawn by Wittgenstein at *PI* I §90, where he writes: 'Our investigation . . . is directed not towards phenomena, but . . . towards the "possibilities" of phenomena.' This passage, as Stanley Cavell has pointed out,[2] affirms the *transcendental* character of the insights we are supposed to gain from the Wittgensteinian study of 'grammar' – as distinct from the *empirical*[3] knowledge we acquire by studying the realm of objects to which the terms of our language refer.

In the light of this distinction, we can say that our Wittgensteinian moral realism accommodates the thought of section 2 by *identifying* the transcendental condition (the condition of the possibility) of a meaningful human life with the transcendental condition (the condition of the possibility) of a certain sort of objective phenomenon: the phenomenon of there being a non-hypothetical point in performing some particular action.

But if my recent remarks about the physicalist theme in Wittgenstein's later philosophy were sound, we can now bring the possibility, or impossibility, of that sort of phenomenon – and hence our capacity, or incapacity, to deal with the problem of moral 'meaning' – into connection with the fact of our acquiescence, or non-acquiescence, in the form of life to which we find ourselves committed. To acquiesce in that form of life, we have said, would be to reconcile oneself to a condition of 'transcendental parochialism'; i.e. it would involve an act of assent to the transcendental constraints which are imposed upon all our mental activity by the contingent facts of our physical existence – the facts of our

---

[2] Cavell in Pitcher (ed.), pp. 175-6.
[3] 'Empirical' here does not, of course, have the same meaning as in the empiricist tradition, but is to be understood in the Kantian sense, i.e. by way of the contrast established in the text: empirical disciplines relate to the *content* of experience, while philosophy (the transcendental discipline) relates to the *possibility* of experience.

'defining situation'.[4] It is this 'defining situation' which locates us – the community of language-users – in our capacity as the (collective) transcendental subject of thought; the eye whose visual field is the world. And so if our problem is one of becoming, or remaining, receptive to the various phenomena of which the world is made up (cf. *T* 1.1) – and especially to one specific class of phenomena, the ethical facts which alone can rationally engage the will – the solution indicated by our proposed moral philosophy is simply that we should learn to occupy without distaste a point of view which, though determinate, has not been rationally determined, but itself determines what can and cannot count for us as a reason.[5]

In this way we can think of Wittgenstein's later thought as reasserting the *Tractatus* doctrine that 'the sense of the world must lie outside the world' (*T* 6.41). True, Wittgenstein's two philosophies diverge in that when he came to restore parity of metaphysical status as between factual and evaluative discourse (cf. sections 6-11 above), he thereby did away with his former grounds for denying that there could be ethical *propositions* (*T* 6.42), i.e. propositions reporting on ethical 'phenomena'. The effect of this change is to re-establish a

---

[4] For the phrase 'defining situation', see Taylor, *Hegel and Modern Society*, p. 160. Cf. also David Wiggins, *Sameness and Substance* (1980), p. 187: 'If freedom and dignity and creativity are what we crave, we shall find more promise of these things in the Heraclitean prediction "You would not find out the bounds of the soul, though you traversed every path: so deep is its *logos*" than in the idea that it is for men to determine the limits of their own nature, or mould and remake themselves to the point where they can count as their very own creation.'

[5] Cf. Nietzsche, *The Genealogy of Morals*, p. 119: 'There is *only* a perspective seeing, *only* a perspective "knowing"; and the *more* affects we allow to speak about one thing, the *more* eyes, different eyes, we can use to observe one thing, the more complete will our "concept" of this thing, our "objectivity", be.'

At this point we are well placed to appreciate the essential unity of the idealist tradition, within which 'value' is accorded ontological primacy over 'fact'. Plato located the Good '*beyond* reality' (*epekeina tēs ousias*, *Republic* 509b): Wittgenstein, by a naturalistic inversion, has human action – and hence, human concerns – 'lying at the bottom' of the language-game with which 'reality' is coordinated.

realm of (intrinsic) value within the world – a realm, as we might say, of *empirical* value; and granted the existence of such a realm, it can make sense, at the phenomenal level, to pursue certain ends for their own sake. Yet the later philosophy, I believe, still displays a conviction that empirical value, 'if it did exist, . . . would have no value.' For it shows us that the mere *existence* of a language-game in which moral facts are recorded is not enough to endow our life with meaning. The only thing which could do *that* would be the advent of a moral language-game which was expressive of ourselves, in the sense explained in section 20; and the only sort of game to which we should be willing to ascribe this quality would be one that we could see, not merely as the expression of some arbitrary set of cultural circumstances in which we happened to be placed,[6] but as grounded in a form of life capable of withstanding critical inspection. Such a form of life would be one which appeared rational to an individual whose perspective was determined, not by any local pre-occupations of the kind which result in (empirical) parochialism, but only by our 'defining situation'.

But that situation, we have said, is the ground of the transcendental constraints upon our thinking: it fixes the 'limits of our world', i.e. of that which we can meaningfully talk about. Wittgenstein's later philosophy, therefore, converges with the doctrine of the *Tractatus* in that it also requires us, in the end, to go 'outside the world' in order to find that which could make the totality of phenomena 'non-accidental' (*T* 6.41). This point may be explained as follows. On one hand, the later philosophy proposes to us the ideal of a language-game free from any merely empirical parochialism; and in this way it suggests a conception of what it would be like for us to find the totality of phenomena 'non-accidental' – namely, the conception of a condition in which our experience of the world was mediated by a (total) linguistic practice that was acceptable to us on critical

---

[6] This being, of course, the pre-critical condition from which we emerge when we come to share the later Wittgenstein's historicist insight about language (cf. sections 27ff.).

reflection. But on the other hand, the same philosophy reveals that in order to understand the mode of operation of the proposed yardstick, we must possess the idea of the human form of life as 'something animal' (*OC* §359, etc.): something on which our (human) categories of rational criticism can get no purchase, because it is 'outside the world' of discourse to which those categories belong. This idea is needed because we have to refer to it in order to specify the limiting case of the overcoming of parochialism – the case where parochialism has been pushed back, as I put it in section 48, to its transcendental limit. And we have seen that within a Wittgensteinian philosophy of language, the attainment of that state of affairs may be identified as the goal of critical thinking about our linguistic, and other, institutions.

 50 ──────

The particular form of moral realism developed in this book may be understood, as I suggested in section 20, as a specialized application of Wittgenstein's 'private language argument'. Just as that line of reasoning leads us to the conclusion that words have meaning for the individual only in so far as he is a participant in a system of shared activities, so the central idea of any moral philosophy which draws on it will be that it is only in so far as he can conceptualize the conduct of his life in the terms laid down by some real system of moral institutions that the individual will succeed in finding a meaning in life as a whole. For it is only on that condition that he will be able to recognize any intellectual authorities in respect of morality; and if he cannot do this, he will be unable to engage in evaluative judgement at all (cf. *OC* §493) – assuming, as in section 15 above, that it is of the essence of judgement to be regulated by the norm of truth. But a world in which, for moral purposes, we were unable to 'find ourselves' – a world in which we were unable to put our minds where 'reasonable' people (cf. section 38 above), in their capacity as moral judges, customarily put their mouths – would be one that offered us no possibility of taking part in objective moral discourse; and this, according to the suggestion of section 2, is as much as to say that in such a world we should be unable to see our life as meaningful.

However, as the argument of these closing sections has indicated, there is another and equally important sense in which our proposed moral realism may be seen as a corollary of Wittgenstein's views on the publicity of language. It may be seen, I suggest, as enshrining an ethical inference from the 'superficial' conception of linguistic meaning which we have seen to be characteristic of expressivist doctrines.

We encounter this conception, in the first instance, in Wittgenstein's view that the putative mental processes of 'meaning' and 'sensation' (pictured as being in principle incommunicable, since they take place 'inside the mind') should be allowed to 'drop out of consideration as irrelevant', since a 'nothing' – a 'grammatical fiction' – will 'serve just as well as a something about which nothing can be said' (cf. *PI* I §293, 304, 307). But the resulting notion of meaning as a 'physiognomy' (*PI* I §568; cf. section 12 above) is also capable of being understood in a more global sense.

It was suggested in the foregoing sections that a rational human form of life would express a system of concerns determined, not by contingent cultural factors whose influence could be transcended through critical reflection, but only by our 'defining situation' – the latter consisting in the fact of our being embodied in a certain way and placed in a certain sort of natural environment. This idea led us to conclude that acquiescence in these contingent physical conditions was the price we must pay in order to be able to 'find ourselves' even in a perfectly rational moral language-game, and hence, also, the price of our discharge from philosophical difficulties about the meaning of life. Accordingly, it would seem that a realist moral philosophy which was based on Wittgenstein's conception of language would represent not just linguistic meaning, but the meaning of life in general, as a 'physiognomy'; namely, that of human existence as such. This is a thought which seems to have been anticipated by Wittgenstein in a passage of the *Notebooks* (6 July 1916) where he writes: 'We could say that the man is fulfilling the purpose of existence who no longer needs to have any purpose except to live.'[1]

Some people may feel that the self-styled 'answer' is unsatisfyingly vacuous, and to them I should like to address the following remarks in its support. First, intimations of vacuity are by no means absent from the non-naturalistic conception of 'moral reality' with which our own proposed theory might be seen as competing. 'The great deaths of literature are few,' writes Iris Murdoch, 'but they show us with an exemplary clarity the way in which art invigorates us by a juxtaposition, almost an identification, of pointlessness and value . . .'; and again, 'The indefinability of Good is connected with the unsystematic and inexhaustible variety of the world and the pointlessness of virtue. In this respect there is a special link between the concept of Good and the ideas of Death and Chance . . . A genuine sense of mortality enables us to see virtue as the only thing of worth . . .'[2]

Secondly, Wittgenstein's own thought supplies a precedent for this negative approach to the question of 'meaning' in ethics. Consider his statement at *T* 6.52: 'We feel that even when all *possible* scientific questions have been answered, the problems of life remain completely untouched. Of course there are then no questions left, and this itself is the answer.' The idea that we discover the 'sense of the world', in so far as that can be an object of discovery, through the progressive – and, ultimately, complete – elimination of *non-philosophical* questions is paralleled in our own construction upon Wittgenstein's later philosophy by the link we have posited between solving the metaphysical problem of life's meaning, and assenting to the (imagined) condition which would result when moral thought and practice had exhausted their dialectical reserves (cf. section 48 above). That would be a condition in which there were, so to speak, 'no moral or political questions left', because all such questions had been 'answered' by the human activity which constructs and reconstructs

---

[1] Cf. Shakespeare, *All's Well That Ends Well*, IV iii *ad fin*: 'Simply the thing I am/Shall make me live.'
[2] Murdoch, *The Sovereignty of Good*, pp. 87, 99.

moral reality over time. (There is also, of course, an analogy with *PI* I §133, where the end of *philosophy* is conceived in terms of the exhaustion of its subject-matter: 'The clarity we are aiming at is indeed *complete* clarity. But this simply means that the philosophical problems should completely disappear.')[3]

Thirdly, it would not be surprising if the later Wittgenstein – having emerged from our discussion as an exponent of 'that Romanticism which is one with the universe'[4] – should turn out to allot a central place in his thinking to the Romantic notion of 'natural piety': the acquiescence of intelligent beings, however far they may have advanced in philosophical (reflective) awareness, in those features of their own mental life which are 'not based on grounds' (*OC* §559). Although this frame of mind is often, and no doubt inevitably, described in negative terms (for example, by reference to the absence of questions), it nevertheless represents a positive moral value within its own philosophical context. Thus Collingwood writes of his older contemporary Samuel Alexander:

> When Alexander said that natural piety should be the clue to metaphysical thinking, he meant to say, as many sound philosophers have said before him, that a metaphysician's business is not to argue but to recognize facts; and he meant to say also that these facts are not recondite or remote, to be recognized only after a long course of special training and specialized research, but simple and familiar, visible to the eyes of a child, and perhaps hidden from clever men because they are too '

---

[3] Cf. also *CV* p. 43, 'Thoughts that are at peace. [*Friede in den Gedanken.*] That's what someone who philosophizes yearns for.'

[4] Cf. Klee, *On Modern Art*, p. 43: 'I will emerge from the oppressively pathetic style to that Romanticism which is one with the universe.'
The specification should not be overlooked. Wittgenstein, too, is a 'modernist' whose Romantic sensibilities are informed by a historically typical course of reflection on language and experience. We might compare that expressivist extravaganza, Joyce's *Ulysses,* which self-consciously draws its own moral in its concluding word – the 'Yes' that rounds off Molly Bloom's monologue.

clever. Certainly, he thought, they must remain hidden from those wise and prudent men who would accept nothing but what was 'proved'; and they were revealed to any babe who would accept them as the child Wordsworth accepted the rainbow.[5]

I believe that if Wittgenstein's later writings are interpreted in these terms it will be easy to grasp the positive content of the specifically ethical idea yielded by our proposed Wittgensteinian realism: the idea that with regard to the meaning of life, as in the case of meaning *simpliciter*, 'what is hidden is of no interest to us.'[6]

But *natural* piety must be distinguished from the kind of 'piety' which consists in being 'content to accept' the dominant language-game, regardless of its merits or defects from a critical standpoint, simply because it is there. The *historical* sense in which the language-game is 'there' must be distinguished from the sense in which it 'is there – like our life', i.e. *naturally* (OC §559). The concept of natural piety as a moral requirement is coordinated, not with that of an established form of life simply as such, but with that of a form of life in accordance with 'universal reason'.

---

[5] Collingwood, *An Essay on Metaphysics*, p. 173. (The phrase 'natural piety' is taken from a poem by Wordsworth.)

[6] I do not expect to escape censure for suggesting that an *ethical* conclusion may be derived from a philosophy which has hitherto been characterized as a linguistic *positivism* (sections 34ff.) I would reply simply that while the distinction between 'describing language-games' and participating in them has its undoubted utility in the quest for a 'perspicuous representation' (*PI* I §122) of the grammar of our language, that quest itself is more than a merely cognitive enterprise; for the 'clarity' at which Wittgenstein's philosophical therapy is directed consists in a state of liberation not so much from false *ideas* as from a false *life*. ('What has to be overcome is a difficulty having to do with the will, rather than with the intellect' (*CV* p. 17). This is why, as Cavell observes (in Pitcher (ed.), p. 184), Wittgenstein's later work 'wishes to prevent understanding which is unaccompanied by inner change'.) The kind of objectivity which makes it possible to rise above linguistic mystification and to 'command a clear view' of human thought and life is not the objectivity of the scientist, but springs from a different demand in which cognitive and ethical impulses find a joint expression – the demand for *philosophical* truth.

The distinction just drawn will help to bring into focus the fourth, and final, part of my reply to the charge of vacuity which might be levelled at our conception of (moral) meaning as a 'physiognomy'. The point which remains to be made is that we – people living today – find ourselves in the historically unprecedented situation in which the *transcendental* ground of the 'meaning of life', as characterized by the moral philosophy developed in this book, is threatened with *actual* destruction or abolition. It is a situation in which the irrationality of our historically specific 'form of life' has grown so acute as to undermine rational belief in the future continuity of our life as a natural species.[7] But it was precisely in terms of our participation in the human 'form of life' in this second, naturalistic sense that we accounted for the 'possibility of the phenomenon' of intrinsic value within the world constructed by human discourse – the very possibility on which we have supposed the meaningfulness of life to be dependent. Thus it can now be of no comfort to us to have learnt the lesson contained in a philosophy which restores reason, or meaning, to our existence by naturalistic means; for since we have no reason to suppose that our collective life will in fact continue, the philosophical position to which our reflections have led us is no longer fortified by that extra-philosophical certainty which ought, in theory, to confer happiness (i.e. *Friede in den Gedanken*) on anyone who gets there.

For us, therefore, the idea of 'meaning as a physiognomy' escapes vacuity in its application to ethics, not only in virtue of the 'aestheticizing' tendency discerned in it above, but also because historical contingency has brought into question the accessibility to ourselves of the immemorial subjective relation of human beings to the 'surfaces' in which meaning is inscribed. This alteration in the experiential background from

---

[7] Cf. Michel Foucault, *The History of Sexuality: Volume I* (1976), trs. Robert Hurley (1981), p. 143: 'For millenia, man remained what he was for Aristotle: a living animal with the additional capacity for a political existence; modern man is an animal whose politics places his existence as a living being in question.'

which academic moral philosophy is supposed to derive its subject-matter presumably goes some way towards explaining the increasingly problematic status of the discipline. For as J.-P. Sartre has observed, 'A poor child does not question itself: ravaged *bodily* by want and sickness, its unjustifiable condition justifies its existence. Hunger and the constant danger of death are the bases of its right to live: it lives so as not to die.'[8]

---

[8] Jean-Paul Sartre, *Words* (1964), trs. Irene Clephane (1977), p. 56.

Bibliography

Adorno, Theodor, *Minima Moralia*, trs. E. F. N. Jephcott, London: New Left Review Editions, 1974.

Anscombe, G.E.M., *Intention*, Oxford: Blackwell, 1957.

Aristotle, *Nicomachean Ethics*, ed. J. Bywater, Oxford, 1894.

Aristotle, *Politics*, trs. Ernest Barker, Oxford, 1946.

Ayer, A.J., *Language, Truth and Logic*, 2nd edn, Harmondsworth: Penguin, 1946.

Ayer, A.J., *Hume*, Oxford, 1980.

Berlin, Isaiah, *Vico and Herder: Two Studies in the History of Ideas*, London: Hogarth Press, 1976.

Bradley, F.H., *Ethical Studies*, 2nd edn, Oxford, 1927.

Callinicos, Alex, *Althusser's Marxism*, London: Pluto Press, 1976.

Collingwood, R.G., *An Essay on Philosophical Method*, Oxford, 1933.

Collingwood, R.G., *The Principles of Art*, Oxford, 1938.

Collingwood, R.G., *An Autobiography*, Oxford, 1939.

Collingwood, R.G., *An Essay on Metaphysics*, Oxford, 1940.

Davidson, Donald, 'On the Very Idea of a Conceptual Scheme', *Proceedings of the American Philosophical Association*, 1973.

Devlin, Patrick, *The Enforcement of Morals*, Oxford, 1965.

Douglas, Mary, *Purity and Danger: an Analysis of the Concepts of Pollution and Taboo*, London: Routledge & Kegan Paul, 1966.

Dummett, Michael, *Truth and Other Enigmas*, London: Duckworth, 1978.

Ehrenreich, Barbara and English, Deirdre, *For Her Own Good: 150 Years of the Experts' Advice to Women*, London: Pluto Press, 1979.

Evans, Gareth and McDowell, John (eds.), *Truth and Meaning: Essays in Semantics*, Oxford, 1976.

Feyerabend, Paul, *Science in a Free Society*, London: New Left Review Editions, 1978.

Foot, Philippa, *Virtues and Vices*, Oxford: Blackwell, 1978.

Foster, M.B., *The Political Philosophies of Plato and Hegel*, Oxford, 1935.

Foucault, Michel, *The History of Sexuality: Volume I*, trs. Robert Hurley, Harmondsworth: Penguin, 1981.

Frazer, J.G., *The Golden Bough*, abridged edn, London: Macmillan, 1971.

Green, T.H., *Lectures on the Principles of Political Obligation,* Oxford, 1895.

Grisoni, Dominique (ed.), *Politiques de la philosophie,* Paris: Grasset, 1976.

Hampshire, Stuart (ed.), *Public and Private Morality,* Cambridge, 1978.

Hare, R.M., *The Language of Morals,* Oxford, 1952.

Hare, R.M., *Freedom and Reason,* Oxford, 1963.

Hegel, G.W.F., *Philosophy of Right,* trs. T.M. Knox, Oxford, 1952.

Hegel, G.W.F., *The Phenomenology of Spirit,* trs. A.V. Miller, Oxford, 1977.

Hobbes, Thomas, *Leviathan,* ed. C.B. Macpherson, Harmondsworth: Penguin, 1968.

Holtzman, S.H. and Leich, C.M. (eds.) *Wittgenstein: to Follow a Rule,* London: Routledge & Kegan Paul, 1981.

Hookway, Chris and Pettit, Philip (eds.), *Action and Interpretation,* Cambridge, 1978.

Hopkins, James, 'Wittgenstein and Physicalism', *Proceedings of the Aristotelian Society,* 1974-5.

Hume, D., *An Enquiry Concerning the Principles of Morals,* ed. L.A. Selby-Bigge, 3rd edn, Oxford, 1975.

Hume, D., *A Treatise of Human Nature,* ed. L.A. Selby-Bigge/ P.H. Nidditch, Oxford, 1978.

Kahn, Charles H., 'The Greek Verb "To Be" and the Concept of Being', *Foundations of Language* (Dordrecht: Reidel), 2, 1966.

Kant, I., *Critique of Pure Reason,* trs. Norman Kemp Smith, London: Macmillan, 1929.

Klee, Paul, *On Modern Art,* trs. Paul Findlay, London: Faber, 1979.

Kolnai, A.T., *Ethics, Value and Reality,* ed. David Wiggins and Bernard Williams, London: Athlone Press, 1977.

Lévy-Bruhl, L., *La morale et la science des moeurs,* Paris: Bibliothèque de Philosophie Contemporaine, 1953.

Lucretius, *De Rerum Natura,* ed. C. Bailey, Oxford, 1922.

Lukes, Steven, *Individualism,* Oxford: Blackwell, 1973.

Machiavelli, N., *The Prince,* trs. W.K. Marriott, London: Dent, 1908.

MacIntyre, Alasdair (ed.), *Hume's Ethical Writings,* Toronto: Collier-Macmillan, 1965.

Mackie, J.L., *Ethics: Inventing Right and Wrong,* Harmondsworth: Penguin, 1977.

McDowell, John, 'Are Moral Requirements Hypothetical Imperatives?', *Proceedings of the Aristotelian Society, Supplementary Volume*, 1978.

McDowell, John, 'Virtue and Reason', *The Monist*, July 1979.

Malcolm, Norman, *Ludwig Wittgenstein: a Memoir*, Oxford, 1958.

Marx, K., *The Revolutions of 1848: Political Writings Volume I*, ed. David Fernbach, Harmondsworth: Penguin, 1973.

Marx, K., *The Poverty of Philosophy* (English trans.), Moscow: Progress Publishers, 1955.

Marx, K. and Engels, F., *The German Ideology*, ed. C.J. Arthur, London: Lawrence & Wishart, 1974.

Mill, J.S., *Utilitarianism*, ed. Mary Warnock, London and Glasgow: Fontana, 1962.

Moore, G.E., *Principia Ethica*, Cambridge, 1903.

Murdoch, Iris, *The Sovereignty of Good*, London: Routledge & Kegan Paul, 1970.

Murdoch, Iris, *The Fire and the Sun*, Oxford, 1976.

Nagel, Thomas, *The Possibility of Altruism*, Oxford, 1970.

Nietzsche, F., *The Genealogy of Morals*, trs. Walter Kaufmann, New York and Toronto: Random House, 1969.

Nietzsche, F., *The Gay Science*, trs. Walter Kaufmann, New York and Toronto: Random House, 1974.

Nietzsche, F., *Twilight of the Idols*, trs. R.J. Hollingdale, Harmondsworth: Penguin, 1968.

Norman, Richard, *Reasons for Actions*, Oxford: Blackwell, 1969.

Nowell-Smith, P.H., *Ethics*, Harmondsworth: Penguin, 1954.

Nyiri, J.C., 'Wittgenstein's New Traditionalism', *Acta Philosophica Fennica, Vol. 28, Nos. 1-3: Essays on Wittgenstein in Honour of G.H. von Wright*, Amsterdam: North-Holland, 1976.

Pears, David, *Wittgenstein*, London: Fontana, 1971.

Pitcher, George (ed.), *Wittgenstein: the Philosophical Investigations*, London: Macmillan, 1966.

Plato, *Republic*, ed. J. Burnet, Oxford, 1902.

Plato, *Protagoras*, ed. J. Burnet, Oxford, 1903.

Platts, Mark, *Ways of Meaning: an Introduction to a Philosophy of Language*, London: Routledge & Kegan Paul, 1979.

Platts, Mark (ed.), *Reference, Truth and Reality*, London: Routledge & Kegan Paul, 1980.

Quine, W.v.O., *Word and Object*, Cambridge, Mass.: MIT Press, 1960.

Quine, W.v.O., *From a Logical Point of View*, 2nd edn, New York: Harper & Row, 1961.

Quine, W.v.O., *Ontological Relativity*, New York: Columbia, 1969.

Rousseau, J.-J., *The Social Contract and Discourses*, trs. G.D.H. Cole, London: Dent, 1913.

Saussure, F. de, *Course in General Linguistics*, trs. Wade Baskin, Glasgow: Fontana/Collins, 1974.

Schiller, F., *On the Aesthetic Education of Man*, ed. and trs. Elizabeth M. Wilkinson and L.A. Willoughby, Oxford, 1967.

Stevenson, C.L., *Ethics and Language*, New Haven: Yale, 1944.

Stevenson, C.L., *Facts and Values: Studies in Ethical Analysis*, New Haven: Yale, 1963.

Strawson, P.F., *Freedom and Resentment and Other Essays*, London: Methuen, 1974.

Taylor, Charles, *Hegel*, Cambridge, 1975.

Taylor, Charles, *Hegel and Modern Society*, Cambridge, 1979.

Thompson, E.P., *Writing by Candlelight*, London: Merlin Press, 1980.

Trigg, Roger, *Reason and Commitment*, Cambridge, 1973.

Walker, Ralph C.S., *Kant*. London: Routledge & Kegan Paul, 1978.

Wiggins, David, 'Truth, Invention and the Meaning of Life', *Proceedings of the British Academy*, 1976.

Wiggins, David, *Sameness and Substance*, Oxford: Blackwell, 1980.

Williams, Bernard, *Problems of the Self*, Cambridge, 1973.

Williams, Bernard, *Descartes: The Project of Pure Enquiry*, Harmondsworth: Penguin, 1978.

Williams, Bernard, *Moral Luck*, Cambridge, 1981.

Williams, Michael, *Groundless Belief*, Oxford: Blackwell, 1977.

Winch, Peter, *The Idea of a Social Science and its Relation to Philosophy*, London: Routledge & Kegan Paul, 1958.

Wittgenstein, L., *Tractatus Logico-Philosophicus*, trs. D.F. Pears and B.F. McGuinness, London: Routledge & Kegan Paul, 1961.

Wittgenstein, L., 'Lecture on Ethics', *Philosophical Review*, 1965.

Wittgenstein, L., *Philosophical Investigations*, trs. G.E.M. Anscombe, 3rd edn, Oxford: Blackwell, 1967.

Wittgenstein, L., *The Blue and Brown Books*, 2nd edn, Oxford: Blackwell, 1969.

Wittgenstein, L., *On Certainty*, ed. G.E.M. Anscombe and G.H. von Wright, trs. Denis Paul and G.E.M. Anscombe, Oxford: Blackwell, 1969.

Wittgenstein, L., *Remarks on the Foundations of Mathematics*, ed. G.H. von Wright, R. Rhees and G.E.M. Anscombe, 3rd edn, Oxford: Blackwell, 1978.

Wittgenstein, L. *Notebooks 1914-1916*, ed. G.H. von Wright and G.E.M. Anscombe, trs. G.E.M. Anscombe, 2nd edn, Oxford: Blackwell, 1979.

Wittgenstein, L., *Culture and Value*, ed. G.H. von Wright in collaboration with Heikki Nyman, trs. Peter Winch, Oxford: Blackwell, 1980.

Wittgenstein, L., *Zettel*, ed. G.E.M. Anscombe and G.H. von Wright, trs. G.E.M. Anscombe, 2nd edn, Oxford: Blackwell, 1981.

Index

236

238